Journeys with Jerry

Robert L. Krogh

Faith in the Forum

Published by: Faith in the Forum

Editors: Bruce Krogh and Bill Henry

Interior design: Robert Krogh

Cover design: Robert Krogh and Catherine Nedley

Library of Congress Control Number: 2021900215

ISBN-13: 978 1 7363500 1 0

Distributed by: IngramSpark

To anyone I ever taught,
I should have shared this with you sooner.

Contents

Preface

In the summer of 2000, soon after the youth group from Hebron Church in Penn Hills, Pennsylvania, arrived at the Safe House Outreach in Atlanta, Georgia, someone uttered the nicest compliment I have ever heard. Having graduated from high school, I knew that this would be my last mission trip as part of the youth group at Hebron Church. We only had enough time to unload the bus, stake out our favorite corner of the carpeted common rooms, and lay out our sleeping bags, before the director of the facility requested that we come together so he could share some information about the week ahead. In his usual quiet manner, our youth pastor, Jerry Zeilstra, called us together and the briefing began.

"Thanks, Jerry," the director started as he placed a hand on Jerry's shoulder. *"I can tell this is a man of great integrity, because when he speaks everybody listens."*

I have never heard a more powerful testament to a person's character or reputation. Nor have I ever heard a better description of one of the greatest youth pastors that has ever lived. And it had come from someone who was merely watching Jerry help unload a bus and settle his crew.

This is not a book that Jerry would have written about himself. He is not prideful or vain enough to assume that anyone might benefit from (or even be interested in) a book about his ministry. His ministry has not been a cult of personality, clever marketing, or theatrical charisma; nor has he ever treated youth ministry as the transient task of an associate pastor biding his time on his way to leading his own church.

Jerry's ministry has simply been the result of a life committed to Jesus Christ and His mission. Jerry has built a network of relationships one student and parent at a time by listening to their questions, sharing his own experiences, and introducing them to the One who made all the difference in his own life. I know of few people in any field who have spent as much time independently studying the latest research and ideas about their areas of expertise. For as long as I have known him, I have had conversations with Jerry that have included his most recent revelations from the ministry books and articles he was reading. As the decades passed, he even kept himself abreast of the latest television, movie, and music trends, all for the sake of relating the gospel to the youth at Hebron Church.

So, when I recently found myself in a season of spiritual confusion, I texted Jerry to see if he would meet me for breakfast. I used the week before our meeting to mull over my thoughts and try to reduce them to relatable discussion points. I was struggling with the current state of my own spiritual growth and ministry as a worship leader, wondering if I had missed some kind of major cultural shift in the church that left me feeling disconnected and behind the times. I knew he would have useful insights from his experiences, but in the process I came to realize that in some ways I might just be missing the simplicity of my time as a student in Jerry's youth ministry.

Every generation warns the next, but I remember adults telling me as a teenager that they couldn't imagine how hard it would be for us to raise kids in the world of the future; it was already hard enough for them in the present. I'm sure that even in their wildest imaginations they could not have predicted the blurring of social, cultural, and moral lines, 24-hour access to friends through social media, or endless entertainment piped through Netflix, YouTube, and cell phones that has become our reality. Sometimes I worry about how my three boys will ultimately navigate this new world when I have trouble wrapping my mind around it myself.

The morning Jerry and I met, I had an idea as I was getting dressed. I wasn't the only one who matured under Jerry's teaching. The stories he told us and the experiences we shared are incredibly valuable illustrations of the promises of Scripture and the importance of the gospel. They have had a lasting impact on hundreds of students and their families. They are worth recording. As a parent, I thought it would be great to have Jerry's lessons available to share with my own kids.

When I pitched this idea to Jerry, he laughed and changed the subject. I decided to forge ahead in an effort to convince him. If I didn't scare him away, I hoped to meet with him regularly so he could correct the details and set my memory straight.

When faith and life are most challenging, I find peace in returning to the simplest truths of the Bible, the fundamentals. If spiritual adulthood was leaving me feeling outdated, perhaps the way forward was to turn back to my youth. Jerry has a knack for communicating biblical truth clearly and in the simplest of terms. The world could benefit from a record of his best lessons. At a minimum, I hope those of us who learned from him will pass his wisdom on to future generations.

"When God wants to teach you something,
He often takes you on a journey."
~Jerry Zeilstra

Introduction

I was entering sixth grade when my parents started hearing about a great church across town. My family had just returned from living abroad for a year and we were eager to reestablish ourselves in the diverse community of Penn Hills, Pennsylvania. Several friends had a lot of good things to say about Hebron Church. The new pastor, Doug Rehberg, delivered excellent, thought-provoking sermons. Hebron also had a thriving children's ministry with Sunday School for all ages and a weekly program on Wednesdays with games, choir, dinner, and Bible lessons. On top of all that, since my oldest sister was now in eighth grade, she would enjoy the vibrant youth ministry led by an experienced youth pastor named Jerry Zeilstra. We decided to visit.

In the several months that followed, I felt like my whole life was in flux. We slowly integrated ourselves into the Hebron Church family. I entered middle school, where five local elementary student bodies merged into one giant group. I endured all the embarrassing effects of puberty. And, my parents decided it was time to move to a new house with a bigger yard and sell my familiar childhood home. I approached all of these major changes with the kind of bitter resentment one would expect from a budding teenager.

I could sense the end of my childhood rapidly approaching, but now I can clearly see the wisdom in my parents' decisions. I never could have imagined the profound impact that Hebron Church would have on my future. So much transition at one time can cause a young man to act out. My first Sunday School teachers at Hebron, Mr. And Mrs. C., weren't particularly fond of my antics. They were very kind to me, but stern enough to corral my arrogance and command my attention. I don't think I made much of a positive first impression on their daughter Michelle, either. At the time, none of us would have ever guessed that Michelle and I would marry eleven years later, and Mr. and Mrs. C would transition from my Sunday School teachers to my in-laws!

INTRODUCTION

The ministry of Hebron Church was so effective in my life because of the steadfast faith of its members. From the senior pastor, to the Sunday School teachers, to kitchen volunteers, Hebron continues today to be a strong community of committed believers who rely on the strength of their heavenly Father, the grace of His Son Jesus, and the guidance of the Holy Spirit. It was a great place for a young man to grow in his faith. This was especially true when I started attending youth group. I already had some exposure to the youth pastor, Jerry, through Wednesday night Kids Club. Over the next decade, he would become a mentor, friend, coworker, and personal hero. The lessons he taught us, both about God and life in general, have been invaluable to me. When I consider some of the confusing cultural changes of the last thirty years, both inside and outside the church, my mind often returns to the now seemingly ancient wisdom imparted to me by Jerry Zeilstra.

1

Mercy in Detention

"That's mercy."

Jerry grew up on a farm in South Dakota. It could be that his rural upbringing appealed to me because of my own frequent family trips across the Midwest as a child. I was raised in Penn Hills, Pennsylvania, a suburb of Pittsburgh, but my dad was from Omaha, Nebraska, and my mom grew up on a farm in central Illinois. So, the wisdom that Jerry shared from memories of his parents, animals, tractors, country roads, and small Reformed church reinforced not only my faith, but also my love for America's heartland. I enjoyed imagining myself in Jerry's shoes, wondering how much closer I might be to God if only I could meet with him in a sea of endless cornfields like Ray Kinsella and his dad in the movie *Field of Dreams*.

"Is this heaven?"

"It's Iowa."

"Iowa? I could have sworn it was heaven."

Something about "fly-over" country makes me long for simpler times. I am fully aware of my overly romantic view of the rural Midwest. The immense sky with its level horizon and white puffy clouds stretching as far as the eye can see over an ocean of corn and beans waving in the breeze reminds me of the beauty of God's creation, the fruits of labor, and my own insignificance in the universe. There is something about this environment that generates honest, grounded men and women who look you straight in the eye with a friendly smile. Their economic success depends on daily discipline, the help of neighbors, and reliance on God's mercy to provide the weather they need for their crops and livestock. Perhaps living at the mercy of God in the fields cultivates a spirit of mercy in Midwestern interpersonal relationships as well. It might also be why the first lesson I remember learning from Jerry was about God's mercy.

Jerry's teaching style was approachable and authentic. He possessed a talent for turning common occurrences into illustrations of Christian thought. He liked to answer questions with more questions, but never with any tone of condescension.

Jerry seemed less like an authority figure and more like a fellow, albeit more experienced, traveler on the journey of life. Stories from his childhood helped us teenagers feel as if we too could glean powerful wisdom from the meaningful life experiences we already had under our belts.

One of the earliest stories I remember Jerry sharing was part of a lesson about mercy. He had a couple of great anecdotes from his childhood that helped to convey the subtle distinction between mercy and grace. Ultimately, Jerry would present grace as the central focus of the gospel, but he started with mercy. Understanding God's mercy laid the foundation for understanding God's grace.

One day in grade school, Jerry forgot to do his spelling homework. When his teacher, Mrs. Johnson, came around the class to check for the assignment and discovered his was incomplete, she reminded him that he would need to stay in the classroom during recess to make it up. Priorities being what they are for an elementary student, when the time came, Jerry chose to ignore her instructions and instead joined his classmates in the schoolyard for recess. As a consequence, Mrs. Johnson informed him that he would now be required to stay after school for detention.

Jerry would stop here to explain that the Zeilstra family had a couple of hard and fast rules. First, with the exception of illness, there was no excuse strong enough to justify missing church. Second, and more important to this story, if your behavior ever resulted in your having to stay after school for detention, you were expected to walk home — a distance of *fifteen* miles! Beyond that, you would still be responsible for your assigned chores when you returned to the farm, no matter how late it was when you arrived.

It isn't hard to imagine the anxiety young Jerry would have experienced as the full weight of Mrs. Johnson's punishment dawned on him. He suffered through the remainder of the school day and stayed in his seat when the bell rang for dismissal. As he watched his friends through the window boarding their buses for the long ride home, he was overcome with emotion. Never once explaining the complete circumstances to his teacher or asking for special treatment, he began sobbing. Mrs. Johnson stood her ground at first, but quickly realizing she would be unable to console him, she spat, "Oh, just go home, you big baby!" Jerry gathered his things and rushed out, wiping the tears from his face, to catch his bus just before it pulled away.

At this point, Jerry would pause and look around the room.

"*That's* mercy," he would say.

After Jerry let his story sink in, he would go on to explain that mercy is *not* receiving the punishment that you *deserve* to receive. Jerry did not have his homework done that morning. Even when provided an opportunity to rectify the situation, he passed. Mrs. Johnson was entirely justified in enforcing her punishment, and he deserved the consequence. Nonetheless, she exhibited mercy by sparing Jerry not only detention, but also a long walk home, lonely chores in the dark, and a late bedtime. Mrs. Johnson's mercy, though, was not motivated by anything more than frustration. It is hard to believe she felt any sympathy for little Jerry given his defiance that day. No, Mrs. Johnson simply decided that after a long day with students, the last thing she wanted to do was to stay even longer with a crying child.

The mercy of our heavenly Father is different. God's mercy is motivated by love and compassion. God is a jealous God, worthy of our very best in all things. Even though we fall well short of that standard every day, He withholds His wrath from us. "[W]e all once lived in the passions of our flesh, carrying out the desires of the body and the mind, and were by nature children of wrath, like the rest of mankind. But God, being rich in mercy, because of the great love with which he loved us, even when we were dead in our trespasses, made us alive together with Christ" (Eph. 2:3-5a).

I have come to realize that the lessons I learned from Jerry in my youth have significantly shaped my worldview. He helped me establish a lot of my personal theology and philosophies about life. He imparted wisdom that steered me safely through early adulthood. He shaped the way I approached my study of social and cultural history in college. He influenced my career decisions. He put me on a lasting path of agreement and unity with my wife. He shaped the way I parent my children. God used Jerry to make me the person I am today. Jerry's biblical teaching and witty mantras have become a major part of how I process the world and digest the many changes that have taken place since my years in his youth ministry. My understanding of mercy is a great example.

In today's "cancel culture," mercy is in short supply. The Internet allows us to pass instantaneous judgment on total strangers in real time. Even the most trivial transgressions on social media can lead to the destruction of a person's life and career in a matter of minutes. All it takes is one misunderstood tweet or a craftily edited video clip for an innocent contributor to become the object of the world's scorn. The anonymity of the Internet empowers both people and programmed responses from "bots" to unleash firestorms of anger and wrath. Gossip news sites are eager to quote vicious reactions to comments of unsuspecting celebrities, politicians, and everyday individuals. Free-lance columnists create titillating water-cooler-discussion pieces out of thin air, citing only a few Twitter comments as evidence of broad public disgust.

Even though social media executives have begun to come forward and shed light on the technological thought manipulation taking place behind the scenes, we continue to fall for the click-bait so as not to be left out of the conversation. If we're honest with ourselves, we are acting like a bunch of junior-high bullies. Criticizing the latest social media faux pas makes us feel better about our own decisions and ideas; it's just one more way social media is addictive.

The public condemnation seen in social media episodes is often an effort to convince everyone else that an otherwise innocuous thought or comment is somehow entirely unacceptable. The person at the center of the contrived conflict is confused by how blatantly he has been misrepresented. Apologies are offered not out of actual contrition, but simply to appease the mob in the hopes of a truce.

When "merciful" responses do arise, they are often motivated by disingenuous virtue signaling aimed at elevating an agenda. Well-meaning idealists, for example, misconstrue concepts like "restorative justice" to make excuses for misbehavior and even crimes in a desire to develop people into contributing citizens. This interpretation assumes that since all people are essentially good, any wrongdoing is a manifestation of some harm that the perpetrator has experienced. Rather than punishing, authority figures seek instead to build relationships, provide counsel, and offer opportunities for improvement. While this approach may appear merciful at first, it ignores the victim and protects the transgressor. The opportunity for actual mercy from the aggrieved party is supplanted by a process that demands acceptance by both the victim and society at large. The perpetrator can effectively avoid any actual consequence for his or her actions and simply be reminded that there is a better way.

As an educator, I have witnessed the result of such policies in our public-education system. Troubled students feel empowered to act however they feel like acting, while teachers and administrators are trained to assume the very best about student intentions and sympathize with the trauma or hardships such students must have endured. Behavior and expectations slowly erode because there is no longer a societal standard into which students are hoping to grow. Students perceive this treatment as weakness and take advantage of the opportunity to act as they please without restraint. In most cases, they experience no remorse as they instead concoct the reasoning behind why they are "misunderstood." This is not mercy. This is enabling.

Making allowances for only those in our ideological tribes gives us a sense of belonging and purpose, but avoids the honest communication required for fulfilling relationships. Imagine the relief we might feel if actual *mercy* was the norm. We could share ideas freely and learn from our mistakes without fear of completely losing our reputation or credibility. We could drop our defensive masks and listen to each other as people rather than opinions. Both the unforgiving nature of social media and the consequence-free pursuit of restorative justice run contrary to the concept of biblical mercy as Jerry taught us.

To truly experience mercy, we must be aware of the wrong we have done and congnizant of the negative impact and resulting consequences. We must embrace fault and seek forgiveness and a restored relationship. The Bible is clear that we were born in a state of sinfulness. The decision of Adam and Eve to eat from the tree of the knowledge of good and evil led to a curse on us all. Even if you are not a person of faith, the evidence is present in each of us. Just like the Apostle Paul, we "have the desire to do what is right, but not the ability to carry it out" (Rom. 7:18).

When we had our first child, my wife and I would sometimes just stand by the crib and stare at him. He was just a tiny, little peanut wrapped tightly in his swaddling blanket and sleeping peacefully. At one point my wife said, "I don't get it. How could he be sinful? He seems so perfect." Well, that was a pleasant thought, but it didn't last! The reality of our son's selfish, sinful nature would emerge quickly as he grew. Pretty much from that moment on, all of our sons (we have three now) have become nothing less than a reflection of our own shortcomings, a constant reminder of how we fail every single day to put God first in our lives. As Ephesians 2:4 says, sin is part of our nature. But, even in our most frustrating and disappointing moments as parents, we have a deep, unwavering love for our boys.

We are sinful. God is *good*. Despite the fact that we were "by nature children of wrath," He has "great love" for us and is "rich in mercy." We are deserving of His wrath, but He withholds it, allowing us to experience this life. Everything we have is a gift from our Creator. We are keenly aware that He could take it from us at any moment. That is why Lamentations 3:22-23 tells us, "The steadfast love of the Lord never ceases; his mercies never come to an end; they are new *every morning*; great is your faithfulness" (emphasis added). We don't just require God's mercy only when we do things we shouldn't do.

We are rewarded with His mercy every day when we wake up in the morning and with every breath we take thereafter. Life itself is the gift of God's mercy. If we, like farmers dependent on the rain, can remember that the blessings in our lives are the result of God's mercy, we are more likely to extend those blessings and that mercy to others. Mercy was a great starting point, but Jerry was just laying the groundwork for the real beauty of the gospel.

2

Grace in the Silage Pit

"That's grace."

Jerry used to say that after so many years in youth ministry, there was nothing we could say that would come as a surprise to him. I remember reacting to that statement by trying to imagine what kinds of terrible things former students had done. Looking back, though, it is more likely that Jerry was just universally convinced of human depravity. Nothing could surprise him because he knew deep down that he was completely capable of the same indiscretions and failures as any of us. And having been saved by grace himself, he offered it to everyone around him. Kids, meanwhile, are kids. We could be very harsh to each other, even to Jerry, but he never retaliated. Jerry approached every student with a spirit of grace.

It would be easy to assume that Jerry's patience and understanding with young people was a practiced part of his profession. A youth pastor is expected to be fun and engaging, giving students space to be themselves. To that end, Jerry had a seemingly infinite repertoire of games to lead and always planned thought-provoking, Bible-focused lessons. He was prepared every week to facilitate a fun and affirming experience for everyone who arrived for Sunday night youth group. He would take special care to make a connection with visitors, get to know their names, and find out who invited them. Cynics, especially these days, might mistake Jerry's zeal for a self-serving obsession with growing a personal following. In fact, I remember peers making jokes about the "Hebron Cult" when Jerry would make his weekly visit to the school cafeteria. But anyone who got to know Jerry quickly discovered that he simply lived what he believed. He was a sinner, saved by grace, seeking opportunities to share that gospel with young people in Penn Hills, no pretense and no expectations.

Some of my friends stepped away from youth group over the years because they felt that others there were too judgmental. To some extent, that perception may have been justified. Since I had grown up in the church, nothing seemed particularly unnerving to me. I have never been a very compassionate person, so I am certain there were times I thoughtlessly made arrogant, alienating comments. On top of that, for teenagers and adults alike, scriptural introspection can give rise to conviction and feelings of guilt. Who would prefer guilt to a carefree pursuit of life experiences?

You don't have to spend much time reading the Old Testament to discover that that particular sentiment has been appealing to people for a long time. Over the last century, though, it seems that our culture has taken it to extremes. There have been undeniable efforts to marginalize Christianity, efforts that are deeply impacting today's youth. The 1990s are my first memory of campaigns like saying "Happy Holidays" instead of "Merry Christmas," court challenges to remove "under God" from the pledge and Christian monuments from public spaces, and a journalistic proclivity toward rebranding certain Christian beliefs and perspectives as "hate." All of these movements have slowly eroded the boldness of believers and muzzled the message of the biblical gospel. Many have rejected the notion of a single source of truth, relying instead on their personal feelings. Simple folks like Jerry, people of great integrity who rely on the age-old consistency of Scripture, seem either to be ignored or to be mocked by "open-minded" critics who reject faith in favor of moral relativism and social-engineering theories.

In the view of the world, Christians are self-righteous anti-intellectuals who just want to believe they are better than everyone else. Many believe that adopting such an archaic value system is nothing but a restrictive hindrance to the pursuit of individual happiness and freedom. Ironically, judgment is used as a club to condemn things that make people feel bad, and mercy is extended only to those who affirm culturally approved viewpoints. For Jerry's part, though, he was intentional about reminding students that there was no reason to impose a scriptural standard on unbelievers. "If you don't believe in the Bible, you might as well eat, drink, and be merry, because when you die, that's it!" Judgment *should* be left to God. The role of believers is to extend *grace* so that others might likewise experience the love of Christ. Regardless of how well we lived up to that model at Hebron Church, the degradation of the church in popular culture continued.

The present societal assumptions are that people are inherently pretty good and that we can eradicate guilt, loneliness, bullying, and all sorts of ills simply by teaching our children every behavior and attitude that is acceptable. There is no need for the judgmental absolutes found in religion if we just learn to embrace diversity. The reality of sin and the bedrock of the Bible have lost a lot of ground to the tyranny of *tolerance,* an arbitrary standard that forfeits future stability for the sake of short-term comfort. It is impossible to explore and appreciate our differences adequately if we are unwilling to discuss them objectively and candidly. Proponents of the tolerance movement love to stress that Jesus said, "Judge not!" But Jesus' response to judgment was *never* tolerance. His answer was *grace.* He extended great compassion and saw value in every person He met, but He certainly was not content to leave people unchallenged in their sinful state. Jesus confronted everyone with truth, convicted everyone of sin, and called everyone to repentance.

Far too often, the church attempts to apologize for its shortcomings and to defend itself against smears from the "tolerant" world. Even worse, churches are quick to identify other churches, rather than the nature of sin, as the source of the bad press. When media culture attempts to isolate religion by highlighting the positions or actions of Christians that can most easily be perceived as judgmental and exclusive, I wonder about their motivations. Some individuals have experienced appalling abuse in the church. Others feel that religion is the root of all bigotry and global conflict. And even regular church attenders can be cynical about church finance, capital campaigns, and the practice of tithing. Regardless, the church should not feel compelled to justify its activities or beliefs to others who do not recognize the authority of Scripture and the redemptive power of the gospel.

Let me be clear. There is no excuse for covering up actual crimes that occur in the church. Church members and leadership who break the law should be reported to authorities and held accountable for their actions. Scripture instructs the church on a process for internal discipline in Matthew 18, but this does not imply that the church possesses its own legal authority in society. Shielding fellow believers from consequences for their illegal actions under the auspices of *grace* does no favors to Christ or His kingdom's work. "[W]hoever resists the authorities resists what God has appointed, and those who resist will incur judgment" (Rom. 13:2).

The church must not forget that its very existence is rooted in the grace of Jesus Christ. For those who profess belief in Christ, failure is not hypocrisy. It is a constant reminder of one's need for a Savior and one's inability to achieve anything without Him. Any good that comes from the church, comes not through strict adherence to the law, but through the free gift of grace through Jesus Christ. This is the reason Jerry made grace the central theme of his ministry, and grace is the reason his ministry was so effective.

For those of us lucky enough to have been a part of Hebron Church, either by the choice of our parents or through the invitation of a friend, Jerry became a mentor in walking with Jesus. His stories gave us insight into his own experiences, but they also laid a practical foundation for understanding our relationships with Christ. For students who had not grown up in the church and were less familiar with the Bible, Jerry's stories made difficult theological concepts simple and approachable. So, he would start with the story of his frustrated teacher, Mrs. Johnson. The schoolhouse encounter that he used to introduce us to mercy likely had something to do with Jerry's spirit of empathy toward students. His next tale, from life on the farm, suggested that Jerry's grounded, gracious personality was also partly the product of his upbringing.

Jerry began this account by recalling the laborious process of making silage. Silage is fermented grain used to feed farm animals. None of us had ever heard of silage, nor did we have any knowledge of how it was made. Jerry briefly explained that to prepare it, a farmer dug a large pit and filled it with fresh chaff from the harvest. Using heavy machinery, he would then compact the plant matter to remove any air that might spoil the silage with mold. On this particular day, Jerry's dad had spent hours driving back and forth with his tractor over the silage pit until it was smooth and firmly packed. The final step required that the pile be covered with a tarp and weighed down with tires to protect it against rain and water throughout the season. But before that could happen, someone needed to make a trip into town to purchase the tarp.

Before he left, Mr. Zeilstra informed his children, Jerry included, that it was very important that they not step foot on the silage pit. Walking on the silage would disturb the compost and create new airspace in the pit that would ruin the feed "this deep" — and Jerry would hold his hands up a good foot and a half apart. His dad was clear, *Do not walk on the silage pit.* Well, Jerry and his siblings did not heed their father's advice. As soon as his dad's truck disappeared over the horizon, they began gleefully running around on top of the squishy silage.

When Mr. Zeilstra returned to discover hundreds of footprints stamped across his perfectly compacted silage, he was furious. He grabbed a pitchfork and began chasing the culprits. The Zeilstra children scattered in terror. Jerry took immediate cover in the silo.

Once his initial rage had passed, Mr. Zeilstra was left alone, without the aid of his former crew, to do his best to restore his work, tarp the pit, and cover it with tires. Jerry, meanwhile, remained concealed in the silo until sundown.

Just as Jerry knew that the consequences would have been in effect had Mrs. Johnson not shown mercy to him at school, so Jerry knew that despite the hour he was still expected to complete his chores before going to bed. He was a little older and stronger now, and his job was to toss thirty to forty bales of hay down from the loft in the barn to feed the cattle. Making sure the coast was clear, he managed to avoid his father's wrath as he sneaked over to the barn and climbed into the loft. Still feeling guilty about the silage and equally concerned about his next encounter with his dad, he began heaving the hay down to be unbaled for the hungry animals.

Partway through the job, as he began to work up a sweat, Jerry caught sight of some activity in the moonlight below. He peered over the edge to discover his dad cutting the twine on the bales and spreading the hay. Without saying a word, his dad worked by his side until the chore was complete. Then they headed back to the house to turn in for the night. His dad never spoke of the incident again.

Jerry would then pause and look around the room.

"*That's* grace," he would say.

With both illustrations in place, Jerry could make the proper comparison, "You see, *mercy* is *not* receiving the punishment that you *deserve* to receive. But *grace*," he would explain, "*is* receiving the *forgiveness* you *do not* deserve."

Jerry and his siblings ruined his dad's day, destroyed the fruits of his hard labor, then disappointed him further by running away instead of owning up to their actions. There wasn't anything Jerry could do to fix the problem he took part in creating, and he hadn't taken any time even to apologize to his dad. But, nonetheless, his dad made the decision to do the extra work alone to salvage the silage and then to meet Jerry at the barn to help him complete his chores. Ultimately, the lesson Jerry learned that day had a far greater impact than Mr. Zeilstra's pitchfork ever could, and it provided him with a glimpse of the grace we receive from our heavenly Father.

Jerry had several verses he encouraged us to memorize. One of them was Romans 5:8, "God shows his love for us in that while we were still sinners, Christ died for us." God pursued us not because we deserved it, but because we failed. Belief in Jesus is predicated on accepting the fact that each of us in incapable of holiness without Him. Romans 3:23 reminds us that "all have sinned and fall short of the glory of God." God, who is holy, cannot *tolerate* our sinful nature and we are therefore in need of a Savior. Jesus did not come into this world to condemn us and then extend only His mercy. He came to save us (John 3:17).

Jerry's dad felt that his relationship with his son was worth forgiving Jerry's transgression, fixing the silage pit, and demonstrating grace, even as Jerry continued to fail him.

Likewise, our heavenly Father felt that His relationship with each of us was worth sending His Son to suffer and die in our place that we might be forgiven, not because we deserved it, but because He loved us.

Jesus was the embodiment of grace. He had no need to compete for attention, defend His reputation, or apologize for His appeals to the authority of Scripture. Jesus did teach His followers to refrain from judgment lest they be judged themselves. He did not espouse an expansion of laws and restrictions to coerce the world into proper behavior. His approach was far more revolutionary. He was the one person in the history of the world who had earned the right to judge others, but instead He offered *grace*. He took the burden of our sin on his own shoulders and carried it to the cross in our place so that we could experience a right relationship with the Father. This is the enduring message of the church.

For centuries the church had no difficulty identifying its vital role in American society. Churches occupied central locations on main streets in every small town. Church buildings served not only as places of worship, but also as town halls and meeting houses. Early Americans, escaping religious persecution in Europe, were taught to read for the primary purpose of understanding and interpreting their Bibles. Children learned to play instruments for worship and sang in church choirs. Calamities were met with the collective effort of church members rather than private-insurance policies. The church's central place in society provided meaningful opportunities to demonstrate the impact of Christ in each person's life and community.

Unfortunately, the scientific and industrial revolutions that swept through the world through the 18th and 19th centuries brought a new emphasis on economic efficiency and a focus on the power of the independent human spirit. These changes not only created a higher demand for empirical evidence in the human experience, but they also spawned a separation of social service from faith. The church today contends with government-provided education, government welfare systems, and enormous humanitarian aid organizations. One can claim to care for the orphan and the widow simply by paying taxes or texting donations to the Red Cross after a disaster.

I can't argue that these incredibly beneficial systems are inherently detrimental. The speed and extent of the services they provide to areas of need are astounding. These efficiently designed networks, however, have allowed us to take credit for God's provision, rather than giving Him the glory. Churches frequently join these organizations in providing help to their communities, but participation in humanitarian efforts no longer sets Christians apart from any other caring individuals. The truth is, it never did.

What Jerry knew, and wanted desperately for his students to understand, is that the saving grace of Jesus Christ is what sets Christianity apart. Grace is the only "selling point" worth repeating. Grace is what has been freely received. Grace is what must be freely given. Jesus demonstrated this emphasis repeatedly during his life. When confronted with the adulterous woman, he challenged the accusers to consider their own sin before casting the first stone, then graciously admonished the woman to "go, and from now on sin no more" (John 8:1-11). In the Sermon on the Mount, He encouraged His followers to turn the other cheek and pray for their enemies (Matt. 5:38-48). And even as He hung on the cross, Jesus prayed "Father, forgive them" (Luke 23:34).

Jerry also understood that the grace found in Jesus Christ was the essential starting point for effective ministry. This is still true for the church today. "For the grace of God has appeared, bringing salvation for all people, training us to renounce ungodliness and worldly passions, and to live self-controlled, upright, and godly lives *in the present age,* waiting for our blessed hope, the appearing of the glory of our great God and Savior Jesus Christ, who gave himself for us to redeem us from all lawlessness and to purify for himself a people for his own possession who are zealous for good works. *Declare these things; exhort and rebuke with all authority. Let no one disregard you*" (Titus 2:11-15, emphasis added).

The grace Jerry received from his father in the silage pit laid a foundation for his future ministry. It prepared his heart to accept the grace of Jesus Christ in his own life eventually, and it also taught him the importance of grace in creating genuine connections with those he hoped to influence. Jerry knew that grace would be fundamental to our life experience, especially through the formative high-school and college years. By leading with grace, Jerry acknowledged that none of us could ever live up to the expectations of Scripture, our parents, or even ourselves on our own. Now, he was ready to expand on the promises of the abundant life available in Scripture to those who choose to acknowledge their sin and rely on this amazing grace.

3

Patience Among Teenagers

"Why'd you do that?"

It was several years before I would have an opportunity to extend grace to Jerry myself. He was really mad that night. It was my final year of high school and the senior boys were gathered around his dining room table for dinner and a Bible study. We listened sympathetically as Jerry explained what had happened. A young man who was down on his luck had been living at Jerry's place for a few days to get back on his feet. That afternoon, Jerry had come home from work to discover that the young man had not only packed up and left, but also stolen Jerry's PlayStation on his way out, most likely to sell it for a little cash. With his face getting a little red, he said, "It just makes me so damn...". Well, that changed the tone quickly. We all burst into a chorus of fake offense and laughter. Did Jerry seriously just swear? Yes! We all felt very privileged to have witnessed an extremely rare event. Jerry had reached the bottom of his seemingly endless supply of patience.

As a schoolteacher, I can say with great certainty that there may be no more beneficial attribute for a youth worker than patience. Jerry possessed it in spades. This is another area where farm life prepared him well. Farmers can't force plants to grow or rain to arrive. They have to be patient. Horses and cows are fairly predictable, but when they decide they don't want to move, pushing and pulling usually causes them to dig their heels in. When machines break down, farmers learn quickly that getting angry at the problem doesn't fix it, and usually makes matters worse. Teenagers present a lot of the same challenges. Sometimes you just have to give them the space to learn and come to their senses on their own. The best you can do is be available, pray, and wait. Jerry learned this early in life.

One day on the farm, Jerry was helping his dad and older brother build a cattle manger, which required the installation of a post. Once the base of the post had been buried deep in the ground, they were using the tractor to roll back and forth over the dirt around it to pack it tightly for long-lasting support. At this point in the project, Jerry was standing aside watching his older brother, Wilmar, operate the machine while his dad shouted instructions over the noise of the engine. "Get a little closer!"

Wilmar backed up and tried again.

His dad watched. A little angrier this time, he yelled, "Get closer!"

Wilmar gave it another go.

His dad shook his head, "No, a little closer!"

Jerry said this scene repeated itself several times until Wilmar had enough, hopped off the tractor, and stormed away. Jerry climbed on to see if he could better meet his dad's demands. He backed the tractor up and took his first run.

"Closer!" his dad yelled.

Jerry backed up and steered the tractor as close to the post as he could. As the rear wheel passed by the post, the protruding axle clipped the top of the post and snapped it in half. He stopped the tractor, looked at his dad, and said, "Did that help?"

His dad looked at him puzzled, "Why'd you do that?"

Jerry shrugged, "You told me to get closer. Isn't that what you wanted?"

As he finished telling the story, Jerry laughed and shook his head. "My dad had a pretty bad temper until he got saved." Jerry shared this story to highlight one of the ways in which he saw his dad become transformed after committing his life to Christ. He said after that he rarely saw his dad become angry and never heard him swear again. Patience had been a part of

Jerry's character for as long as he could remember, but seeing that change in his dad was confirmation that the Holy Spirit had taken hold of his dad's heart.

Jerry taught us that our relationship with the Holy Spirit is what effects noticeable change in our lives. Once we surrender our lives to Christ, our hearts begin to change through the process of sanctification. Evidence of that relationship can be seen as our lives begin to bear fruit. "But the fruit of the Spirit is love, joy, peace, patience, kindness, goodness, faithfulness, gentleness, self-control; against such things there is no law" (Gal. 5:22-23). All of these qualities have become part of Jerry's character by the grace of God. They are available to every believer led by the Spirit. Patience, in combination with a whole lot of kindness, goodness, gentleness, and self-control, was a powerful tool in Jerry's ministry.

There were several times when I remember Jerry being patient with me. In fact, I'm sure before I graduated to junior high, word had reached him that I was pretty obnoxious. In my nonstop effort to draw attention to myself and make people laugh, I drove youth-club volunteers and Sunday school teachers nuts. I doubt I was the first troublesome kid Jerry ever met. He was more than prepared to help me work on my character.

The first prolonged period of time I spent with Jerry was during the summer after sixth grade. I was finally old enough to attend the week-long summer camp at Surf City. Surf City was a camp experience organized by the Pittsburgh Youth Network. Mostly Pittsburgh area churches took buses out to Camp

Miniwanca, situated between Stony Lake and the coastline of Lake Michigan near the town of Shelby, Michigan. It is a great camp with lots of water activities, hiking, miles of sand dunes, great food, and rustic cabins. Each day was packed with Bible study, meals, music, games, and club sessions with skits and a keynote speaker. It was a great place to spend a week in the summer, but of course, I found a way to ruin it for myself. I am still a little embarrassed by the first impressions I made on Jerry and my peers.

Surf City was a lot of fun, but the experience could be a little uncomfortable for the uninitiated. The cabin areas had limited electricity. Instead of windows, the cabins had large openings on the sides covered with canvas tarps. They were more like enclosed pavilions filled with bunk beds. Not being a huge fan of community showers, I spent most of the week pretty dirty, covered in sweat and sand most of the day. I was uncomfortable and homesick, and I wasn't ashamed of letting everyone know about it. I think I spent as much time crying as I did participating in the days' activities. I wasn't as cool, fun, fit, or athletic as most of my classmates. So, remaining emotional was my best shot at attracting any attention.

Several leaders and classmates came to my rescue, offering support and advice. When they asked how I was doing, I would sniffle and say I was still homesick. I was being ridiculous. Jerry was wise to avoid me. He was undoubtedly aware of my carrying on because the leaders met daily to discuss how things were progressing, and he at least acknowledged me from time to time. But in his wisdom, he knew that patience was the key. It would do no good for him to reward my strange behavior by giving me the attention I sought or by offering to call my parents to pick me up. The best approach was to sit back and wait for me to work through my issues and grow up.

Jerry's patience paid off. I blubbered my way through the week and grew increasingly engaged the closer we got to the end of the week. I was happy to get home, but I looked back on the week regretting some of the decisions I had made to sit out on all the fun. I realized that five days is a very brief period of time. If I could learn to remain a little more present, the future would arrive in due time. Jerry never chastised me for my stubbornness. He let me come to my senses and remember the good times, and he encouraged me to make the trip to Surf City again the next year.

By the following summer, I had expanded my circle of friends at youth group, invited some of my school buddies, and knew exactly what I was getting into. I went to Surf City every year I could. I still participated in my typically reserved way. I never had the full confidence in my body image to take my shirt off at the beach in front of junior-high girls. I also felt too self-conscious to dance or jump around much during the music. I enjoyed it anyway and have a lot of great memories, with the possible exception of another first impression I made. One of my many "great ideas" gone awry.

There are two things I need to explain for you to understand clearly what happened. First, climbing the sand dunes at Camp

Miniwanca was a big part of the Surf City experience. The dunes were tall and steep, especially the one closest to camp known as Mount Baldy. With every step you took up the dune, it felt as if you slid two steps back down. Once you reached the top of a ridge, it was fun to leap from the top and land softly in the sand below. Another enjoyable activity, especially for the boys, was to pick out a friend coming up the dune, barrel down toward him, jump into the air, and land just short, spraying a giant plume of sand into your friend's face.

Second, during my final week at Surf City, the keynote speaker was Glenn Campbell from Atlanta, Georgia. This was the second time I had heard him speak at Surf City. He was an engaging communicator and, having heard him before, I already knew most of his stories and therefore felt as if I knew him pretty well. Of course, that feeling was based a lot more in adolescent assumptions than in actual reality.

After club on the final night of camp, all the campers are directed to head up Mount Baldy for a campfire and storytelling. As the campers set out from the clubhouse, some friends and I ran ahead with the brilliant idea of ambushing others with sprays of sand as they trudged up the dune. We landed a couple of good sprays on some friends near the top and the excitement was starting to wear off when I spotted a prime target.

Glenn Campbell was halfway up the dune with his head down. Never to miss an opportunity for accolades, I set my eyes on the prize and headed straight for him. At just the right moment, I sprung into the air and waited for my legs to hit the sand. But they never did. I had miscalculated and instead collided directly with Glenn's legs, hyperextending his knee. He tumbled backward in agony while I began apologizing profusely.

I suddenly became keenly aware that this was the only actual one-on-one interaction I had ever had with Glenn Campbell, and I was ready to call it a night and head back to the cabin to hide. Glenn was extremely gracious. Luckily nothing was broken, and he was able to continue the journey up the dune. He hobbled into place next to the fire and stood with his weight on his uninjured leg to tell his stories to the group. I was grateful he didn't single me out or tell the entire camp what had happened on the way up. My guess is that he was also a great, patient youth pastor.

Jerry's patience in this situation was a little more subtle, but just as valuable. I told him about the incident and explained that I had already apologized. I'm sure my remorse and embarrassment were evident on my face. Jerry shook his head and smiled a little, but that was the extent of his response as I remember it. As far as I know, he didn't bring it up with Glenn, my parents, or anyone else. Jerry was well aware of his own flaws and had realistic expectations for teenagers. This wasn't the first dumb thing one of his students did, and it wouldn't be the last. It also wasn't a situation that necessarily involved him, and he saw little benefit in interfering. His ability to remain patient, even when the behavior of kids may have reflected poorly on him, reminded us that we could trust him.

A few years later, I was riding shotgun with Jerry in the front of a rental van. Every January and February, Jerry organized ski trips to Seven Springs, a resort about an hour away. This week, students filled the entire bus, and Jerry had rented the van to add seats. We were approaching the mountains on the Pennsylvania Turnpike when the snow picked up. Jerry wanted to use the windshield wipers, but some ice had piled up in the bottom corner of the windshield. He asked me to reach out of the window to clear it with my hand, but I had a better idea.

Why open the window and make my hand cold? Just a little nudge would surely knock the ice loose and the wind would send it sailing. I leaned forward, made a fist, and with the side of my hand gently pounded on the bottom of the windshield in front of me. I learned a lesson that day. When it is below freezing on the outside and there is heat blowing out of the defroster on the inside, the integrity of the glass is compromised. On the second bump of my fist, we heard a crack. The windshield split all the way across.

I looked over at Jerry with a nervous chuckle. He stared back at me with a look of resignation, as if he were replaying in his mind the moment when he declined the insurance at the rental agency. Jerry's patience allowed him to take these situations in stride and formulate thoughtful, measured responses. I filled his silence with my apologies and questions about how much it would cost to repair the windshield. Jerry said there wasn't much to do about it at that point and he would deal with it when he returned the van.

I felt pretty silly about the windshield the rest of the night and on the return trip. Jerry was probably kicking himself for even asking me to clear the windshield in the first place, especially given my history of clumsiness and things turning out differently than I planned. Despite my insistence, Jerry never brought up the windshield again. By not reacting harshly to my stupidity, he allowed me to save face and turned the incident into an opportunity to extend grace.

Jerry's example of patience helped to shape me as a teacher and a parent. I am not always as consistent as I wish I would be, but I have found the same strategies work well with my school students and children. Sometimes kids just need space and time to mature. Browbeating and reprimanding children for acting like children is a great way to drive a wedge between you and them. Waiting for growth can be frustrating and sometimes expensive, but providing patient direction instills trust and a record of genuine concern.

It is very difficult for parents and teachers not to worry about how a young person's actions reflect on you as the responsible authority. Jerry knew he had no power to change anyone else and focused instead on his response to students. He didn't enable poor behavior. He always addressed it when necessary, but never in a way that belittled or drew attention to the student. By speaking with students privately he also avoided rewarding anyone with an audience. Jerry helped me understand that mistakes are part of the learning process. Patience is essential to teaching and to learning from our mistakes.

Patience is required to respond appropriately to kids of all ages. I have discovered when acting as the disciplinarian that my reactions are often rooted in selfishness. I will lash out spontaneously either to end obnoxious behavior quickly or to assert my personal expertise about the situation. Neither of those interactions is beneficial to the relationship I have with the child involved. It is good to recognize that there is usually time to walk through an issue together with the student. We have all been advised to count to ten before acting. A little patience goes a long way not only in building relationships, but also in setting a great example to kids on how to react to their own struggles. Or, as the Bible puts it, "Train up a child in the way he should go; even when he is old he will not depart from it" (Prov. 22:6).

4

Sin and Holiness in South Dakota

"How do you define sex?"

Jerry's friendly Midwestern demeanor broke through to students, and his family and boyhood farm were never far from his mind. He organized a trip for ninth-grade students every summer so they could meet his family and connect with his roots. The trip itself, however, had a far greater purpose. As students in his ministry entered their high-school years, he knew they would face a slew of alluring temptations that would challenge their identities and beliefs. He used this annual South Dakota trip to encourage students to set personal standards.

By ninth grade, students in Jerry's ministry had been exposed to the gospel message several times. Weekend retreats to a local camp called Laurelville and summer excursions to Surf City provided frequent opportunities for teens to wrestle with their faith. There was no confusion at Hebron Church about the power of sin in our lives, and our need for Christ.

I remember a powerful moment in the van during my own class trip to South Dakota as we drove across the plains of Iowa. One of my buddies remembered a dirty joke and whispered it to me. The rest of the boys in the van just happened to fall silent at the very worst moment, as he delivered the punchline.

I don't know if Jerry heard the joke, but I'm sure he could tell by the whispering and my nervous laughter (I didn't really get the joke at the time, but I pretended I did to impress my friend) that whatever had been shared was inappropriate. In his wisdom, Jerry didn't ask what was said or require us to tell everyone. He simply said, "You know, it is interesting that we use the same mouths to sing praise songs to God as we do to tell dirty jokes." Nothing more needed to be conveyed. We were busted. And whether we knew it or not, he had just set the stage for the rest of the trip. In one sentence, Jerry had challenged us to consider within ourselves the line between sin and holiness.

The Big Three

In South Dakota, the discussion about standards centered on the three very consequential temptations we were sure to encounter in high school and college: drugs, sex, and alcohol. Jerry wanted all of us to understand that a commitment to Christ involves a commitment to holy living. He saw these specific vices as the first major challenges to our faith as we entered adulthood. Beyond the challenge they were as personal decisions in my life, though, I remember these three vices as becoming a wedge between myself and many of my peers. For some, just the discussion of trying to avoid drugs, sex, or alcohol reeked of arrogance. American culture is pretty clear that our late-teen years are a carefree opportunity to experiment without fear of lasting consequences. There is an assumption that anyone trying to pursue holiness at that age is a judgmental prude who wouldn't want to hang out with normal kids. I took a lot of Jerry's advice to heart, but I remember the constant struggle of feeling that I might be missing out on something. Ultimately, my life experience during those years fell somewhere in between, as I succumbed to temptation at times and discovered grace on an even more personal level.

Jerry, however, understood that this discussion involved a battle for each of our hearts and he didn't shy away from it. The South Dakota trip included meals with his family, games, work projects, and daily lessons about these consequential topics. My class was part of the "Just Say No" generation. Avoiding drugs was not a new idea. One of my friends, whom I greatly admired, intended to pursue a career in law enforcement. He had very strict standards for himself already to avoid any criminal record. We were all used to hearing from adults that we shouldn't do bad things, but Jerry approached the topic differently, with several wise, scriptural observations.

Our Bodies Are Temples

"Or do you not know that your body is a temple of the Holy Spirit within you, whom you have from God? You are not your own, for you were bought with a price. So, glorify God in your body" (1 Cor. 6:19-20).

The Bible tells us that our bodies are temples of the Holy Spirit. God requires that believers be good stewards of their bodies. In 1 Corinthians 6, Paul warns about the significant implications of sexual sin because of the intimate involvement of the body. Drugs and alcohol have a similar impact on our bodies. God has plans for our prosperity, but faith in his plan and purpose for our lives is required. Reliance on drugs for escape or happiness is nothing more than rejection of God's plan. Jerry taught this not as a harsh judgment of those who use drugs, but as a means of defining the choices we face. He reminded us that the abundant life promised by Jesus can be found in contentment and enjoyment of life as it is; supplements aren't necessary.

Sin Loves Company

"A man of violence entices his neighbor and leads him in a way that is not good. Whoever winks his eyes plans dishonest things; he who purses his lips brings evil to pass" (Proverbs 16:29-30).

We have all experienced a time when someone encouraged us to participate in an activity that we knew was wrong. There is also a good chance that we have encouraged someone else to do something that was morally wrong. After all, "What happens in Vegas, stays in Vegas." Jerry made it clear that the allure of sin — from the smallest of indiscretions, like a dirty joke, to the most offensive crimes — has a lot to do with the acceptance we experience from others. "Sin loves company," he would say. We already knew that to be true, especially after the story of Jerry and his siblings on the silage. Eve ate the fruit to experience the approval of the snake. Adam ate the fruit to keep the acceptance of Eve. If you're going to explore questionable behavior, it's easier if you know that someone else will travel down that road with you. With the help of the Holy Spirit, we have the power not only to pass on sin, but also to pursue positive alternatives. Jerry reminded us that by simply refusing to join people in sin, sometimes you can keep them from pursuing detrimental behavior themselves.

Sin Has Consequences
"For the wages of sin is death, but the free gift of God is eternal life in Christ Jesus our Lord" (Rom. 6:23).

There is a reason Jesus had to die to forgive us our sins. Sin has consequences. "The wages of sin is death." In Christ, we are already forgiven and saved from the eternal consequence of sin. That is a wonderful promise, but it does not excuse us from the life-altering natural consequences that come as a result of our decisions. Jerry had two great illustrations for this point. The first one was toothpaste. Once toothpaste has been squeezed out of a tube, it is nearly impossible to put it back in and restore the tube to what it once was. Likewise, when we make a decision to cross a boundary in our lives, we leave a realm of innocence that cannot be restored. This is true for every new experience: eating solid foods as a baby, reading a book, climbing a mountain, trying a cigarette, having sex, looking at pornography. Some experiences are beneficial to achieving maturity, some are completely unnecessary, but all have consequences.

In his second example, Jerry told how his dad once punished him for saying something mean to his sister. He provided Jerry with a board, a box of nails, and a hammer. He gave him the task of driving the nails into the board. When Jerry had finished, his dad asked him to remove the nails and return them to the box. Each nail represented a decision. Each nail was able to be taken back out, but there would still be a hole in the board. Participation in sin has consequences, but as James 3 reminds us, so do the words we say to others. Jerry stressed that before we reached a point of no return, there is great benefit in establishing some personal principles to govern the limits of our speech and actions.

Choose Your Friends Wisely

"Whoever walks with the wise becomes wise, but the companion of fools will suffer harm" (Prov. 13:20).

"The righteous choose their friends carefully, but the way of the wicked leads them astray" (Prov. 12:26, NIV).

"Iron sharpens iron, and one man sharpens another" (Prov. 27:17).

My mom used to say, "You can pick your friends and you can pick your nose, but you can't pick your friend's nose." Jerry's message on friendship dovetailed well with that philosophy. Well, at least the "pick your friends" part. He had three important points when it came to friends. The first was that friendship takes work. As is the case for most kids, we were forced together in school for the majority of 180 days every year. Youth group and trips like South Dakota brought us together even more frequently. But Jerry wanted us to understand that after graduation, when we went our separate ways, maintaining these relationships would require a tremendous investment of time and energy. Of course, that was before Facebook, but even so, I have come to experience the difficulty of developing and keeping close friends as I have grown older. Jerry's second observation on friendship was that the friendships that would last would be the friendships centered in Christ. Or as he put it, "A friend in Christ is a friend for life." Having a relationship with Jesus already turns a person's focus toward eternity. Christians have a strong bond in their faith and are confident that no matter what happens on this Earth, they will encounter each other again in their eternal future. Third and finally, Jerry noted that "a friendship that ends badly, never really ends." I remember this theory throwing us for a loop. Even now, I don't feel like I fully understand. Why would a friendship end unless it did end badly? I guess he meant that the relationship would leave lingering feelings of regret.

Throw Fun Parties

"They are not of the world, just as I am not of the world. Sanctify them in the truth; your word is truth. As you sent me into the world, so I have sent them into the world" (John 17:16-18).

In fourth grade, I can recall a health teacher telling my class that when older kids talk about "partying," they weren't talking about birthday parties. Jerry didn't pull any punches in describing how attractive and exciting high-school and college parties could be. Sex, drugs, and alcohol would all play a part in the get-togethers in which we might participate. Given our sinful nature, no matter what personal boundaries we set, we would ultimately experience feelings of temptation, envy, and regret. In some cases, we would wrestle with the desire to try things we knew we shouldn't. In other cases, we might be left feeling that we missed out on the fun that others experienced. Either way, he challenged us to consider throwing parties ourselves that were exciting and fun without the need for the big three.

Every Date Is a Potential Mate

"Do not be unequally yoked with unbelievers....[W]hat portion does a believer share with an unbeliever?" (2 Cor. 6:14-15).

I can still remember the emotional tension of my teen years, shifting gears from one crush to the next as I discovered that most girls just weren't into me. In one of Jerry's most influential lessons on my life, he asked a very straightforward question.

"How do you define sex?"

Say what?

"How do you define sex?"

He had us write our answers on a piece of paper and then share them with the group only if we felt comfortable. It's hard to imagine a youth leader being this brazen these days. Even then, the question caused a lot of nervous laughter. It was pretty ironic really. The dirty joke my friend told me on the road was far more embarrassing!

I don't remember any of the specific responses that day, but Jerry went so far as to suggest that holding hands is a first step. We, of course, ridiculed him for suggesting that, but he was making a larger point. It was Jesus, after all, who said that even looking at a woman lustfully was the same as having an affair with her.

Jerry could safely assume that we all understood, believers or not, that the Christian standard was to wait until marriage to have sex. What he was forcing us to consider was where we actually drew the line between "our parts" and our hearts. If we were with someone we truly cared about, what would constitute saving ourselves for marriage? It wasn't until much later in life that I would realize how much I valued that conversation. Much to the benefit of both of us, my wife would have the same discussion with her class the following year.

Beyond establishing the physical boundary for ourselves, however, Jerry also taught us that "every date is a potential mate." Even more important than choosing friends wisely, it was important that we not approach intimate relationships too casually. The Bible teaches us that there is danger in believers being yoked with unbelievers. I cannot fault anyone for falling in love. Jerry helped us realize, though, that love, especially young love, can cause us to overlook many differences. Some of those differences can cause great stress later in a relationship. His word of caution was not meant to condemn someone as an unworthy partner, but simply to encourage us to consider matters of the heart, especially concerning those to whom we would allow the closest access.

Needless to say, for a group of high-school freshmen, these meetings led to a lot of joking and awkward silences as we struggled with our ignorance and the gravity of these issues. Jerry was always patient and open to our questions and willing to laugh right along with us. During one of our discussions, Jerry kept stressing that if we ever found ourselves in an intimate situation with a significant other, it might be good just to head home and take a cold shower. He must have mentioned the benefits of a timely cold shower a handful of times before my friend Jon couldn't take it anymore. "Jerry, does it have to be a cold shower? Couldn't we at least take a lukewarm shower? I hate cold showers." In a way, Jon was illustrating Jerry's point. These boundaries we were grappling with needed to be all or nothing.

I can't speak for all my classmates, but by the end of the South Dakota trip, I had a pretty firm sense of how I planned to make these decisions throughout my high-school and college years. Jerry had provided me with a healthy dose of confidence in the Word of God to back up my positions. I was bolstered by the knowledge that my peers and I would face these challenges together. And, I was reassured knowing that every generation of believers before me had to make the same kinds of decisions.

The years that ensued were not without their challenges. Making the best decisions in the face of temptation and peer pressure is much easier said than done. My own struggle with holiness became a struggle with guilt. I wondered if setting personal boundaries wasn't self-defeating. It is difficult to separate our own ability to "stay holy" from our reliance on Jesus to walk beside us. I'm pretty sure my own lack of understanding on how to deal with falling short cost me friendships as I reacted poorly to the situations of others and failed to be open about my own.

A college friend once offered to join me for church on a Sunday morning if I got drunk with him at a party first. I prudishly passed on the opportunity. I still wonder if that was the right call. South Dakota was empowering and informative at a pivotal time in my life, but as my own kids approach those same years, I am even more aware of the importance of personal boundaries and full reliance on the wisdom only God can provide.

5

Identity in the Rainbow Room

"Remember, you are the only Jesus some people will ever see."

One of the things I have always admired about Jerry Zeilstra is his confidence. Teenagers are quick to point out every little thing they notice about others. A lot of that is a defense mechanism to keep the attention away from their own flaws, but kids tend to forget how mean they can be, even if they are "just joking." Jerry was an easy target. Compared to all of us at the time, he was older, heavier, and hairier, and he had several quirky mannerisms, especially his unusual South Dakota dialect, leaving the "d" out of common words like "din't" and "shouln't," and his endearing habit of singing more loudly than everyone else in the room. Jerry graciously met every criticism with a smile and a laugh. It all rolled right off his back. Maybe some of this resilience came from age and years of youth-ministry experience. We would learn, though, that above all else, Jerry was certain about the love of his heavenly Father and completely comfortable with exactly who God created him to be.

I will never forget my wedding day. The weather was perfect. Over two hundred close friends and family members attended, and a great time was had by all. Following Jerry's South Dakota advice, we threw a fun party. But in the midst of the celebration, I was keenly aware of an identity crisis within myself. For the first time in my life, all my different personas had to be on display at the same time. My extended family members and old family friends, who still called me "Robbie," were there. My church friends, who knew me as both a rambunctious kid and their worship leader, were there. My high-school buddies, who I constantly tried to entertain with crass humor and foul language, were there. And my college friends, who knew an only slightly more mature version of my high-school self and seemed a little confused that I was marrying so quickly after college, were there too. I was very concerned that someone might catch a glimpse of me "not being myself." In a way, this was good for my very young marriage. My wife was the one person who had already seen all of my sides in all of the different contexts. She was my singular focus and safe haven throughout the day.

The concept of identity has changed quite a bit since my youth. Back then, American culture encouraged you to explore your feelings and experiment with discovering yourself. Today, it seems one's personal quest for self-discovery can be hijacked by groups that desire to add you to their particular cause. Beyond that, there is a growing acceptance of people "identifying" as anything they can imagine, adopting gender, ethnic, and racial groups despite their actual genetic makeup. Regardless of how traditional or revolutionary the approach, though, every person struggles throughout his or her life with the same questions: "Who am I?" and "Why am I here?"

In elementary school, several years before I met Jerry Zeilstra, I had a couple of friends whose parents gave them a lot more freedom than mine ever gave me. They were tougher than I was, played video games I wasn't allowed to play, watched movies and TV shows I wasn't allowed to watch, and even wore cool t-shirts, like the classic "I'm Bart Simpson, who the hell are you?" At that age, I was certain that all my friends had the same life experience as I did. Surely, we all went to school during the week, watched cartoons on Saturdays, went to church on Sunday mornings, and spent at least one week each summer at Vacation Bible School. I assumed that, deep down, the kids with more freedom also loved Jesus and wanted to do the "right thing." I was completely oblivious to the fact that my parents really just sheltered me from a lot of worldly things.

Ignorance was bliss. I would talk about my faith with them as a matter of course, never wondering if it was unwelcome or unusual. Some of my friends were even receptive to the idea of a "good-language club," where we would call each other out for swearing and track our failures and successes with a point system. No matter how their life experiences differed from mine, it seemed we at least had a similar set of values and beliefs. Several decades ago, that might have been closer to the truth, but not anymore.

For most of its history, the United States was a nation in which churches were some of the strongest social institutions in every town. There was a pervasive awareness of at least basic Christian doctrine. Religious values were reinforced in literature, media, blue laws, and holiday celebrations. America had a more universal sense of right and wrong based on Judeo-Christian beliefs. Today, the majority of people still know that Christians celebrate Christmas, follow the teachings of Jesus Christ, and believe in heaven. And whether people know it or not, the American conscience is still largely grounded in a Judeo-Christian moral framework. My generation, however, witnessed a shift through the post-modern era, when media content began to blur the lines between right and wrong and even Western and Eastern spiritual thought. "Live and let live" has become more than a motto. We have expanded that vision to, "Live and validate the way everyone else wants to live, or else." We determine what is right and wrong by how we feel. If it feels good in the present, it must be right. If it feels bad, it must be wrong.

Television, movies, and literature have been very successful in setting the pace of cultural change, and the church has been very unsuccessful in keeping up. It is not uncommon now for pastors to encounter adults who haven't heard the story, let alone the gospel, of Jesus Christ — ever. It is not surprising that our individual searches for identity have become so broad and extreme. We have strayed from our truest identity as children of God. Grasping that fundamental truth lays the groundwork for self-discovery and self-acceptance. This is another area where Jerry was ahead of his time. He had two approaches to helping us discover our identity. One was a matter of biblical truth, the other an exercise in introspection. Both were lessons that he taught us in the Rainbow Room.

Perhaps it was appropriate that the youth group met in the Rainbow Room. This basement annex was a large carpeted room filled with hand-me-down sofas. One continuous roller-coaster-style rainbow stripe had been painted around the entire perimeter of the otherwise sky blue, cinder block walls. For decades, the rainbow has been recognized as a symbol of diversity and identity, especially for those who have felt most marginalized. Of course, well before that, God promised Noah that he would never again destroy the Earth with a flood. He gave the rainbow as "the sign of the covenant that I have established between me and all flesh that is on the earth" (Gen. 9:17). The Rainbow Room could serve as a dual reminder of both the broad diversity in our community and the enduring faithfulness of God throughout the generations. Jerry used this space on a weekly basis to share truth with teenagers and shape our identities with fun conversations about God's Word.

The Rainbow Room occupies a prominent place in my memory of youth group. I can still smell the dusty old couches, feel my butt sink low into the weak springs, and picture the worn student Bible resting almost at eye-level on my knees. This is where we met on Wednesday evenings for confirmation classes with Jerry through seventh and eighth grade. It was the room where junior and senior high met together to sing worship songs during Sunday night youth group. I would eventually spend Sunday afternoons there too, preparing to lead that music with the praise team. The junior high would leave after music and have a separate lesson in another room. None of us left the Rainbow Room without feeling some envy toward the senior-high students who got to stay for Jerry's lesson. By the time I reached ninth grade, that space was a sanctuary for my soul. The rest of my week just didn't feel the same if I didn't spend my Sunday evenings in the Rainbow Room.

Knowing Who You Are

Jerry's lesson started with another verse worth memorizing. "But you are a chosen race, a royal priesthood, a holy nation, a people for his own possession, that you may proclaim the excellencies of him who called you out of darkness into his marvelous light. Once you were not a people, but now you are God's people; once you had not received mercy, but now you have received mercy" (1 Pet. 2:9-10). Jerry explained to us the identity that we already have as believers in Jesus Christ:

First, we are "a chosen race" and "a holy nation" claimed by God to be set apart from those who have chosen not to obey his Word. God has established Jesus as the cornerstone of the church, "and whoever believes in him will not be put to shame" (v.6). But to those who choose not to believe, Jesus becomes, "a stone of stumbling and a rock of offense" (v.8). Earlier in the same passage, Peter explains that as we come to know Jesus, we are like "living stones... being built up as a spiritual house" (v.5) around Him. Jerry was reminding us that we have a place in God's kingdom because Jesus is the sure foundation on which we can build our lives and that as we do this, we will be recognizably different from those around us.

Second, we are "a royal priesthood," who by the blood of Jesus Christ can enter the presence of God. Jerry unpacked the significance of these words to the Jewish people. In the tabernacle and then the temple of ancient Israel, the area where the ark of the covenant was kept was called the Holy of Holies. This was the dwelling place of God among his people. A curtain separated this space from the rest of the temple, and it was accessed only once a year. At that time, the high priest, sprinkled with the blood of a sacrificial lamb, would enter the Holy of Holies to atone for the sins of the people of Israel. When Jesus died on the cross and declared "It is finished!" the curtain tore from top to bottom. Now we, a royal priesthood, sprinkled with the atoning blood of Jesus, can enter the presence of God with confidence. Jerry wanted us to know that we have the ability and access to worship Jesus freely and to know Him personally.

Third, we are "a people for his own possession," giving us a purpose far beyond ourselves. Using this moment as an opportunity to review the mercy and grace we have received, Jerry taught us that we were bought for a price. God's desire for us is to "proclaim the excellencies of him who called [us] out of darkness into his marvelous light" (v.9). The passage continues with Peter urging his readers to attempt to live blameless lives. Jerry wanted to be sure we understood that our true identity — as a people set apart, with access to God the Father, and a calling to represent Him to the world — is tied directly to our witness for Jesus.

Knowing Who You Represent

I heard a story once about a man who was in a hurry driving his car. Another driver cut him off as he approached a traffic signal just turning yellow. He slammed on his brakes as the other driver barreled through the intersection and left him stuck, irate, at the red light. As the rage swelled within him, he began yelling profanities and gesturing his arms in frustration. He was so mad he hadn't noticed the police officer who pulled up behind him. The officer chirped his siren and pulled the man to the side of the road, only adding to his fury. As the officer approached his driver-side window, the man vented, "What did you pull me over for? I didn't do anything wrong! That other driver cut me off! You should have pulled him over instead!" The police officer politely replied, "I'm sorry sir, but there is a Jesus bumper sticker and a fish on the back of your car. When I saw how you were behaving, I thought that perhaps the vehicle had been stolen." This story gets to the heart of Jerry's other lesson on identity.

Jerry's lesson on 1 Peter 2 taught us some of what Scripture has to say about our identity, but understanding what the Bible says is much easier than living it out. Jerry never let us off that easy. So, he had a question to catch us off guard: "If being a Christian was a crime, and you were brought before a jury of your peers to stand trial, would there be enough evidence to convict you?" Now that is a question that will quickly flood your mind with detailed memories of how you spent your last few days! It was also a great conversation starter. Jerry asked us to consider what kinds of evidence might demonstrate that someone is a follower of Christ and explore some practical ways to approach our identity as Christians.

For one thing, he reminded us of the South Dakota lesson on choosing our friends. Those different identities that haunted me on my wedding day were each borne of the company I was keeping. In each circle of friends, I began to take on the qualities of that group. In youth group, it wasn't hard for Jerry to find examples to demonstrate this. For the most part we wore the same style of clothing, used the same slang, played the same sports, and listened to the same music. We become more like those with whom we spend our time. If our desire is to represent Jesus, we need to spend time with Him. At the simplest level, Jerry added, the word "Christian" actually means "little Christ." The more time we spend with Jesus, the better we will understand His character and the more we will begin to look like Him. The first verses of the Gospel of John tell us that Jesus Christ is the Word of God made flesh. So, how can we spend time with Jesus both to better understand who He is and to begin to see evident change in ourselves? We can spend time in His Word.

The fruits of the Spirit, that Jerry mentioned when talking about his dad, become evident in all believers. Love, joy, peace, patience, kindness, goodness, faithfulness, gentleness, and self-control are found not in trying to be like Christ, but in allowing Christ to live through us. We don't become more loving, joyful, or peaceful by trying harder to follow his Word. Rather, as we spend time with Jesus, he transforms our hearts to express His own love, joy and peace as we rely on Him. We adopt His identity as our own.

To drive it home, Jerry turned again to Scripture. "But our citizenship is in heaven, and from it we await a Savior, the Lord Jesus Christ, who will transform our lowly body to be like his glorious body, by the power that enables him even to subject all things to himself" (Phil. 3:20-21). When traveling abroad, we, as American citizens, represent the United States. Jerry wanted us to understand that, in the same way, as citizens of heaven living in this world, we represent Christ. But God calls us to an even greater role in His kingdom. "Therefore, we are ambassadors for Christ, God making his appeal through us" (2 Cor. 5:20a). Beyond representatives, we are called to be His messengers of reconciliation. Jerry closed with a powerful reminder. "Remember, you are the only Jesus some people will ever see." Once again, Jerry made the concept easy to grasp. When we identify ourselves as followers of Christ, the way we choose to live our lives will have eternal consequence.

These days, young people are encouraged to root their identity in their feelings. In extreme but well-publicized cases, parents refuse even to "assign" their children a gender at birth, hoping to avoid the imposition of societal expectations. They would prefer to allow their children freedom to decide for themselves, and they expect the rest of society to conform to their child's personal inclinations. The desire is normalization and tolerance, but these kinds of social experiments have serious implications for the child's life experience. Ultimately, these ideas are nothing more than child-centered parenting. Raising a child without a fundamental sense of identity leaves him with only his feelings as his guide, but a young person grounded in God's Word can face all kinds of adversity with peace and strength.

Jesus said it this way: "Everyone who comes to me and hears my words and does them, I will show you what he is like: he is like a man building a house, who dug deep and laid the foundation on the rock. And when a flood arose, the stream broke against that house and could not shake it, because it had been well built. But the one who hears and does not do them is like a man who built a house on the ground without a foundation. When the stream broke against it, immediately it fell, and the ruin of that house was great" (Luke 6:47-49).

Jerry knew that as we matured the simplicity of life would fade and each of us would encounter times of uncertainty and chaos. He aimed to help us build our faith on the solid foundation of the gospel of Jesus Christ. When the excitement of organized youth events, conferences, and mission trips became nothing more than a memory, Jerry wanted to be sure that we remembered who we are and why we are here. In the midst of all the identities I had constructed for myself, Jerry helped me discover my truest identity — the one that will last forever. I am a child of God.

6

Humility in Question

"The best way to learn is to ask questions, then listen."

Jerry took his job seriously. He was an avid reader and a student of his vocation, always aware of the latest research and hot topics in youth ministry. One of the most popular areas of discussion among teachers and youth leaders during the 1990s was "postmodernism." Jerry explained the postmodern era to us as a time of great skepticism, when people questioned not only authority figures, but the existence of any absolute truth. The attitude of the postmodern generation was that just because someone claimed to be an expert didn't mean he or she had thought of everything. Each of us is, after all, an expert on the sum of his own experiences. For my generation, postmodernism wasn't something new; it was all we knew. Consequently, Jerry's ministry during this time required both patience and confidence as he dealt with our doubts and "intellectual" challenges to the truth. As with most things, Jerry took our postmodern perspective in stride. He knew that if Scripture had withstood the test of time to this point, it would survive the scrutiny of late-twentieth-century teenagers.

Following the example of Jesus, Jerry pursued a spirit of humility that enabled him to teach with authority in a time when authority and absolute truth were shunned. Humility is yet another character trait of Jerry's that I sought to emulate, but never fully understood until much later in life. There were two valuable aspects to Jerry's humility. The first was his non-confrontational submission to others. Though most full-time ministers seek the role of senior pastor, Jerry remained content to make a powerful impact by quietly working with and for others. The second valuable aspect of Jerry's humility was his acceptance of the identity and role prepared for him by his heavenly Father. He invested heavily in his area of influence, studied his craft, and strove for excellence in his work.

Jerry has always been an incredibly agreeable person. No relationship was ever worth compromising for the sake of being right. As students, we often had questions about his more stinging ideas. One time, he told me and a group of my male friends that the way we treat our mothers was a good indication of how we would treat our wives someday. Thinking back, it is actually pretty funny how defensive we all became. I guess our authority-challenging was alive and well at home, too. We objected pretty seriously to Jerry's claim, but he was happy simply to let it stand, no need to argue. He just let that thought sit in our brains, knowing we would run our own internal experiments as we matured.

I had opportunities to watch Jerry interact with fellow church-staff members in similar ways. When church leadership discussed expenditures, service times, or ministry programs, Jerry sometimes had very strong, well-justified opinions, but it was not in his nature to push back against challenges aggressively, especially against those which came from authority figures. I can remember a particular meeting in which Jerry was visibly shaking as he calmly, yet emotionally expressed his displeasure with a particular decision. I don't remember the specific topic; I just remember his incredibly steady commitment to keeping peace with his brothers and sisters in Christ.

Fast forward to today. When everyone is keenly aware that a Google search will quickly yield dozens of supporting articles and polls for almost any position, Jerry is steadfast as ever in prioritizing relationships over his ego. He will gladly share his thoughts about the latest news or political issue but is equally enthusiastic to listen to yours. Even in these situations, he is happy to cede his level of expertise to yours, because he knows that a little humility goes a long way in gaining perspective into who you are as a person rather than a position.

Jerry was always willing to explore difficult questions with students. He drew his inspiration from reading the stories of Jesus in the Bible. He spoke often about how great Jesus was at patiently guiding others through conversation. One of his best examples was the story of the Samaritan woman at the well in John 4. Jesus challenged her, in a loving way, to think deeply about her faith. Several times, she reveals her entrenched view of the world. Jesus never tells her she is wrong; he just points her to the truth in his responses.

"The Samaritan woman said to him, 'How is it that you, a Jew, ask for a drink from me, a woman of Samaria?' (For Jews have no dealings with Samaritans.) Jesus answered her, 'If you knew the gift of God, and who it is that is saying to you, "Give me a drink," you would have asked him, and he would have given you living water'" (John 4:9-10).

Jesus put the relationship before the argument. Jews and Samaritans were not supposed to associate. Yet here he was, a Jew, asking a Samaritan for water. It is clear from the ensuing conversation that Jesus wasn't interested in debating racial relations, demanding obedience, or even getting a drink. In that moment, he simply wanted the woman to know that he valued her as a person. He wasn't just acknowledging her presence. He was hoping to engage directly with her soul. The whole conversation was about her relationship with Him.

"The woman said to him, 'Sir, you have nothing to draw water with, and the well is deep. Where do you get that living water? Are you greater than our father Jacob? He gave us the well and drank from it himself, as did his sons and his livestock.' Jesus said to her, 'Everyone who drinks of this water will be thirsty again, but whoever drinks of the water that I will give him will never be thirsty again. The water that I will give him will become in him a spring of water welling up to eternal life'" (vv. 11-14).

When the woman attempted to bring pragmatics and traditions into the debate, Jesus turned to things of greater significance. His asking for a drink was just a conversation starter that led to a discussion of matters of eternal consequence. He didn't just notice the woman there by the well; he cared sincerely about her future. He was carefully helping her consider a whole new perspective on life, offering her a lasting peace and purpose well beyond the mundane chores and restrictions of the day. She was intrigued.

"The woman said to him, 'Sir, give me this water, so that I will not be thirsty or have to come here to draw water.' Jesus said to her, 'Go, call your husband, and come here....' Many Samaritans from that town believed in him because of the woman's testimony, 'He told me all that I ever did.' So when the Samaritans came to him, they asked him to stay with them, and he stayed there two days. And many more believed because of his word. They said to the woman, 'It is no longer because of what you said that we believe, for we have heard for ourselves,

and we know that this is indeed the Savior of the world'"
(vv. 15-16, 39-42).

The cynic might view Jesus here as nothing more than a salesman. Perhaps he targeted this desperate woman just to promote His brand and proselytize not only her, but also as many of her friends as possible. Jerry wanted us to see the situation differently. Jesus had just revealed Himself to this woman as the Messiah. She had this experience with him alone. If she were to return to her village and tell people about the encounter, they would have surely written her off as a dreamer. But when the woman left to find her friends, Jesus stayed to validate her story. Beyond that, in a really cool demonstration of his prophecy to her, His Jewish disciples joined this collection of Samaritans to sit at Jesus' feet together, for two days! Jesus focused all his energy on this one Samaritan woman, pointed her to eternity, and supported her as she told others. As a result, the harvest was ripe and bountiful (v. 35). Jesus humbled Himself to the situation at hand and turned a passing conversation into a two-day revival meeting.

Jerry demonstrated this same kind of humility with his students. He engaged us where we were and led us to Jesus without argument or condescension. He allowed the truth of Scripture to permeate our conversations and made room for the Holy Spirit to convict our hearts. In his letter to the Romans, the Apostle Paul puts it this way, "For by the grace given to me I say to everyone among you not to think of himself more highly than he ought to think, but to think with sober judgment, each according to the measure of faith that God has assigned" (Rom. 12:3). Jerry never took advantage of his position of authority over us. He put the relationship first, pointed us to truths of eternal significance, and stood by us as we wrestled with our faith and shared it with others.

The other way that Jerry exhibited humility was in his full acceptance of his God-given identity. He never taught us this lesson directly. This is part of Jerry's humble character that became clearer to me later in life as I contemplated Jesus' parable about servants left in charge of their master's affairs. To each servant, the master entrusted a certain number of talents while he was away. When he returned, two of the servants had taken the talents and used them to produce more for the master. The master gave each of them additional responsibilities and praised them saying, "Well done, good and faithful servant" (Matt. 25:23). But, the third servant feared failure. In his false humility before his master, he buried the talent while his master was away so that he could safely return the amount he was given. To this servant, the master said, "You wicked and slothful servant! You knew that I reap where I have not sown and gather where I scattered no seed? Then you ought to have invested my money with the bankers, and at my coming I should have received what was my own with interest. So, take the talent from him and give it to him who has the ten talents.... And cast the worthless servant into the outer darkness. In that place there will be weeping and gnashing of teeth" (Matt. 25:26-30).

This parable puzzled me for a long time. It was difficult for me to understand why God, whom the master in the story represents, would be so harsh toward the servant who first tried to do no harm. This servant was clearly humble in recognizing that he could never be as shrewd as his master. He made the decision to protect his master's belongings and keep them safe from loss, and his reward for this safekeeping was eternal damnation! How could a loving God be so vengeful toward one of His servants?

I would not understand this aspect of Jerry's humility until someone helped me redefine my understanding of the word itself. For decades I lived with the understanding that humility meant not being too prideful. So, in my own endeavors, I brushed aside compliments and developed a habit of making self-deprecating comments. I became my own biggest critic and fought hard against pride to the detriment of my general confidence. I used "humility" as an excuse to stand on the sidelines, even when I knew God had given me talents and insights that could be used to contribute. My misunderstanding of humility cost me many years in which I could have been considerably more productive for the kingdom.

In graduate school, I met several fellow musicians, songwriters, and pastors who had published music and books and had developed significant followings. It was difficult for me, with my limited definition of humility, to view their success as anything other than the result of unbridled, selfish ambition. When I asked them how they addressed pride and humility in their ministries, a new definition emerged. Each of these artists and thought leaders expressed a similar sentiment. Humility has little to do with governing pride.

True humility is submitting yourself to God's design for your life. It requires an acknowledgment of the gifts He has given you and an effort to develop and use them for His glory. In that context, the elite athlete named MVP of the Superbowl who thanks God for his success is exceedingly humbler than the man who passes on an opportunity to serve his neighbor because he doesn't want to appear prideful. Though I wouldn't realize it until later, Jerry's unwavering commitment to youth ministry set a remarkable example of humility for his students, but there is no better picture of humility before God the Father, than Jesus Christ.

"So if there is any encouragement in Christ, any comfort from love, any participation in the Spirit, any affection and sympathy, complete my joy by being of the same mind, having the same love, being in full accord and of one mind. Do nothing from selfish ambition or conceit, but in humility *count others more significant than yourselves.* Let each of you look not only to his own interests, but also *to the interests of others.* Have this mind among yourselves, which is yours in Christ Jesus, who, though he was in the form of God, did not count equality with God a thing to be grasped, but emptied himself, by taking the form of a servant, being born in the likeness of men. And being found in human form, *he humbled himself by becoming obedient* to the point of death, even death on a cross. Therefore God has highly exalted him and bestowed on him the name that is above every name, so that at the name of Jesus every knee should bow, in heaven and on earth and under the earth, and every tongue confess that Jesus Christ is Lord, to the glory of God the Father" (Phil. 2:1-11, emphasis added).

The Bible tells us that each of us has been blessed with spiritual gifts that are to be used for the glory of God the Father. There is an expectation that we will replace our fear and doubt with faith in Jesus Christ, that we might rely on the power of the Holy Spirit to pursue boldly the life God intends for us. Just as his students benefited from Jerry's humble commitment to his calling, so future generations depend on ours. The world offers more opportunities for fame and material success than ever before, but God has called us to pursue Him first. Sure, He is looking for humble pastors and youth leaders, but also humble businessmen, humble teachers, humble police officers, humble engineers, humble doctors, humble cashiers — you get the idea. God will gladly use, and richly bless, all who are willing to commit their effort and work to His kingdom's purpose.

The Bible encourages us to root ourselves in the authoritative truth of Scripture. "Blessed is the man who walks not in the counsel of the wicked, nor stands in the way of sinners, nor sits in the seat of scoffers; but his delight is in the law of the Lord, and on his law he meditates day and night. He is like a tree planted by streams of water that yields its fruit in its season, and its leaf does not wither. In all that he does, he prospers" (Ps. 1:1-3). That is quite a promise in contrast to the postmodern path of self-discovery.

Despite Jerry's best effort, the postmodern movement persists. It is not surprising, with the emphasis on personal experience over authority, that we seek insight only from those who validate our views and feelings. Rather than coming to our senses and recognizing the valuable wisdom possessed by our elders and ancestors, we have replaced tested truths with the loudest voices. We continue to erode trust in our institutions, search for historical grievances, and mock belief in biblical principles.

Many people seem convinced that the world's problems can be solved by collectively focusing on a vague spirit of love and kindness. The conflicts of the past, in their view, were simply due to a lack of enlightenment and self-awareness on the part of humanity. The most noble calls for tolerance and inclusiveness have become the opposite of humility. The desire is to be recognized as a "good person." Today's selfie culture and obsession with social media branding has generated a mob-like moral competition, where individuals and corporations race to demonstrate their commitment to the most popular tribal mantras. Young people present themselves online as flatteringly as possible in an attempt to mask their shortcomings and keep up with the image of happiness they covet in the social lives of their peers. Humility has become a relic of the past.

In the PBS documentary "A People of Preservation," the narrator explains the importance of humility in Amish culture. The plain clothing and architecture of the Amish stem from a desire to exhibit Demut, the German word for humility. According to their teaching, no one should strive to stand out or consider himself higher than the community. They accept only minimal displays of self-expression among their youth and during courtship. In the rest of American society, we prize standing out. Clothing and personal possessions are used to attract attention and express importance and superiority. The Amish call this Hochmut (pride). Our culture expects everyone to care for himself. The Amish care for each other intensely. When a family barn burns down, rather than filing an insurance claim, the community meets the need together and erects a new barn within days. Few people who are not already part of the Amish church would be willing to adopt their level of austerity, but we could all benefit from considering their impressive display of humility before God and their fellow man.

Humility was a virtue that Jerry taught primarily by example. His personal practice of humility showed us what was attainable for someone who committed to putting his relationships with God and others before his own interests. He acknowledged God's call on his life to be a youth pastor and aspired to be the best youth pastor he could be. He made no apologies for his effort, accepted compliments and accolades with simple gratitude, and humbly served at Hebron Church for decades. His vision for his students, however, did not stop with the town of Penn Hills. One relationship at a time, Jerry built a thriving ministry that would grow to have an impact around the world.

7

Mission in Modes

"Don't you know what Jesus did for you?"

Having grown up in the relative isolation of the South Dakota countryside, Jerry understood the importance of helping his students expand their view of the world. He had himself experienced a life-changing trip to Haiti, where he saw true poverty for the first time. In addition to the spring and fall weekend retreats, summer camps, and ninth-grade trip to South Dakota, which largely focused on our personal relationships with Christ, Jerry planned annual "work camp" trips. Their purpose was to help us all develop an outward gaze and a heart for missions. In a stroke of genius, Jerry designed a program of work camps that rotated through a four-year cycle. His desire was that students, as they transitioned from ninth through twelfth grade, would have the opportunity to serve in four different settings: urban, rural, local, and international. Most of his former students will tell you these trips were the most transformative of all our experiences at Hebron Church. Of course, this was Jerry's intention from the outset.

There are so many great causes to support in the current age. Nonprofit organizations raise millions of dollars for very specific missions, from supporting military families to fighting animal cruelty. Crowd-sourcing platforms like GoFundMe have given people the opportunity to contribute mightily to those in need with incremental donations. Political organizations lobby for an endless variety of special interests. Nongovernmental organizations have grown into powerful global-aid networks. Businesses have shown a trend toward including charity as part of their marketing campaigns. Even our local grocery store now asks customers if they would like to round their bill up to the nearest dollar to support hospitals or cancer research. One needs to look no further than the pink ribbon of the Susan G. Komen Fund to be reminded of the powerful response humanitarian causes can solicit and the impact they can have.

Charity, important and wonderful as it is, has become big business. The unfortunate consequence of this growth is how easy participation has become without any significant involvement or sacrifice on the part of the supporter. Sending a small amount to support a cause or adding a clever hashtag to an Instagram post makes us feel altruistic and involved. Then we quickly set our phone back down on the couch, return to our favorite show on Netflix, and wait for the notifications to alert us to the fact that other people "like" the good thing we have done.

Jerry knew that true involvement required sacrifice, and sometimes, a journey. We needed to forgo the expectation of entertainment, physically experience different environments, meet people from different backgrounds, do some actual work, and expect nothing in return. We needed to learn what it means to be the hands and feet of Jesus. I cannot say with any confidence that these trips made me an expert in mission work, but I learned valuable lessons on each one.

Clairvaux Farm, Maryland

As the cycle fell, the first work camp trip in which I had the opportunity to participate was a week on a farm in Maryland. Clairvaux Farm serves as a halfway house for men and women experiencing homelessness. One of the most important requirements for employment is possession of a permanent address. This place provided an address for individuals looking to rebuild their lives. They could seek jobs and pursue careers without the stress of finding affordable housing or transportation. As their situations improved, they could return to full independence. I don't have many vivid memories from this trip aside from our shared dormitory, a couple of trips to the local dump in a pickup truck, and learning the basics of rugby from some of the older kids during our free time. What I will never forget is the scolding I got from Jerry when I made a simple little joke.

One afternoon, Jerry and I were assigned the task of repairing and tightening the hardware on some bunk beds at the facility. It wasn't a long job. There were a handful of beds in the room and the ratchet made quick work of it. As Jerry secured a bolt on the final bunk, he asked, "Is that it?" I quipped back with a smile, "Yep, that's good enough for who it's for!" Now, I know it sounds bad, but this was a joke my dad often made when we did projects around the house. It was quickly apparent to me that it made a lot more sense in the context of home, where "who it's for" is yourself! Jerry was not amused. His brow instantly furrowed and he let me have it. "Hey, don't ever say that! Don't you know what Jesus did for you?" Yikes. I blushed, "I didn't mean it like that!" Jerry was gracious of course when I explained where the phrase came from, but his response that day will echo in my brain as long as I live.

Jerry's verbal smackdown forever changed my thoughts about work and missions. The memory of that moment visits me often and affects the way I serve my church, my family, and my community. Just imagine how empty all the work and ministry we had accomplished that week in Maryland would have become if just one member of that community would have heard me say, "That's good enough for who it's for!" No amount of apologetic explanation could ever have made up for it. And when I consider the beauty of things in my life, my undeserving self, and the extent of the grace required to make sense of it all, I am certainly thankful that Jesus did not take that attitude.

When it comes to missions, your work is your witness. Jesus called his disciples to "let your light shine before others, so that they may see your good works and give glory to your Father who is in heaven" (Matt. 5:16). Jesus demonstrated this sense of purpose in everything he did while He walked the Earth. The goal was to bring glory to His Father. Any spirit of complacency or obligation will quickly be obvious to those we serve. Jerry wanted to be sure that I remembered the reason for our work that week: to bring glory to God because of the wondrous grace we have received through Jesus Christ. This was a powerful reminder in preparation for the trip the following summer.

Reynosa, Mexico

My second summer as a high-school student was our international trip to Reynosa, Mexico. Our job involved building small 9'x12' homes for poor Mexican families and leading VBS (Vacation Bible School) for the village children. This experience brought all kinds of eye-opening life lessons. The people we met were remarkably joyful despite their material poverty, which perplexed us American teenagers. We looked forward to our midweek day off to shop in the Mexican market. We joined other church groups for evening services and slept each night at a compound in Texas with air-conditioned dormitories. Even in our "sacrificial" mission work, we expected a certain minimal level of comfort. In our evening small-group discussion sessions, Jerry reminded us of the abundant blessings to which we were accustomed and how easy it was to take them for granted.

In Maryland, Jerry had taught me to *give* my very best effort for others to bring glory to God. Mexico offered the opportunity for Jerry to teach us all how to *receive* gifts properly from others for that same purpose. About halfway through the week, we were told by our leaders that the local-community members desired to prepare a meal for us to express their gratitude for our service. I had a pretty weak stomach and was not a huge fan of Mexican food to begin with. So, needless to say, I was not particularly pleased that our regularly scheduled bagged lunches that day would be replaced with local fare cooked in unsanitary conditions and with water we had been cautioned all week not to drink. Jerry knew this plan probably created at least a little anxiety in our minds.

The night before our last day of work in Reynosa, Jerry addressed his group of students. He shared the story in Luke 10 of Jesus sending his followers out to minister to others. Jesus instructed them, "Whenever you enter a town and they receive you, eat what is set before you" (Luke 10:8). Jerry then said something along these lines. "Tomorrow, the families we have been serving will be making us lunch. I want to remind you that these families feel very grateful to you for the work you have done. They don't have a lot of resources to express that gratitude, and this meal is going to cost them a great deal. So, whatever they serve you, and however you feel about it, say 'gracias,' and eat as much of it as you can. We don't want to waste their effort or take away their opportunity to give. This is their opportunity to give glory to God, and we should not deprive them of it." Jerry had a knack for anticipating our behavior and arming us with wisdom and truth in advance.

So, when the time came for lunch the next day, I lined up with everyone else to receive a plate of tamales and boiled cactus. I don't know if I was alone in feigning a smile when thanking our hosts, but the meal actually turned out to be delicious and I happily scarfed it down. I have no memory of the effect it had on my gastrointestinal system, but I will never forget the valuable lesson Jerry taught us in receiving gratitude. God calls his children to be givers, just as John 3:16 tells us He is. If we stand in the way of others in their desire to give, we not only exude a spirit of condescension, but we also stifle their ability to do what God has called them to do. This lesson, like the lesson about hard work in Maryland, has been transferable to all my relationships.

Camp Aldersgate, New York
Camp Aldersgate was a summer-camp experience for kids in the Adirondack Mountains in upstate New York. This was the least glamorous of my work-camp trips. There was not a lot to write home about other than a log cabin on the property that was so

infested with termites you could actually hear them chewing on it from several feet away! But as someone who loved to travel and brag about my unique experiences, the local work-camp year was the most unexciting and the least memorable. All we were doing was serving as helpers and counselors for a week-long summer camp. If that sounds self-centered, it's because it is! You have already figured out the lesson I learned that summer. As with all his planning decisions, Jerry intentionally included a short-distance trip every four years to remind us that "mission trips" aren't always exciting or a long way from home. There is work to be done all around us. And the point of work camp in the first place is not about us; it is about Jesus.

In the case of Camp Aldersgate, this lesson did not come directly from Jerry. I can certainly credit Jerry with setting the scene for that week, but it was the example of a fellow student from Hebron that year that has stuck with me more than anything else. Aaron was a year younger than me, but he always exhibited a great deal of maturity. Early in the week he took a liking to a camper with some pretty significant emotional and behavioral issues. For the sake of this story, we will call the camper Jack. Aaron took on the responsibility of shadowing Jack for the week. He would keep him company and help manage his behavior.

By Tuesday, things weren't going well for Jack. He had caused disruptions on more than one occasion, and the camp directors were considering expelling him from camp for the remainder of the week. This information did not sit well with Aaron. He expressed his displeasure to anyone who would listen about why they shouldn't send Jack home. I can remember sitting with Aaron on the camp lake shore one afternoon as he ranted about the camp's treatment of Jack. I had never personally encountered Jack, so I really didn't have a strong opinion one way or the other. I assumed Aaron had just formed a bond with Jack and felt defensive for his friend. In my own self-centeredness, I completely missed the genuineness of Aaron's deep, Christ-centered compassion.

The debate didn't last long. By Wednesday, Jack's parents had been called, and Aaron would never see him again. He was devastated. As we walked through the camp together during some down time, Aaron, near tears, explained to me the reasoning behind his anger. Jack had confided in Aaron over those couple of days. Aaron understood that Jack had experienced rejection in almost every social context he had ever been in, his entire life. And here, a Christian camp had only a few days of Jack's life to demonstrate to him the unconditional love of Jesus. God's love was big enough for Jack, no matter his struggles. To Aaron, it was absolutely unconscionable for the camp to tell Jack that he wasn't worth the trouble.

I was dumbfounded. Aaron was younger than me, but clearly more spiritually mature and wise beyond his sophomore status. I had no power to change the situation and no words to console him. He was right. And unbeknown to Aaron, I was embarrassingly aware of my selfishness. Much like the camp directors, I was more concerned about my own enjoyment. I had sulked around, wondering why friends had gotten more exciting assignments or why I gave up a week of summer for this mundane trip. Aaron arrived eager to share Jesus with others. He was given the least desirable assignment of us all and was sincerely upset when he was relieved of the responsibility.

In Maryland, Jerry taught me to give my best effort to bring glory to God. In Mexico, Jerry taught me to be grateful while giving others the opportunity to give. At Camp Aldersgate, I don't remember learning anything from Jerry. I was too obsessed with myself that week. Luckily, Aaron snapped me out of it with his amazing example of compassion. Aaron brought me back to the reality of missions. The primary purpose of missions is to share the gospel of Jesus Christ with others. Work camp was not supposed to be about me; it was supposed to be about Jesus. I had it all backward and was consequently missing the point, but Aaron understood this truth on an even deeper level. The camp directors that week were so concerned that Jack's behavior might keep other campers from learning about Jesus that they forgot how their actions might be perceived.

To be fair, I can't speak for Camp Aldersgate. There may very well have been extenuating circumstances or even safety concerns involved in their decision to send Jack home. I don't, in any way, mean to condemn the leaders that week. Having worked in education for many years myself, I am aware that these kinds of decisions are difficult and involve many factors. Certainly, spiritual considerations weighed heavily on their hearts as they made their determination. Nonetheless, I appreciated Aaron's insight. A decision to keep Jack at camp, share the gospel with him, and encourage other campers to pursue kindness and empathy would have spoken volumes about the depth of the love of Jesus.

A similar situation arose during Jesus' ministry. When people brought children before Jesus, the Bible says His disciples rebuked them. They likely had the same kinds of concerns, that the children would be a distraction or weren't yet old enough to understand Jesus' teachings. Jesus responded by saying, "Let the little children come to me and do not hinder them, for to such belongs the kingdom" (Matt. 19:14).

No matter what went into the camp's decision surrounding Jack, Aaron had called me out personally. My spirit all week was exactly the opposite of what it should have been. I was concerned about how I was experiencing Jesus throughout the week. I wasn't interested in suffering through any distractions or hardships. Aaron adopted the attitude that the Apostle Paul called for. "For by the grace given to me I say to everyone among you not to think of himself more highly than he ought to think, but to think with sober judgment, each according to the measure of faith that God has assigned.... Bless those who persecute you; bless and do not curse them. Rejoice with those who rejoice, weep with those who weep. Live in harmony with one another. Do not be haughty, but associate with the lowly. Never be wise in your own sight. Repay no one evil for evil, but give thought to do what is honorable in the sight of all. If possible, so far as it depends on you, live peaceably with all"

(Rom. 12:3,14-18). I am grateful for Aaron's heart that year, and I hope that Jack has since found a place of love and acceptance.

Oklahoma

The summer after my senior year of high school, Jerry took us to work camp near the Kiowa Indian Reservation in Oklahoma. This was a deviation from the urban, rural, local, international cycle, but the missionaries working with the Kiowa needed some renovations on their church and youth center that year. I was excited about this trip because I had never been on a reservation before. Working with Native Americans brought together both the rural and the international feel, so I was sure to have new experiences to talk about. Even more exciting was the prospect of a week away with my girlfriend, Michelle, who would also be on the trip. Jerry used the opportunity to offer another tidbit of wisdom on leadership and relationships.

I had turned eighteen that February, but Michelle would still be seventeen until September. Jerry pulled me aside on the bus before we even arrived. He reminded me of a few things. First, from a legal perspective, I was now an adult and Michelle was a minor. He wanted to make sure I knew that public displays of affection would not be tolerated. As far as he was concerned, as an adult, I was considered a leader on the trip and Michelle was a student. He was also clear that aside from the example we might set for the rest of the group, he wanted our hearts to be focused on the task at hand. We had both a team purpose and a spiritual purpose in Oklahoma. Work camp trips were not designed to foster young love. Besides, he pointed out, any relationship worth its salt ought to be able to withstand a week apart.

Michelle and I did pretty well. In the age before cell phones we took a few opportunities to pass notes to each other. Part way through the week Michelle received news that her dog had to be put down. I at least had the chance to console her in that. We also had a few chances during breaks to catch up and chat. If Jerry ever felt that there was any lingering, a knowing glance was all it took to get us back on track. When it comes to our testimony, Jerry knew the importance of pursuing holiness. As the King James puts the words of Paul, "Abstain from all appearance of evil" (1 Thess. 5:22, KJV).

I know that to many this all may sound prudish, but I remember the lesson of that week for a couple of reasons. First, by not having the pressure of keeping each other's attention every moment of every day, we both were more participatory and developed even deeper friendships with our classmates. Michelle took a risk on an unforgettable quad ride with one of the local kids that I probably would have discouraged. I hung out with my buddies more during this last summer that we would spend together. Second, we had the opportunity to realize that we didn't need to sacrifice everything else in life, like friendships or faith, to be in a meaningful romantic relationship. Lastly, by heeding Jerry's advice, we modeled a healthy relationship to others and avoided becoming a distraction to the team.

A lot of young people in relationships are so caught up in their feelings that they lose sight of how little attention they are giving to the rest of their relationships. Michelle and I were never very public with affection anyway, but Jerry helped us avoid that behavior. Ultimately, the moments we did share on that trip were more special, and we had space to grow in our relationships with Christ even as we grew closer together. It is not surprising that this idea resurfaced in the Scripture passage we chose for our wedding five years later.

"For this reason I bow my knees before the Father, from whom every family in heaven and on earth is named, that according to the riches of his glory he may grant you to be strengthened with power through his Spirit in your inner being, so that Christ may dwell in your hearts through faith—that you, being rooted and grounded in love, may have strength to comprehend with all the saints what is the breadth and length and height and depth, and to know the love of Christ that surpasses knowledge, that you may be filled with all the fullness of God" (Eph. 3:14-19). Our marriage is successful today because Jerry helped us put Christ at the center of our relationship from the very beginning.

When it comes to missions, your walk is your witness. If the purpose of our team was to demonstrate the love of Christ to the Kiowa community by giving up a week in the summer to improve their facilities, it was imperative that our own hearts be focused on Jesus. Focusing on myself could have ruined the team's witness in Maryland by my making fun of the work there.

Focusing on myself could have ruined my witness in Mexico by my rejecting the hospitality of the community there. Focusing on myself in New York could have ruined my witness by my showing no compassion or care for the students there. Focusing on myself in Oklahoma could have ruined my witness by my showing everyone that I valued Michelle more than Jesus. You would think these lessons in conjunction with my newly minted high-school diploma would suggest I had finally matured. One more work-camp test remained.

Atlanta, Georgia

The mission trip to Atlanta would be my last with Hebron's youth group. I returned after my first year of college to make the trip as a leader. Jerry had long been at work to develop leadership qualities in me, and Atlanta would provide a unique opportunity for me to learn about myself in the mission field. The Safe House Outreach provides clothing, meals, and services to Atlanta's homeless population. The people serving there used each interaction as an opportunity to share the gospel. The director who oversaw our group was a man of great faith. On our day off that week to explore the local mall, he encouraged us to keep our eyes and our wallets focused on "things that would be pleasing to the Lord." His statement resonated with us because after only a few days working among the poor, we were about to walk back into the pit of material desire, a shopping mall. When we arrived at the mall, Jerry stressed what the director said and turned us loose to enjoy our time wisely.

The mall was somewhat of a proving ground for me personally that week. As an official leader for the first time, I was beginning to consider the needs of the students with me rather than my own, but I was still relatively timid as an authority. So, I spent the time shopping alongside some of the younger kids, joking with them, and getting to know them better. I'm sure Jerry felt pretty comfortable with my ability to chaperone a few students walking around the mall. I was feeling pretty good about my effort. When the time came to show them true leadership, though, I failed pretty miserably.

Near the end of the week, the facility director explained that we would spend a day in face-to-face ministry with the homeless on the streets of Atlanta. We would depart the Safe House in groups of three or four students, seek out homeless men and women, and look for opportunities to share the gospel with them. The one directive he gave us was to go out with empty pockets. The people we would encounter, he said, would likely ask if we had any money, and it was better if we could answer honestly that we did not. The story of Acts 3 was playing in my head:

"Now Peter and John were going up to the temple at the hour of prayer, the ninth hour. And a man lame from birth was being carried, whom they laid daily at the gate of the temple that is called the Beautiful Gate to ask alms of those entering the temple. Seeing Peter and John about to go into the temple, he asked to receive alms. And Peter directed his gaze at him, as did John, and said, 'Look at us.' And he fixed his attention on them, expecting to receive something from them. But Peter said, "I have no silver and gold, but what I do have I give to you. In the name of Jesus Christ of Nazareth, rise up and walk!" And he took him by the right hand and raised him up, and immediately his feet and ankles were made strong. And leaping up, he stood and began to walk, and entered the temple with them, walking and leaping and praising God. And all the people saw him walking and praising God, and recognized him as the one who sat at the Beautiful Gate of the temple, asking for alms. And they were filled with wonder and amazement at what had happened to him" (Acts 3:1-6).

I had the perfect plan. If anyone asked us for money, I would respond like Peter, look him or her in the eye, and say, "We don't have any money to give you, but we do have Jesus!" This man or woman would then ask for a full explanation of the gospel, which I would clearly convey. He or she would then immediately acknowledge a need for Christ, and I would be a missionary hero to the teenagers under my direction. I would make the same kind of impact on them that Jerry and other former students of his had made on me! Yes, I had the perfect plan.

Jerry assigned a small group of students to me that morning, and we took to the streets. Once again, I was certain of Jerry's confidence in me, even though I hadn't shared my plan. We set out toward the center of town to confront the homeless with the life-changing gospel of Jesus Christ.

We hadn't gone very far when a man approached us on the sidewalk. We were wearing our Safe House Outreach t-shirts. Throughout the summer, visiting youth groups walked the streets for Safe House on the same assignment. The man was filthy. His shirt was stretched out and covered in paint stains. He was missing several teeth and hadn't shaved in weeks.

"Hey, you got any money? I could really use your help. Whatever you can give, man."

This was the moment I had been waiting for. All eyes on me. Mind running wild. The Holy Spirit clearly whispering, "Go on, Rob. 'We don't have money, but we have Jesus!' Say it. Go on."

As the visions of missionary glory flashed before my eyes, I fumbled, "Uh, no sorry, no money. Come on guys." And my small group of students shuffled along behind me.

Now, thankfully, given this evangelism drill occurred on a weekly basis, we probably weren't the first or last group from the Safe House that this man encountered, but I was instantly ashamed of my lack of courage. My faith had been challenged, and I had failed the simplest of tests. As we continued down the street, I saw other teams engaged in conversation with men and women. I have little memory of the next couple of hours. We wandered around making small talk with people we passed, waiting for the time to be over. I could not get past my inability to step up to the plate and vocalize my faith. Jerry had faith in me to lead others that day, and I couldn't even muster enough faith in Jesus to share Him with a stranger. I felt like Peter hearing the rooster crow, exposed as an impostor.

If I could travel back in time, I don't think I would trade that moment, but I should have talked more with Jerry about it. Maybe others had similar experiences that day. At a minimum he would have given me some understanding words of wisdom. Instead, I returned home deflated without that benefit. I have learned a lot about evangelism since that summer. I have built upon the experience that Jerry gave me to learn some important lessons.

As I had learned from prior trips, missions are about Jesus, not ourselves. It is impossible to participate in mission work and not learn something about oneself and the broader world. More often than not, those returning from mission trips will talk about all they learned and saw, much as I have in this chapter. When we are on mission for Christ, it cannot be about ourselves. I failed in Atlanta because I had a plan to bring glory to myself through my work. My goal was to prove that I had the same knowledge as the apostles. I discovered that true faith would have caused me to leave the results to Jesus. I could have viewed that man with the compassionate eyes of Jesus rather than my own self-conscious eyes. I could have shared the love of Jesus and left the burden of conviction to the Holy Spirit.

Missions are also about relationships and not objectives. When Jesus sent His seventy-two disciples out to prepare the way for His ministry, he told them to find those who were receptive and then, "remain in the same house, eating and drinking what they provide.... Do not move around from house to house" (Luke 10:7). Jesus didn't want His followers to simply travel around shouting, "Repent, the end is near!" He encouraged them to build real relationships and invest in the lives of others. The downside to short-term mission trips is the limited time in which you can truly get to know other people. Perhaps my plan to force the gospel on the man in Atlanta would have impressed him, but more than likely he would have shrugged me off as someone who really didn't care about him in the first place.

Missions are more than humanitarian effort. The day we were sent out into the streets to meet homeless people and speak with them about Jesus was unique. Most mission trips and organizations have a stated desire to spread the love of Jesus, but a direct focus on evangelism is minimal. We rely heavily on doing good works and hope that the gospel will be caught by onlookers. But with the growth of secular humanitarian organizations, good works have become a more generic expectation of a virtuous life. Involvement is encouraged for everything from improving your mood, to your college applications, to your personal or corporate brand. What sets missions apart is the motivation that we are called to witness to the power of Christ in our lives as the sole motivation for our good works.

During my work-camp trips we repaired bunk beds, painted buildings, and constructed homes. Facilitating Vacation Bible School for the Mexican children at least allowed for a group presentation of the gospel. But in Atlanta, when the time came to, "make a defense to anyone who asks you for a reason for the hope that is in you...with gentleness and respect" (1 Pet. 3:15), I discovered I was woefully unprepared.

Jeff Vandersandt, in his book *Gospel Fluency,* stresses the importance of telling people about Jesus as the reason for your good works. The world is filled with people who are disappointed in themselves and feel that something is missing in their lives. They have read the same articles about changing their attitude or performing random acts of kindness. If we don't explain what Jesus did for us as our motivation, those we encounter are left to assume that they are still just flawed folk, unable to live up to the example of other more disciplined, more prosperous, or simply more fortunate people.

Jesus Christ was the ultimate humanitarian, who has given us the opportunity to participate in His cause. The Bible tells us that "all have fallen short." "There is no one who is good, not even one." We are all sinners, separated from God. That is the feeling of lacking that we all share. But God demonstrated his love in this. While we were still sinning Christ died for us. He didn't give us his spare change. He didn't build us a house. He didn't chat with us for a while on the street. He died for us. Despite our undeserving nature, He died to give us the opportunity to be reconciled with God and to satisfy the eternal longing in the hearts of all humanity.

Those of us who have received His grace know that there is nothing more valuable or life changing. Jesus did not spend his time on earth working to raise people's standard of living or challenge political structures. He spent His life pointing others to His Father. We are motivated to do the same because of what He did for us. No matter how many mission trips we make to improve the lives or facilities of others, if we leave Jesus in the background, we rob Him of the glory He deserves and deprive others of eternal peace and security.

Jerry hoped that work-camp trips would take students beyond our fun, fellowship-focused youth-group meetings and outings. He wanted us to see how we could be active ministers of the gospel to others, not just church consumers. In my case, this turned out to be a challenging proposition. I am grateful for Jerry's persistence. These trips confronted my selfishness head on and taught me valuable lessons about service, graciousness, compassion, teamwork, and the necessity of the gospel of Jesus Christ at the center of it all.

8

Leadership and Discipleship Over Dinner

"Walk with me."

I can still remember where I was standing, in the hallway just outside the Rainbow Room, when Jerry gave me the speech. After a typical evening of my goofing off at youth club, the weekly program for first through eighth graders, Jerry pulled me aside and made sure he had my undivided attention. "You know, Rob, it bothers me when you act up during our lesson times because I see great leadership potential in you." Now, I'm not sure I have ever fully embraced that belief about myself, and I know for a fact I wasn't the only student who received Jerry's "leadership speech" over the years, but I do know that Jerry's blunt remark sparked a sense of responsibility in my heart and, maybe for the first time in my life, inspired me to consider taking some steps toward emotional and spiritual maturity.

There is a temptation today to view leadership as simply developing a personal following. The world is smaller than ever. YouTube, Facebook, Instagram, and Twitter give everyone the opportunity to broadcast their thoughts and personalities to the entire planet. This level of connectivity generates a desire in each of us well beyond Andy Warhol's predicted fifteen minutes of fame. We want to have a global impact. Personal branding is the name of the game. Each of us wants to give voice to a unique message that cuts through the noise, catches someone's attention, and goes viral. Then we might secure our place as a *thought-leader,* an *influencer!* This style of modern influence, though, could be better characterized as a desire for celebrity. Digital platforms create the false impression that every opinion, no matter how uninteresting, is meaningful and important. The emphasis is on being seen and heard rather than truly being followed.

Jerry taught us a view of leadership that was clearly evident in the words and actions of Jesus: leadership through service. Jesus said that He came to do the will of His Father (John 4:34, John 6:38). He submitted Himself fully to the Father's plan for His life. He left His place in heaven to come to earth as a baby. He prioritized His heavenly Father's authority over the authority of his earthly parents when they found Him teaching in the temple (Luke 2). He never sought attention for His own sake. He credited the Father for the miracles He performed. His teaching pointed people to the glory of the Father and His kingdom (Matthew 5-7). And, He subjected Himself to the cross to fulfill the Law. Personal influence and celebrity were never Christ's objectives, but because of His submission to the Father's will, His name has been exalted above every other name (Phil. 2:1-11).

Jerry did his best to model servant leadership. He never drew attention to himself, but always pointed our focus to Jesus. In his teaching, he focused on Scripture. In his demeanor, he embodied a spirit of grace. In his correction, he demonstrated love. In his expectations, he encouraged holiness. Jerry wielded influence with us not through personality or charisma, but because we witnessed his authentic steadfastness and faithfulness in following his personal Lord and Savior. We desired the same kind of faith we saw in Jerry, a fellow disciple of Jesus. When Jerry affirmed leadership qualities in me that day, I was eager to prove myself, but I soon discovered that I had a lot to learn about being a leader.

Jerry had a specific leadership role in mind for me. He knew my parents had recently bought me my first guitar and I had started taking lessons at the local music store. Jerry had a vision for a youth praise team and thought maybe I could be one of the guitarists. Youth group included a time of music and worship that focused our hearts and bridged the gap between the high-energy games and the quiet lesson time. When I first started attending youth group, Jerry would project the lyrics on the wall with transparencies and we would sing along to recordings on compact discs played through a stereo. Jerry had a strong desire to switch to live music because he believed that our worship should be an authentic expression of the body of believers gathered in that room. God created us as we were and wanted us to raise our own joyful noise to Him. So, Jerry was willing to take a risk on a few very novice musicians and singers to lead the youth group in worship.

We weren't very good. We would arrive a little early for youth group, select a few songs, and practice playing them together as the other students arrived and started playing games in another part of the church. When we felt ready, we would join everyone else for the tail end of "Birdie on the Perch" or "Upset the Fruit Basket." Some weeks we would still be rehearsing when the games ended and a crowd of students gathered outside the door. That made us feel even more special. The responsibility gave us all a sense of importance and an active role in Jerry's ministry, but it also provided additional opportunities for mistakes and lessons on leadership. It doesn't take long for a little attention and power to inflate a teenager's ego. Having the power to choose the songs I liked, deciding when to open the doors to the youth room, and enjoying the rapt attention of a crowd of my peers made me believe that not only did I deserve Jerry's generous assessment of my abilities, but *I* was also really *someone worth following!*

Leading music quickly became a pursuit for more attention. Even as I pretended to be humble by deflecting compliments, I enjoyed receiving them. Anytime we attended a youth retreat, I would rush to learn the most-popular songs from that weekend and demonstrate that I could figure them out and play them too, after only a few hours of being home. I developed feelings of jealousy toward my fellow musicians and arrived at the assumption that I could do it all. At most youth conferences, the lead singer played the guitar at the same time. I practiced that skill until I was able to do both and take over singing on Sunday nights. I imagined our little band playing at youth retreats, writing music, recording albums, and touring the country. I lusted after the accolades of adults and peers alike as they noticed my improvement and contributions, and I struggled with bitterness when people acknowledged talent in others. Worst of all, though, was my propensity to criticize other worship services and leaders. I did my very best to maintain a godly veneer, but Jerry was wise enough to see through it and call me out.

Jerry used my role in leading worship to teach me two very important leadership principles. First, just as Jesus pointed to the Father, the object of our worship should be Jesus Christ alone. One Sunday, we selected a popular song that we had sung several times as a group. I never really cared for it, but others on the team did. When we finished singing it together, in the middle of the worship set, I asked the whole group of kids, "Do you guys even like this song, or should we stop singing it?"

I was looking for validation of my personal opinion, nothing more. There was no question about the truth of the lyrics or its appropriateness for the moment. No, I was just blatantly redirecting the focus of fifty people from Jesus to myself. Jerry found me near the end of the night and took me to task in his typically kind and gracious way. He recapped what happened, laughed, and asked, "What was that about?" He reminded me that no one in the room was there to worship me and that I was offering my gifts to an audience of One.

I learned the other principle of leadership as part of a lesson that Jerry taught to the group on Romans 12. Music was an important part of our weekly gatherings both with the youth and also for Sunday services. I am not really sure how exclusive it was to the 1990s, but a trend developed among Christians to refer to music itself as "worship." My fellow youth musicians and I were known as a "worship team." We called the lead singer of a "worship team" the "worship leader." When we discussed the quality of "the worship" at a camp or after youth group, we meant the music, and only the music. This is still very common today, especially when people debate their preferences for "traditional worship" (meaning mostly mid-nineteenth century hymns) or for "contemporary worship" (meaning all kinds of different things, but probably involving a drum set).

Music is a valid, biblical expression of praise and worship, but Jerry wanted to dispel the notion that our worship began and ended with the weekly music set. He began the lesson by asking us what our definition of worship was. We provided the predictable responses: singing, prayer, giving thanks, admiring creation, going to church. Then he had us turn in our bibles to Romans 12, and we read, "I appeal to you therefore, brothers, by the mercies of God, to present your bodies as a living sacrifice, holy and acceptable to God, which is your *spiritual worship*" (Romans 12:1, emphasis added). He asked us what we thought it meant to present our bodies "as living sacrifices." We fished for the words we thought Jerry was waiting to hear. "Staying pure?" "Letting God work through us?" "Trying to do the right thing?" He quietly affirmed our responses, then explained that he wanted us to understand that we don't worship God by being religious, going to church, and singing. True worship involves a relationship of surrender to Jesus. Jerry's second lesson complemented the first.

If I had any hope of developing as a leader of worship, not only would I need to remember to keep Jesus the central focus, but I would also need to strive to do that all the time. Even as a young man, I had already noticeably compartmentalized my life. In my search for identity, it was easy to think of my leadership role as a temporary position of importance during the music time. Scripture calls all of us to a higher standard. Jesus desires us to present all of who we are to Him as a living sacrifice. I would come to discover that not only were Jerry and Jesus paying attention, but that my peers also noticed when the person I was during the week didn't match the "leader" I was on Sunday. As a worship leader and a young man, I needed to consider how much I had truly submitted to Christ in all areas of my life. Otherwise, I was guaranteed to squander any influence or impact I might have.

As I transitioned into my high-school years, Jerry created a new program as a part of his ministry that he called Leadership/ Discipleship, or "LD." This was a core group of around thirty hand-picked students grades nine through twelve. He met with the group once a month to dig deeper into Scripture, discuss the business of the youth ministry, and have us hold each other accountable. In addition to the monthly meetings, Jerry led an annual retreat to a farm in West Virginia where we had the opportunity to discuss some long-term plans for the youth calendar and set goals for our own growth and development.

LD meetings started with prayer and dinner together. Then we would gather around in the living room to discuss life and God's Word. Most of the time, we met at Jerry's house, but sometimes one of our families would host. It was in the context of these gatherings that I remember hearing some of Jerry's wisest insights.

During one of the first Leadership/Discipleship meetings that I attended, Jerry stood up after dinner and said, "Walk with me." Then he walked right out his front door. The rest of us halted our conversations and shared puzzled glances, then stood up and followed him outside. Jerry lived on an old farm of several acres in the middle of Penn Hills. He strolled out along the driveway, around the barn, up a path, across a small clearing at the top of the hill, then down the hill back to the front door.

He didn't say another word after his initial invitation to join him.

Jerry was a pretty active guy, so he hiked at a brisk pace. Several students kept up with him from start to finish. Others straggled way behind, lost in conversation with one another. As I recall, some of the guys were running back and forth tossing a ball or Frisbee to each other as they leapfrogged along. When everyone finally returned to the house, we took our seats around the living room again. Most of us were a little befuddled by the exercise that seemed like some kind of warm-up lap around the yard. Jerry quickly hinted at an explanation.

"What do you think it means to walk with Jesus?" This was the first Jerry had said anything since, "Walk with me," so it didn't take us long to make the connection. Jerry proceeded to break down the different ways in which we had "walked with him" for the previous fifteen minutes. Some of us stayed by his side, attempting to match his pace and remain within range of his direct influence. Some of us kept Jerry in view just enough to stay on track while keeping enough distance to maintain some level of privacy. And, some of us squeezed as much fun as we could out of the adventure with only a loose connection to the rest of the group.

Much like the parable of the sower, Jerry's "Walk with me" illustration placed people into categories. Those who stuck with Jerry were like faithful disciples of Jesus, intentional in their pursuit of Christ. Those who lagged a bit behind, out of Jerry's earshot, were like Christians eager to follow Jesus, but not willing to surrender their entire lives over to His guidance. The group playing Frisbee, who took the longest to make it back to the house, represented those who didn't want to miss out on "the good life," enjoying their own pursuits, but complying closely enough with the general direction of Jesus' teaching not to be considered morally bad.

Truth be told, I had heard about this demonstration a year before from my older sister. I had intentionally stayed right by Jerry's side so I could proudly claim to have walked with Jerry, "the right way." I did not admit this openly that evening, but I had inadvertently created an additional category. The metaphor found in my actions was possibly the worst.

I knew the plan and manipulated the illustration in an effort to make *myself* look good. I shunned my fun-loving friends playing Frisbee so they could shamefully realize that I better understood what it meant to "walk with Christ." How embarrassing. I represented the Pharisees, the crowd of believers who expend great effort to be viewed by others as righteous. There was no actual surrender in my walk that evening. I thought I could earn merit through my own actions, but instead I demonstrated to myself that I still had a lot more growing up to do.

As the years progressed, Jerry used Leadership/Discipleship to challenge us directly with the Word of God. He helped us graduate from our childhood understanding of Scripture as a collection of great stories and restrictive rules, to viewing it instead as a direct source for wisdom and relationship with

Jesus Christ. He taught from hard-hitting scripture passages that pushed us to consider the implications of walking with Christ. Many of these passages stand out in my heart today because of Jerry's willingness to tackle these ambitious topics with argumentative teenagers. His goal was to create leaders by discipling us through God's Word.

On my first Leadership/Discipleship retreat, Jerry centered his lessons on the theme of integrity. "What does it mean to be a person of integrity?" he asked. The group came up with answers like honesty, reliability, and trustworthiness. Jerry had us turn in our Bibles to Psalm 15.

"O Lord, who shall sojourn in your tent? Who shall dwell on your holy hill? He who walks blamelessly...does what is right...speaks truth in his heart...does not slander with his tongue...does no evil to his neighbor...honors those who fear the Lord...does not put out his money at interest...does not take a bribe against the innocent. He who does these things shall never be moved" (Psalm 15).

We worked through this checklist of attributes to self-assess. Jerry explained that to be a leader, one had to be a person of integrity. But before we assumed he was just offering another list of lofty expectations, Jerry wanted us to understand that with the ambition for integrity came the promises of dwelling on God's holy hill and never being moved.

At one memorable LD meeting Jerry asked us if we could say that we were truly "sold out for Jesus." Again, he let the

Bible do the talking. "Whoever does not bear his own cross and come after me cannot be my disciple" (Luke 14:27). After all, "Greater love has no one than this, that someone lay down his life for his friends" (John 15:13). Were we really prepared to give up our lives for the sake of others? Jesus calls us to complete surrender.

At another meeting Jerry pressed the issue of holiness. If we were truly a people set apart by God, he wanted us to consider if we actually looked any different. He wanted us to think about what kind of fruit was evident in our lives thanks to the influence of Jesus. "[B]ut as he who called you is holy, you also be holy in all your conduct, since it is written, 'You shall be holy, for I am holy'" (1 Pet. 1:15-16). And the best way to pursue holiness, he explained, was to read, study, and memorize God's Word. "I have stored up your word in my heart, that I might not sin against you" (Ps. 119:11).

Jerry certainly didn't want us to miss the fact that God loved us. "See what kind of love the Father has given to us, that we should be called children of God; and so we are" (1 John 3:1). He wanted us to know that God sent His son even though we didn't deserve it, "but God shows his love for us in that while we were still sinners, Christ died for us" (Rom. 5:8). And, he loved the illustration of God rejoicing over his children: "[H]e will rejoice over you with gladness; he will quiet you by his love; he will exult over you with loud singing" (Zeph. 3:17b). Even as we wrestled with sin and doubt, Jerry reminded us that

Jesus didn't come to condemn, but that we might "have life and have it abundantly" (John 10:10).

In addition to scriptural lessons, Jerry developed us with more practical training. He taught us to reflect and evaluate our efforts. He asked for our input on recently held events, and we discussed ways to improve in the future. He taught us to lead by example. The Leadership/Discipleship team was expected to arrive early to youth group and also be the last to leave. Oftentimes, that meant a few of us would linger for deeper conversation about the evening's lesson. He taught us to empathize. Knowing that we were a bunch of self-obsessed adolescents, he encouraged us to "listen with your eyes." People aren't always going to verbalize their need for love and acceptance. It was up to us to notice those needs and make attempts to meet them through ministry.

Jerry grew his youth ministry by training a small army of students to minister alongside him. He ended each meeting with the same question: "Anything else for the good of the order?" Even in asking that question, Jerry made us feel valued and integral to the program. Working as a team brought us closer together. We encouraged each other at school, invited friends to join us for youth group, and took ownership over the experience. As we approached our senior year, he asked us to begin training our replacements. He used to say, "You can tell how big an impact you have had, by how much you are missed when you are gone." As a practical matter, he wanted to make sure the ministry could continue from year to year, but he also wanted us to consider our influence on the younger students. Jerry had helped us identify our gifts and roles in God's kingdom. Now it was our responsibility to do the same for others.

9

Love Under a Tractor

"When God wants to teach you something,

He often takes you on a journey."

Jerry often told us that he loved us. Sometimes at the close of a lesson. Sometimes when the group returned from a summer trip. Sometimes when it was time for lights out after a late night on a retreat. Unfortunately, in our present age of fear and suspicion, I will admit that probably sounds a little creepy. I never read any nefarious motives into these words though, because there weren't any. Throughout his years in ministry, Jerry had seen students walk away from the faith, die in car accidents, overdose on drugs, and commit suicide. This wasn't fluff or manipulation. He wanted each of us to know that he cared about us, that we mattered, and that we were genuinely loved.

Far too often in popular culture, love is associated with physical attraction. We live in a highly sexualized society. Sex is used to ignite our passions in advertising, music, and movies. An attractive man or woman on a billboard naturally catches our eye. Song lyrics cause our minds to drift to memories of emotional experiences and dream up new desires. We know that two characters in a movie have made a real love connection when their first date goes so well they head straight for the bedroom. Television series targeting teenagers make sexuality the central theme. Even Disney classics teach every princess to find her "Prince Charming," as if appearance and romance are the hallmarks of a great relationship. All of this sets us up for major disappointment when we discover that our temporary feelings are only part of the equation.

Jerry taught us how to understand the multidimensional concept of love properly. To begin, he wanted us to understand that love is more than just a feeling. The romantic love depicted in media is all based on people's feelings. Jerry explained how feelings are fleeting and romance is very difficult to perpetuate. He offered the sound dating advice that we shouldn't set any precedents we didn't plan to maintain. First impressions like opening the door for a girl or buying expensive gifts on Valentine's Day are romantic gestures that are sure to fan the flames of young love, but if you forget to meet that same expectation in the future, you are digging your own grave of disappointment. So, just be yourself from the beginning and your relationships will be more genuine.

True love, Jerry said, is not a feeling; it is a decision. Love is not a decision about whether or not one feels attraction for another. Love is a decision to put the interests of another before your own. The trouble with relying on feelings to identify love, especially as a young adult, is the powerful hormones filling your veins with lustful desires. It is easy to confuse these new kinds of thoughts for something meaningful because we have been conditioned to identify love as an emotional sensation. Viewing love as a decision, however, helps a young man clearly identify the difference between love and lust. Jerry wouldn't shy away from the importance of romantic feelings, but they were not at the core of a loving relationship.

Jerry's teaching on love went deeper than just the juxtaposition of feelings and decisions. During one season of youth group, Jerry led us through an exploration of the four loves as defined by the Greeks and popularized by C.S. Lewis. Each of us already has some natural awareness that love is a deep and complex topic. Obviously, there are differences between the way we love our parents and siblings, our friends, our partners, and our children. The Greeks helped break this down with unique terms for each: *storge, philia, eros,* and *agape.* I have since come to discover there are even more forms of love, but Jerry ensured that we had a solid understanding of these four.

We first learned about *storge*, the kind of love that is shared between those with a common bond, especially within families. This is the love that parents have for their children and siblings have for one another. A great way to understand this kind of love might be to consider the jokes that people make about Thanksgiving gatherings. If we haven't done it ourselves, we have all encountered someone who rolls his eyes and laments having to survive dinner with the family. We complain about the idiosyncrasies of our extended family members and the inevitable conflicts that we can expect when everyone feels comfortable enough to be himself. To put a more positive spin on it, *storge* love is the source of our freedom to say anything among family. We know that we can let loose and they "have to accept us because we are family."

Philia, the second form of love, describes brotherly love. This is the feeling of goodwill and true friendship that we experience with our fellow man. William Penn, the founder of the Commonwealth of Pennsylvania, named his first planned city Philadelphia, "the city of brotherly love." He envisioned a place characterized by friendship and kindness, both staples of his Quaker religious beliefs. Jerry pointed us to the example of David and Jonathan in 1 Samuel. The two men were fast friends who cared greatly about the well-being of the other. *Philia* love could use a comeback. Our cultural messaging makes it difficult for young people to form strong bonds with same-sex friends without questioning the nature of those relationships and their own identities. Jerry stressed the importance of such relationships and often reminded us that our "longest lasting relationships would be those rooted in Christ."

The third form of love required the least explanation and commanded our most rapt attention. Eros is the Greek word for romantic love. Jerry walked us through Scripture to show us God's plan for sexual love. God told Adam and Eve, "Be fruitful and multiply" (Gen. 1:28). He used his creation of Adam and Eve to set the precedent that "a man shall leave his father and his mother and hold fast to his wife, and they shall become one flesh" (Gen. 2:24). Jesus set the high standard for marriage when He taught on this same verse in Matthew 19 and when He addressed the topic of adultery in the Sermon on the Mount (Matt. 5:27-32). Jerry never married, but he made sure that we knew that *eros* is an essential part of every marriage relationship. He encouraged each of us to remain pure for the sake of experiencing the kind of marriage relationship God desired for us in the future.

In a way, each of these forms of love is added to our life as we mature. As children we are content in the *storge* love of our family. As we grow up and engage in our communities, we search for *philia* in the form of great friendships. Then, as we approach adulthood, *eros* fuels our desire for greater intimacy. The final form of love, however, is the kind of love we seek in the deepest caverns of our heart. To explain *agape* love, Jerry had us turn in our bibles to Paul's first letter to the Corinthians.

"Love is patient and kind; love does not envy or boast; it is not arrogant or rude. It does not insist on its own way; it is not irritable or resentful; it does not rejoice at wrongdoing, but rejoices with the truth. Love bears all things, believes all things, hopes all things, endures all things" (1 Cor. 13:4-7).

This passage is often read at weddings because its description of love appeals to our highest ideals. Each of us desires to be fully known, yet accepted despite our flaws. *Agape* love is unconditional.

Agape is the truest form of love that we can experience or express. It transcends emotions and responsibilities. Ultimately, *agape* is the decision to put the life of another ahead of one's own. Jesus put it this way, "Greater love has no one than this, that someone lay down his life for his friends" (John 15:13). Jerry provided a couple of illustrations of that kind of love over the course of my time with him. One was his personal testimony of the love of his sister that led to his decision to follow Christ. The other was an heroic, selfless act of his own that demonstrated to me how much he loved his students.

On a fall evening in October 1970, the Zeilstra kids were preparing to depart for youth group. Thirteen-year-old Jerry hadn't finished his homework for the next day and wasn't particularly excited about going, but a friend was arriving soon to pick him up along with his sisters Joyce and Ethel. Their parents were visiting the farm of their aunt and uncle to help attach the corn picker to their tractor for the harvest. Shortly before it was time to leave, Jerry noticed the gate separating the milking cows from the dry cows was open and the animals had escaped.

Partly eager to take advantage of this legitimate excuse to avoid youth group, Jerry lit out for the family's Case tractor, fired it up, and tore off into the pasture. He shifted quickly through first, second, and third gears to head off the cattle. In his excitement, he took the bend on the terrace too quickly. The narrow front tires couldn't handle the torque of the top-heavy machine. The tractor rolled over. In an instant, Jerry found himself in extreme danger, trapped underneath the tractor between the seat and the axle. He could hear his sisters yelling from the yard as they realized they had just witnessed a likely fatal accident.

Joyce and Ethel arrived as quickly as they could to find Jerry pinned and unable to move. He had suffered a broken collarbone and ankle, and the top half of his left ear had been torn off. The throttle knob pressing into his stomach had, very fortunately, missed crushing his chest or pelvis. Oil and fluids were already pooling around his head, and his sisters knew the situation was dire. Jerry was conscious enough to provide instructions. They would need a jack and chain to lift the tractor and water in case a fire broke out.

Joyce hurried back to the house to call for help. The neighbor was already on the party line and agreed to bring his loader tractor over at once to help. Joyce then called for an ambulance. Meanwhile, Ethel remained by Jerry's side as he slipped in and out of consciousness. Jerry pleaded, "Ethel, you have to get away. This thing could explode at any second." Ethel wasn't having it. She said, "No, I love you too much. If something happens to you, it will happen to me, too." Ethel stayed until the neighbor arrived to right the tractor and Jerry was safely loaded into the ambulance.

Jerry spent the next several days in the hospital recovering from his injuries. He spent a lot of that time pondering his miraculous survival. He thought about Christ's death on the cross. He considered his sister's willingness to die with him under that tractor. He wondered why he was spared. He never made it to youth group that night, but his friends still gathered, prayed for his safety, and sent him cards that he still has to this day, stored with photographs of the incident.

About a year later, during a weekend retreat at the Zeilstras' church, several people shared their testimonies. That Saturday evening, with the tractor accident and the decision of his sister Ethel still fresh in his memory, Jerry stood to declare his desire to commit his life to Jesus Christ. And as evidence of God's work in his life, his father also made a commitment that night. Jerry remembers that before he went to bed that night, his dad stopped in to tell him that he loved him.

Most conversion stories center on the revelation of sin and repentance. As a young man, I often found myself feeling a little jealous of people with powerful testimonies of God rescuing them from hopeless situations like drug addiction or great personal loss. Their stories seemed far more exciting and effective than my boring tale of growing up in a Christian home and deciding at a young age to follow Jesus. Life has been pretty comfortable for me, and while I have come to know Jesus more and more, God spared me the experience of ever hitting rock bottom. I have, of course, come to view this as a great privilege.

Jerry's testimony is unique in my mind because of its basis in the *agape* love of Jesus. His focus in accepting Christ was love and grace rather than guilt and sin. Any decision to follow Christ will involve both of these revelations. First, we must realize that we are sinners worthy only of separation from God. And second, we must understand that God loved us so much that He sacrificed His Son to pay the penalty for our sin. The love expressed through the free gift of grace found in the death and resurrection of Jesus, on behalf of His undeserving people, is *agape* love. It is unconditional. Jerry experienced that love directly through the actions of another believer.

Jerry nearly killed himself on that tractor. He made some well-meaning but bad decisions and placed himself in a position that should have resulted in his death. In that moment, Ethel painted a picture of grace and love for a scared thirteen-year-old boy. Her brother's life, despite his mistakes, was worth giving up her own. Jerry heard the story of Jesus differently the next time he heard it thanks to Ethel. Jerry's testimony is not only a reminder of Jesus' love for us, but also the impact of offering *agape* love to others. It's like what Jerry says, "You may be the only Jesus some people ever see."

Jerry illustrated this same *agape* love in his own way years later. In the summer of my freshman year, I joined Jerry and several students on a backpacking trip on the Laurel Highlands Hiking Trail in southwestern Pennsylvania. I was not especially fit, so my parents were happy to encourage any interest I showed in physical activity. They bought me a brand-new pair of K-Swiss boots for the adventure, and I borrowed one of the church's backpacks to carry my share of the load. I enjoyed long walks in the woods, but I wasn't particularly looking forward to living in the woods for three days without the benefit of my usual creature comforts. I did my best to match the excitement of my friends.

We loaded into a couple of vans, and the drivers dropped us off at the trailhead in Ohio Pyle. It was explained to us that we would take it easy on the first day to break ourselves in. The first campsite was only six miles into the woods. Jerry passed out some of the canned food to add to our packs and spread out the weight. We prayed together and set out on our journey.

The Laurel Highlands Hiking Trail is a rugged seventy-mile trail through the Laurel Highlands mountains in western Pennsylvania. It runs northeast through the wilderness between the Youghiogheny River and Conemaugh Gorge. The woods, ridges, and giant rocks provide spectacular views. As you hike along, you feel immersed in the nature around you and disconnected from the distractions of civilization. The campsites have permanent lean-to shelters; each is basically a slanted roof with walls on each side and a wooden floor. A stone chimney and fireplace protect the open front side but leave plenty of space for the breeze to pass through. For a lot of folk, this all adds up to an exhilarating, challenging experience that brings a great sense of accomplishment and pride. By about twenty minutes in, I was hovering somewhere between discomfort and bitter anger.

I had a lot to complain about. For starters, no one told me that four of the first six miles of the trail were uphill with a total climb of over 1500 feet. My quads were killing me. Secondly, I wasn't aware that it would be frowned upon for me to take a water and snack break every half mile or so. Third, my brand-new K-Swiss boots were not comfortable and I was pretty sure I was developing.... Yes, during one of my frequent rest breaks near the top of the first hill, I removed my boots and socks to confirm that I indeed already had blisters. Fourth, I'm pretty sure my pack was heavier than it needed to be. Maybe I was given too much of the food. Fifth, why did everyone else seem so jovial in the midst of this torture? Did they just have better equipment? They were making me look bad. I spent most of the day being coaxed along by very patient chaperones who I'm sure were rolling their eyes at me behind my back. It was well deserved either way. I was clearly dead weight.

By the time we finally reached the lean-tos that afternoon, I was exhausted both physically and emotionally. I surveyed the primitive shelter I would be sharing with the others for the night and laid out my sleeping bag. I tried climbing the chimney stones. I played with the water pump a little. I cringed when I checked out the pit toilets. The last thing I wanted was to continue this trip, but now I was stuck in the woods, miles from civilization. The best I could do was fake it. There was still a lot of hiking left. Even after my lame attempts to kill some time, it was still only late afternoon. Dinner, the final potential bright spot in my day, was still hours away.

Feeling lonely and miserable, I wandered over to the edge of camp and looked out over a valley we had passed through to enter the camp. That's when I noticed Mike Hayes running up the path toward me. Mike was a year older than I was. He had considerably more experience in the wilderness than most of us and was greatly admired by his peers for his confidence and friendly demeanor. At this moment, though, he did not look well. He was moving very quickly and gripping his hand. His face was pale, and he locked eyes with me as he came up the hill.

"What's wrong?" I asked.

He didn't say anything. He just came closer and extended his hand so I could see. His middle finger was crushed and sliced wide open from the base to the tip. The gash was very deep and filled with a pool of blood. Consumed with my own concerns, I just winced and stared as he rushed past me to find someone more helpful.

It didn't take long for the leaders to realize something was terribly wrong. They gathered around Mike and worked quickly to apply a tourniquet and a makeshift sling out of bandanas. You could read the concern on all their faces. This was before the age when every adult and child was carrying a cell phone.

It wouldn't have made much difference anyway, given that we were so far from good reception.

I did my best to stay quiet and out of the way. The other guys who were with Mike when the accident happened followed closely behind him and shared the story. Rather than sulking in boredom the way I was, they had gone down to a small creek to see if they could dam it up with some rocks. One very large rock they had chosen to move was beyond their capability. They had lifted it enough to get a good grip, but it began to slip. When it became clear they couldn't hold it, they yanked their hands away. Mike waited just a moment too long. His finger was smashed. As he instinctively pulled back, it caught on something sharp enough under the rock to lay it open.

The first-aid supplies that we had with us were not adequate to fix the damage, and there was no way to call for help. It quickly became apparent that someone would have to return to Ohio Pyle for help. All of us had just trekked the six-mile, uphill trail to get there that day. I'm sure that even the fittest among us was not eager to do it again. Mike certainly was in no condition to make the trip himself. He did not look well. Jerry knew he was in a race against time. The sun would be setting soon, and he could make no assumptions about Mike's condition. He grabbed a bottle of water, and he and Mike's friend Barrett left everything else and began running.[1]

---

1   Mike recalled that Barrett stopped at the creek on his way out of camp to make sure they hadn't left any pieces of Mike's finger on the ground.

The remaining chaperones propped Mike up against a tree and made him comfortable. There was some concern that he might be slipping into shock, but as time passed, the color slowly returned to his face. He began making quiet conversation, even cracking jokes, trying to keep from thinking too much about the throbbing in his hand. All any of us could do was wait.

By the time Jerry and Barrett made it back to town, the stores and restaurants were beginning to close for the day. They found a place to call 9-1-1 and solicited the help of a park ranger. Since the accident took place at the first set of shelters, it turned out there was an access road directly to the camp. Around sunset, we heard a vehicle approaching.

A jeep pulled up. Jerry and Barrett hopped out with the ranger. He talked briefly with Mike to assess his condition. Then they loaded Mike and his pack into the jeep and headed for the nearest hospital. Jerry made the trip with him. Once they were closer to the city, he was able to get in touch with Mike's parents. The local hospital stabilized his hand and transferred Mike to Pittsburgh for reconstructive surgery.

Jerry left us under the leadership of his college intern, Tom, and the other chaperones. We continued the hike the next day, and Jerry met us at the second camp that evening. He had good news. Mike was doing well. They had acted quickly enough that Mike would keep his finger. Fortunately, the doctors told them, the nerves are positioned on either side of the finger, so the wound along the centerline would not impact his ability to move or feel his finger normally once it healed. We were all glad to hear that Mike had avoided greater damage.[2]

The rest of the backpacking trip had a very different feel for me. Until that afternoon, I had literally thought only about myself. I wondered how I could possibly survive such an arduous experience. I hated being the least experienced, least knowledgeable, least equipped hiker. I resented the fun the others were having and assumed they were faking it. And, I tried to figure out how to make others feel sorry for me.

All of my excuses fizzled after Mike's incident. He had gotten hurt working with and supporting his friends. He actually sustained an injury that could have been life-threatening, and one that he would still be dealing with long after we were done hiking the rest of the way. He was genuinely disappointed that he couldn't continue and finish the journey. And, he still aimed to make others laugh and enjoy themselves even as he waited for help.

Jerry added another layer to that. He had demonstrated his competence and courage to do whatever was necessary to protect us. I wouldn't judge Jerry if there were moments on his run back to town that he might have considered the inconvenience of all of this. If those boys had just been more cautious and less adventurous, maybe the whole situation could have been avoided. But, with Mike's safety on the line,

---

2   The doctors had to fuse the final joint on Mike's finger so it no longer bends. He feels certain this is the reason he was not permitted to enlist in the U.S. Navy during his senior year of college, shortly before the onset of the Iraq War.

Jerry wasn't concerned about casting blame or arguing about decisions. He dropped what he was doing and did what needed to be done.

Once he was back with us, Jerry led us in Bible lessons around the campfire and sometimes during lunch breaks on the trail. I don't remember any of the lessons specifically, but he had a phrase that he repeated often during youth trips, especially backpacking: "When God wants to teach you something, He often takes you on a journey."

This was a journey I would never forget because it taught me the difference between being a self-obsessed little boy and a Christ-obsessed mature man. With little forethought, Jerry, much as his sister Ethel had done, had instinctively demonstrated *agape* love to Mike and the rest of us. To a lot of people, running six miles is a walk in the park. To me that afternoon, though, after trudging along all morning for six miles, the idea of turning around and running the same distance, even if it was mostly downhill, struck me as superhuman. In a way, it was.

Jerry has served the youth and families at Hebron Church for over thirty years now. I am certain that any youth pastor you ask would probably rather hike six miles and run six more in the same day than make that kind of commitment. Ask Jerry and he would probably remind you, "I can do all things through him who strengthens me" (Phil. 4:13). Jerry was shown *agape* love by his sister, he recognized its source in the grace of Jesus Christ, and he has allowed that to permeate his own nature.

Before the Apostle Paul begins describing the characteristics of love in 1 Corinthians 13, he emphasizes its outright importance. "If I speak in the tongues of men and of angels, but have not love, I am a noisy gong or a clanging cymbal. And if I have prophetic powers, and understand all mysteries and all knowledge, and if I have all faith, so as to remove mountains, but have not love, I am nothing" (1 Cor. 13:1-2). The *agape* love of Jesus can take any one of our lives, no matter our past, and transform it into something effective and powerful for His glory. Jerry's impact was the direct result of his surrender to this *agape* love. Jerry would be the last to take the credit, too, because as he reminded us on several occasions, "We love because he first loved us" (1 John 4:19).

10

Legacy

"You can tell how big an impact you have had,

by how much you are missed when you are gone."

Near the end of my senior year of high school, Hebron Church held a celebration for Jerry's ten-year anniversary at the church. I wasn't going far from home for college, but the finality of high-school graduation weighed pretty heavy on my heart. I was going to miss the well-established rhythm of school, church, and hanging with friends. During the event, there was an opportunity to stand up and share kind words and memories of our time with Jerry. As I listened to several people tell their stories, a song began to form in my head. I grabbed one of the offering envelopes and a golf pencil from the back of the pew and began scribbling down lyrics.

Every now and then, a person comes along
That can teach you a lesson, sing you a new song
Well, in you I found, a helping hand
And I wrote this song, just so you'd understand

If no one else listened, if no one else cared
If no one was affected by the things that you said
I want you to know that you left an impression
I want you to know how grateful I am

This is my last year, time flies by
It's so hard to believe that was ten years of our lives
Well, I'm heading off, but you'd better stick around
'Cause there's so many people who need you in this town

When the opportunity arose, I grabbed my guitar and shared the song with the congregation and Jerry. There is no doubt I was expressing the sentiments of everyone in the room. Jerry's influence in the church extended well beyond both me and the rest of the youth. He had used his position in youth ministry and Christian education to build relationships with the youngest families to the elderly. Even today, some of his fondest memories involve connections he made with older members as part of his grass-cutting ministry.

Penn Hills is not an affluent town. Sometimes the expense of youth trips and events exceeded the means of local families. Jerry knew there were many elderly congregants and widows who were unable to care for their yards. He purchased a couple of lawn mowers and developed a list of folks who needed their grass cut throughout the summer. Jerry always invited one or two students along to complete the work and visit with people. Jerry credited the money earned to each student's account to cover the cost of summer trips. The homeowners welcomed the company and were delighted to contribute to youth-ministry experiences.

Jerry typically tried to schedule the day so his last stop would be at Mrs. Davies' house because he enjoyed spending time with her. She would offer Jerry and his helpers stale doughnuts and fried SPAM. Students were sometimes uncomfortable with accepting the food. SPAM was unappealing enough on its own, but to make matters worse, Mrs. Davies' eyesight was failing, and her stove was usually pretty dirty. With the same gracious spirit Jerry encouraged in Mexico, he told students as they drove to her house, "If she feeds us, we are eating." Jerry says she made up for it with the drinks. After a long day of cutting lawns, he knew nothing was more refreshing than her iced tea mixed with a can of frozen lemonade. "That was one thing that was very good."

Jerry always made it a point to develop multi-generational connections within the church because he understood the importance of legacy. Older believers have a lot to offer to the youth in a church. For one youth event, students were dropped off in groups of three at the apartments and homes of shut-ins from the church. We shared a snack, played board games, and got to know each other for a few hours until the leaders made the rounds again to pick us up. Throughout the confirmation process, Jerry paired each student with a sponsor, a senior member of the congregation. Each dinner table at youth club had table leaders, usually an older couple from the church patiently supervising the behavior of six youngsters. Those kinds of connections strengthen the fabric of any community, especially a family of believers. In reminding us about the power of legacy, Jerry was slowly adding to his own.

During my first year of college I tried connecting with some of the campus ministries and churches, but it was difficult to replicate the belonging I felt at Hebron. High-school graduation was my first real struggle with physical mortality. The idea that this world of friends and interests that I had constructed could suddenly end was a little devastating. Trying to start over and do the same again in college seemed like a waste of time, especially since it would all end in another four years. Once again, my inward focus caused me to miss out on a broader experience.

The following summer, I attended youth group one Sunday as a returning college student. I relished the familiarity of it all. I reconnected with friends, played some ultimate Frisbee, and sang songs I hadn't heard for months. At one point during Jerry's lesson, I remember looking around the room and feeling a deep sense of admiration and comfort. I was now a welcome outsider, viewing Jerry's ministry in a whole new retrospective light. In the midst of all kinds of change and concerns, Jerry provided a consistent, safe, and caring place for this room full of kids year after year. I couldn't help but wonder how his words were affecting their hearts for the future.

In today's fast-paced culture, it is difficult not to feel the pressure to move from one opportunity to the next in the pursuit of influence and prestige. Jerry took a different approach by staying put and equipping students for kingdom work in which he would never directly participate. His ministry has generated several pastors and missionaries.

- Dan and Kelly Weightman, who participated in a college mission trip with Jerry to the Bahamas, decided to return there after they married. They founded the Caribbean Youth Network to serve and develop young Bahamians.

- Barrett Hendrickson, the guy who ran six miles alongside Jerry to find help for his friend, returned to Hebron himself as a worship and youth pastor. He and his family have joined the expanding mission work of the Weightmans.

- Dave Hendrickson, Barrett's older brother, is senior pastor at

Longview Community Church in Longview, Washington.

- Tom Hughes is co-lead senior pastor of Christian Assembly in Los Angeles, California. In his book *Curious*, Tom shares some ways Jerry influenced his ministry.

- Mike McDonald is the senior pastor at Grace Anglican Church in Fleming Island, Florida.

- Joshua Brown pastors Bellefield Presbyterian Church in Oakland, Pennsylvania, and also previously served as Moderator of the Presbytery of the Alleghenies for the Evangelical Presbyterian Church.

- Dan Bender currently serves as the Kids and Youth Coordinator at Hickory United Evangelical Presbyterian Christian in Hickory, Pennsylvania.

- Rob Gage is the Family Ministry Director for Northbridge Community Church in Pittsburgh, Pennsylvania.

- Andrew Churchill ministers to at-risk youth on Pittsburgh's North Side as the Assistant Director of Athletic Operations for Urban Impact.

Jerry also taught youth-ministry courses as an adjunct professor at Geneva College for several years, where he spoke into the lives of countless other young men and women from around the country. Church ministry isn't the only way to serve

God, though. Jerry's students have pursued a wide variety of career fields and live around the globe. Many of us carry Jerry's wisdom around in the back of our minds as we live our daily lives, parent our children, and volunteer in our local churches.

Jerry's far-reaching influence did not have the same effect on everyone. Some students attended youth group sporadically. Many never participated in the summer trips. Students whose families didn't also attend Hebron for church, or who were invited by friends closer to the end of their high-school years, developed more peripheral relationships with Jerry. Bottom line, Jerry was a flawed man working with a team of flawed, emotional teenagers. It makes me sad to remember the times when my own words and actions were detrimental to other students, but such missteps were inevitable. Every one of us arrived with his or her own personality, background and baggage. Jerry's biblical teaching didn't sit well with everyone.

Thankfully, it is the Holy Spirit who convicts the heart of an individual. It is left to us simply to walk faithfully, read God's Word, and testify to the work of Jesus Christ in our own lives. Jerry set a great example for us in this. Even for those students who never fully accepted the gospel, I think most at least left with a positive impression of Jerry Zeilstra. He accepted us for who we were, but he knew that Scripture possessed promises for life abundant and free. He encouraged us toward new life in Christ.

There are a couple of reasons why people decide to avoid or leave the church. To some people, the Christian walk appears judgmental, restrictive, or hypocritical. Others have left the church because of emotional of physical hurt caused by other believers. Many simply reject the notion of religious faith as simplemindedness. I am thankful to have experienced Jerry's authentic, consistent ministry. I hope anyone reading this today who has had negative experiences with the church will consider a path of grace and forgiveness in pursuit of a relationship with Jesus Christ. There is no greater love available than that which we find in Him. Don't let the shortcomings of His people stand in your way.

Jerry taught us in our Leadership/Discipleship meetings, "You can tell how big an impact you have had, by how much you are missed when you are gone." So far, his own legacy has been difficult to measure by that standard, because he hasn't left. Twenty years later, Jerry remains a steadfast servant of Christ and minister to the people at Hebron Church. His role has changed over the years, but students still benefit from the ministry structure that he put in place three decades ago, including the annual trip to South Dakota to visit his now aging parents. The congregation relies heavily on his faithful service, enduring friendship, and great wisdom.

Jerry's life has been a testament to the extraordinary impact one person can have when he yields to the authority of his heavenly Father. The events and people that shaped Jerry's heart — an angry teacher, a forgiving dad, a tractor accident, a selfless sister — were part of God's plan to use him in mighty ways. By submitting himself to God's purposes and faithfully walking with Jesus, the influence of this South Dakota farm boy now reaches around the globe. There will come a day when Jerry will hear the Father say, "Well done, good and faithful servant" (Matt. 25:21). But the same invitation is available to each of us. We need only turn our focus away from ourselves and onto Jesus. Life exists to bring Him glory in the first place. Make the most of it.

Afterword

Reflections From the Author

To Students:

Wherever you are in your faith journey, I hope the lessons
Jerry taught me are useful to you in your life as well. If you
are not currently part of a church body, I encourage you to
find one with a youth program that is grounded in the Word
of God. This was the source of Jerry's wisdom and has become
the source of my own wisdom as well. Ask your parents to
help you identify a mentor who can hold you accountable in
your spiritual growth. If you are a believer, regular practices of

reading God's Word, praying, and participating in worship will give you an increasing knowledge of God's character.

Your life is going to bring challenges, seasons of doubt, and pain. Faith and a keen awareness of God's promises are essential in difficult times. The people of Israel faced periods of great distress throughout the Old Testament. They often recited the historical record of God's faithfulness to remind themselves of their security in Him. Today is a great time to begin developing your own history with God. Ask Him to show you ways in which He is faithful to you. Store those memories deep in your heart and rely on them when life weighs you down.

If you do not have a personal relationship with Jesus, know that He loves you. No matter how you have spent your life to this point, He has a plan and a purpose for you. His Word is reliable for meaning and direction. His death was sufficient to atone for your sins. His resurrection provides us with eternal hope for the future. His love will motivate and sustain you in your relationships with others. If you want to learn more about Him, grab yourself a copy of the Bible, connect with a church near you, and find your Jerry.

To Parents:

You will always be the most powerful influence in the lives of your children. If you are a parent of very young children, begin to think about the values you want to impart and the kind of character you want to cultivate in them. Teach them with love and grace from the Word of God. Study it yourself. Fight fiercely for love and kindness in your home. Know that you will fail on your own and entrust your children's future to their Creator.

One of the ways you influence your children is by choosing who you let into their world. God has placed you in a position of authority over your children for a reason. I am grateful for my own parents and their intentional approach to childrearing. They made the decision for our family to join Hebron Church. We were taught from the Bible, engaged in the church community, heard Rev. Doug Rehberg's weekly, thoughtful, Christ-centered sermons, and participated fully in Jerry's youth ministry. My time in that church, with the support of my parents, gave me the opportunity to learn how to ski, play the guitar, install A/V equipment, make videos, and write music. I made friends who will be friends for eternity, including my wife and mother of my own children.

So, if you haven't already, find a gospel-centered church for your family. Build relationships with other families who are following Jesus. Get involved in the church and get to know the staff members. One of the primary reasons Jerry's ministry was so well attended and effective was because he had the strong support of families. Parents knew Jerry and trusted him. Some parents even volunteered their time to help on Sunday nights and chaperone summer trips and weekend retreats. Be supportive and honest with your church leaders to further their mission to bring young people to Christ.

To Youth Pastors:

Kids are busier than ever. At the same time, your work is more important than ever. Thank you for following God's calling on your life. He is using you to help kids over the bridge between childhood and spiritual maturity. The world changes very quickly, and students are constantly connected to friends and distracting entertainment. One thing that never changes, though, is the power of a relationship. Build relationships with your students. Build relationships with their families. Encourage them to build relationships with their friends and invite them to church. Build relationships with your students' friends and their families. Bring them all to the feet of Jesus.

Remember the power of leading by example. Your long-term impact will be the result of your investment in your present relationships. To bring others to Jesus, you must develop your own relationship with Him. You are not the focus of your ministry; Jesus is. The time you spend with Jesus is a necessary source of stamina and patience, a hedge against pride, and a constant reminder of His glory and grace. Jerry is a great leader because he is a great follower of Jesus.

Youth events should be a lot of fun. Students should feel free to express themselves. Be wary of focusing too much on the entertainment aspect of youth ministry, though. Your students are intelligent, questioning, budding adults. They are eager to think deeply about their beliefs. Provide plenty of time to encourage conversation about Scripture. Don't shy away from questions, even the ones that might stump you. Your authenticity in those moments will draw students into an honest relationship with Christ. They will strengthen your faith and sharpen your communication skills. Remember, you will always have more to learn about the infinite attributes of God.

To Pastors and Church Leaders:

A body of believers is always only one generation away from losing faith in God. As you lead your churches, remember the importance of the youth in carrying the gospel message into the future. When hiring youth pastors, resist the temptation to focus on personality and technical knowhow over spiritual maturity and passion. Students are not wanting for entertainment. Genuine connection and biblical truth are in much shorter supply.

Your church's youth pastor must be confident of your support in order to perform his job well. The church must be prepared to bear the burden of accepting all students and visitors. Teenagers need space to act silly and be themselves. Whether this manifests itself in insulting language, sacrilegious comments, or property damage, the church should be ready to approach student offenses from a position of grace, remembering the desire to lead students to an understanding of what Christ did for them on the cross. If issues arise that are within the control of your youth pastor, address them directly with the goal of professional development and improvement.

Encourage your youth pastor by providing necessary feedback, resources, and support. The senior pastor should have both a working and personal relationship with the youth pastor. Know that you can speak freely with each other about concerns and hold one another accountable spiritually. You are on the same team. The church should provide adequate resources to fund youth activities and make major events more affordable for students to participate. Most importantly, the pastor and the church should regularly pray for the youth pastor, the youth program, and the students. Pray that God might use your church's youth ministry to bring new families to the church and carry the gospel out into your community.

"Jerry-isms"

"Hey, Sister!"

"Hey, Brother!"

"That's mercy."

"That's grace."

"Treat every date as a potential mate."

"A friendship that ends badly, never really ends."

"A friend in Christ is a friend for life."

"The only way to do it is to do it."

"The only way not to do it is not to do it."

"You are the only Jesus some people will ever see."

"The way you treat your mother is a good indication of how you will treat your future wife."

"Sin loves company."

"Anything else for the good of the order?"

"If you really want to see God working in your life, you need to start giving Him the credit."

"The best way to learn is to ask questions, then listen."

"Be bigger than life."

"I'm perfect, in God's eyes."

"You don't need to ask Jesus to be with you, He already is!"

"Good, better, best, never let it rest, 'til your good is better and your better's best!"

"You are a saint, live like one"

"Learn to listen with your eyes."

"You can tell how big an impact you have had by how much you are missed when you are gone."

"When God wants to teach you something, He often takes you on a journey."

Faith in the Forum

faithintheforum.org

GUNPLAY WAS THE LAST THING SLOCUM WANTED . . .

Eddie's eyes, like a hawk, were fixed on Slocum. There was a gun on the ground, but the man's gun was still in Eddie's belt, and he believed Slocum had forgotten about it. Slocum looked mind-wandering. Now he was turning to White Flower, as if to tell her something important. The perfect moment for Eddie, and his hand swept to his belt and he had the gun coming up, feeling a surge of confidence, because the polecat was still looking at White Flower, when it happened; a *blur of movement*, a gun spurting flame, and Eddie's body hurtled back and he stumbled to the earth, a bullet in his heart.

OTHER BOOKS BY JAKE LOGAN

JAKE LOGAN

SLOCUM AND
THE BLOOD RAGE

B

BERKLEY BOOKS, NEW YORK

SLOCUM AND THE BLOOD RAGE

A Berkley Book/published by arrangement with
the author

PRINTING HISTORY
Berkley edition/January 1988

ISBN: 0-425-10555-5

A BERKLEY BOOK ® TM 757,375
Berkley Books are published by The Berkley Publishing Group
200 Madison Avenue, New York, N.Y. 10016.
The name "BERKLEY" and the "B" logo
are trademarks belonging to Berkley Publishing Corporation.

PRINTED IN THE UNITED STATES OF AMERICA

10 9 8 7 6 5 4 3 2 1

1

The sun slanted off the canyon, painting the time-
less crags a light bronze as Slocum, on his powerful roan, looked lazily down from a crest of rocks.
Then he heard the thud of hoofbeats bouncing off
the rocks, and saw the girl, her red-banded hair
streaming, her bare legs gripping the brown mustang as it raced around a massive boulder. Behind
that bulking rock, someone had put deadly fear in
her.

Slocum's eyes narrowed as he watched her kick
wildly at the haunches of her pony; from the buckskins she should be Apache, but she didn't look it.
Her features were white and, from this distance,
striking.

Slocum tensed when the reason for her terror
came into view, a powerful Apache, the muscles

under his bronze skin rippling as he goaded his black stallion, showing it no mercy in his fierce desire to catch the girl.

The distance closed between the riders and, as Slocum watched, the girl hopelessly zigged and zagged her pony.

The Apache, in a burst of speed, grabbed the pony's mane, bringing it to a snorting halt. The girl leaped clear and raced toward the crags, not yet aware of Slocum.

With long, powerful strides, the Apache caught the girl by her arm, spun her, and she whirled and fell.

Though jarred, she came instantly alert and leaned on her elbow to watch the Apache. Stony-faced, he walked calmly to her pony and pulled a belt from its neck. His eyes gleamed when he glanced into its pocket.

Slocum, about thirty yards from them, watched hypnotized. What the hell was happening? Did she steal something? Or did it belong to her? And why so fearful, though, from the look of her she seemed to have plenty of iron.

Possession of the belt didn't seem to completely satisfy the Apache, for he let it drop and walked toward the girl.

Now, for the first time, the stone face of the Apache cracked and an almost devilish grin spread over his features. He spoke in quick harsh tones. The girl's voice was just as harsh. What she said infuriated him, for he leaned down and slapped her. She struck back and he grabbed her, pulled at her buckskins. Her breasts came into view, and

Slocum, watching in anger, couldn't help but be impressed.

The Apache's moves were unmistakable as he forced her down and back. She understood quick enough, for with a sudden movement, she brought a knife from her boot and thrust at him. He caught her wrist, twisted the knife from her hand and staring in her eyes, raised the knife to plunge into her heart.

Slocum's hand was a streak of lightning as his gun barked, the bullet hitting the side of the Apache's head, hurtling him off her body; he staggered up crazily, then fell in slow motion, his face to the ground.

The girl stared at the dead Apache, then looked up to see Slocum. He was smiling at her as he holstered his gun. He nosed the roan down toward her. She looked confused, not knowing whether to run or stay and thank him. She covered her lovely breasts, carefully picked up the belt and tied it to her pony.

When Slocum came closer he was astonished at the beauty of the girl. Her features were regular, smooth, her nose acquiline, her skin light, her eyes astonishingly bright blue. Yet she had something about her that was Apache, a powerful, well-shaped body. She seemed to Slocum to combine the best qualities of white and red.

She watched him warily from glowing blue eyes, and he smiled. She calmly picked up the knife that had dropped from the hand of the Apache and slipped it into the holster of her boot. She looked so white that it didn't surprise him when she said, "White Flower offers you thanks."

He nodded gravely, pointed to himself. "I am Slocum."

She studied his face, trying to read if he would be threatening as the white men often was to a beautiful half-breed.

He looked down at the Apache, at his brutal features that even in death, looked cruel. "Not a friend to White Flower, was he?"

A small smile creased her lips "Red Thunder? No, no friend. Bad man."

"I will bury him," he said.

She bit her lip; something on her mind, he thought. He pulled the shovel from his saddle and dug a hole in the soft earth near a flat-sized boulder, dragged the Apache to it and dropped him.

She watched, her face calm and untroubled, wondering what he'd do after. All he did was put the shovel into its saddle holster, look at her one more time.

With a hard glint in his green eyes, he said, "One less mangy dog spoilin' the earth." He said it more to himself than to her.

He swung over his saddle, waved, then headed the roan south.

She seemed bewildered, as if his departure, after such an encounter, was the last thing she had expected.

He rode slowly along the edge of the canyon, looking at its massive cliffs climbing steeply and beyond the rim of stone to the glowing blue sky. Not long after, he heard fast hoofbeats. The girl was riding quick-paced on her fine, broad-chested pony. She rode erect, proud, and he couldn't help admire the sight of a beautiful girl on a fine horse. He pulled up and waited. Her face was calm, but her eyes showed concern.

"White Flower," she said, "must warn Slocum that two braves will seek out Red Thunder. When they find him in the grave, they will search to avenge him."

He shrugged: you did one thing, thinking it was the end, but every act had consequences. "Slocum will take care," he said. "And what of you? Will White Flower be in danger?"

A small smile creased her lips. "White Flower is always in danger."

What did she mean? Because of her beauty? Or was there another reason? She looked as if she had thoughts on her mind. "White Flower rides southwest, too."

Slocum rubbed his chin. Was she asking to ride with him? Why?

"What about your tribe? Shouldn't you go back. Would it not be safer?"

Her jaw firmed and her bright blue eyes gazed into the distance, as if she were seeing something. "I go to find Sean O'Brien," she spoke slowly.

He gazed at her puzzled. A half-breed, going to find a white man? Slocum swung off the saddle. "Why does White Flower go to O'Brien?"

"There is a reason." She looked away.

He patted the muscular haunches of the roan. "Would it not be better to go to your tribe, to your people?"

"There is no place in the tribe for me," she said solemnly. "Not anymore. I go to find O'Brien." She paused, with lips tightened. She'd say no more, that was clear to Slocum, though there seemed plenty to tell.

He glanced at the great expanse of boulders and brush, the cliffs, the huge, towering canyon. "This is bad country. There are drifters and desperadoes, and wild bucks—your people." He grinned. "A girl like you—must be careful."

She smiled. "White Flower can defend herself."

But she hadn't done that well with Red Thunder. He thought of White Flower making the trip alone; it seemed most foolish.

He'd ride partway with her, and see what came of it. Her tribesmen, she had said, might be looking for Red Thunder. They'd track Red Thunder to his grave, and if he knew the Apache, they'd reconstruct what had happened; a bullet in Red Thunder, tracks of White Flower's pony, tracks of a paleface who had put Red Thunder with his ancestors. What then? Something to think about. *They might try to make her pay for his death. Him, too.*

Plenty of trouble ahead, and he'd be smart to expect it.

Still the girl, as a companion, was better than many a riding mate he could think of.

They rode south and the descending sun cast deep shadows in the canyon. He picked a path through huge boulders that bulked on either side and stayed alert. A girl like her, in this wasteland, could be honey to the drifter and desperado, and a couple might just creep out from under a rock. But the sun kept sinking and nothing much happened. He decided it was time for dinner and when he saw a bit of fluff move in the bush, his gun barked. The jackrabbit jumped in the air and dropped. Slocum made a fire smothered in a pit and they ate fried meat and drank coffee.

She sat cross-legged, and ate with surprising delicacy; she had white, even teeth and fully formed lips. She seemed always to be calm until the moment came when her head turned and her blue eyes stared at a faraway boulder. His senses alert, Slocum listened, and finally heard the sound. After a while the man appeared. He was hatchet-faced, with strong features and a sinewy body. He wore a short black hat, black shirt with a blue bandanna, dusty boots. He looked at White Flower and his eyes glittered, then at Slocum. He looked confident, as if there was nothing in this world to fear.

"Howdy, pardner. Heard the sound of your gun. Reckoned you were hunting. I was headed for Tombstone and lost my bearings." He stood there, waiting, his gaze flicking to White Flower, astonished at her looks.

Slocum stroked his chin; he'd seen lots of drifters, scouring the territory for a piece of luck, but this one might not be a drifter. Probably knew the way to Tombstone, but now that he'd seen White Flower, he might get other ideas.

"Brady's the name." He looked sharp to see if it was recognized by Slocum, but it wasn't. "Been draggin' my tail north since sunup."

Brady had taken a side stance, which a gunman took if he wanted his gun fast. His hard gray eyes were studying Slocum, his lean, strong face and powerful body. Brady looked easy—a man with a lot of confidence. When his gaze shifted to White Flower his tongue came out to lick his lips. Then looking at the heating coffee pot, he eased up, as if his thoughts had changed.

"What's your handle, mister?"

"Slocum."

"Where from, Slocum?"

"Calhoun county, Georgia." Slocum glanced at White Flower. Her face was impassive—she wasn't going to reveal what she felt, though he sensed she wasn't happy about Brady. But that could be discomfort in the presence of any pale-face.

Brady's hatchet face twisted in a mirthless grin. "I been through Georgia. You rebs were a tough bunch to beat. But I got no grievances. Who'd you fight under?"

"General Pickens."

Brady measured him. "You look like you did a bit o' damage to our boys. But it's over." He glanced at the girl. "You're mighty lucky, Slocum. Where'd you find the breed? Never saw anything like her."

Slocum's eyes were cold. He didn't like anything about Brady.

Brady picked up Slocum's dislike, but it didn't faze him. He just went on calmly. "Real nice-lookin' filly. Tell yuh, I'm mighty weary, been runnin' hard, wouldn't mind a bit o' your coffee."

"Help yourself." He watched Brady pour coffee from the steaming pot and sip it, leaning against the nearby boulder. "That tastes good. Had a pardner with me, but we ran into a coupla sneaky bucks. They picked him off. I made things hot and they vamoosed." He glanced at White Flower. "Couple of *her* friends."

"*Why* are you runnin' so hard toward Tombstone?"

Brady sighed. "Been tryin' to catch up with Doc Holliday. That low-down dog put a bullet in Eddie Gleason, my good friend. I aim to pay him off for that." Brady said this casually.

Slocum had to smile. "You're a man with nerve, Brady. Doc Holliday is a hard man to beat."

Brady shrugged. "Lotta bull. Remember this, Slocum—*a rep don't mean a man's a hot gun*. I seen Doc pull his Colt. He ain't the nearest thing to lightning. And he can miss the side of a barn door, too." Brady sipped his coffee, his hatchet face in a grim smile. "And I don't mind sayin', Slocum, there's more than one way to skin a cat."

Slocum's eyes narrowed. Brady was probably a fast gun, but he wasn't above shooting a man in the back, if he had to.

Brady walked to his horse, pulled whiskey from the saddle and poured it into his coffee. "Tell you, Slocum, a lotta polecats get a big rep, live off it for years. Then someone good comes along and puts 'em in boothill—like that." Brady talked as if he knew all about it.

"Who'd you fight under, Brady?"

Brady's eyes dropped. "Fought under Sherman." His voice went harsh. "We went through Atlanta. Might as well say, I hated rebs. Killed my share." Then he smiled quickly. "No offense, pardner. No point fightin' that war again. Bloody enough. But it's over." He gazed at White Flower.

"You sure know how to find the girl, Slocum. This half-breed must be a lotta fun on a cool night. What'd you take to sharin' a bit o' this fancy stuff?"

Slocum's green eyes iced, and he glanced at her. Though her face was still impassive, he could read hard thoughts.

He stood up. "Brady, I been tired of you for quite a time, but you're a mighty ignorant man, and I won't hold it against you. Whyn't you just get on your horse and start travelin'."

Brady looked surprised. "Why—what'd I say?"

Slocum almost had to grin. "To be honest, pardner, I'm sorta surprised you're still drawin' breath, considerin' the *mean* way you talk."

Brady smiled good-naturedly. He was a mighty confident cowboy. "That's the truth, Slocum. I talk mean. Heard some polecats say it often. But no polecat who ever said it—*repeated it*. Fact is, you're lucky I let you say it." He leaned forward, his sinewy body tense. *Reckon you don't know who I am.*"

"Don't know. Not sure I want to."

Brady's face was granite hard. "But I'm gonna tell you. 'Cause I want you to think about it when you're lying down there. They call me *Quick-Draw Brady*. My gun has killed fourteen men." His smile was almost good-natured. "Now lemme tell you what's gonna happen. I'm gonna put a bullet in you, then take this pretty little squaw. We're going to have a hot time. Pity is you won't know. 'Cause you're going to be the fifteenth man I shot."

He took his position and waited, his body lean and sinewy, every inch a gunfighter.

Slocum stared into the gray eye depths of this joker as he bragged, until he saw the flicker—signal of the brain's command. Slocum's hand flashed, and the fire spurted from his gun a split second before Brady's gun fired—the sound tore through the canyon. A frozen moment, then Brandy glared amazed at his gun hand: it was bloodied, the bones shattered. As if hit by a thunderbolt, he looked at Slocum. He was realizing he'd been beat in the draw.

Finally he found his voice. "God blast you. You broke my hand." He gazed again at his hand. "Might as well be dead."

Slocum smiled, his voice satirical. "Think of yourself as lucky, ole Quick-Draw." He bent to pick up Brady's gun, slipped it into his gunbelt. Then he slowly poured the coffee on the fire, watched the steam come up.

"And remember this, Brady, *a fast mouth can't beat a fast gun.*"

2

As they rode, Slocum looked at the broken rocks, the soaring cliffs, at a peak stabbing at the sky. Hit with glancing light by the sinking sun, it looked like a holy lance used against the heathens. They rode in silence until the sun went down, the land darkened, and the canyon became vast and mysterious.

Slocum picked a camping spot against a huge boulder, which gave protection, and built a fire in a pit. They ate rabbit and afterward he poured whiskey into their cups.

White Flower, since leaving Brady to lament his wounded hand and pride, had spoken little. Slocum couldn't help think that a man like Brady would have done miserable things to a woman like

13

her. He'd think of all the damage done by the Apache, use it as the excuse to make *her* pay for it.

She sat cross-legged in front of the fire, and sipped the drink. Her blue eyes glowed in the flickering light and the night shadows played on the fine planes of her face.

"Slocum is quick—a good warrior," she said.

He smiled. A quick gun was the secret of survival in the territory, where danger could strike from anywhere.

"That polecat, Brady, didn't have nice plans for you," he said.

She touched the knife in her boot. "White Flower would die before she'd let him take her."

A lotta spunk in the girl. He shook his head. "One need not die if one is smart as the fox. Better that the bad one die."

She gazed at him, thoughtfully, lifted the cup to her lips.

He listened to the cry of a nighthawk soaring overhead, and looked at the sky, now dark blue and studded with millions of big white stars. She seemed melancholy.

"Why," he asked, "does White Flower not wish to go back to her tribe?"

"The mother of White Flower is dead." Her voice was toneless. "It was Red Thunder who did it."

Slocum was astonished. "He did it? How?"

"The juice of a poison herb. To make her sick."

Slocum frowned. "Why?"

She looked quizzical. Not sure she could trust him. "The heart of Red Thunder was dark."

Slocum pondered. Her mother had no protection—she had mated with the detested white enemy and given birth to a half-breed. But what made Red Thunder so vicious? He seemed mighty interested in her wampum. And maybe more. "Was it because Red Thunder wanted you, and your mother stood in the way?"

White Flower's glance was cool. "He had reasons." It was all she said. Then she scowled and stared into the dark at the corner of the cliff fifty yards off. He turned sharply, but saw nothing, heard only the howl of a coyote. The sky glittered with stars and a golden moon hung low on the horizon. "What does White Flower see?" he asked.

Her nostrils dilated, but she stayed silent.

He strained and listened, heard nothing; she was part Indian and could pick up stuff that he couldn't.

He crouched low, gun in hand, moved quickly forward, hugging the side of the rocks. He did not believe, if they were Apache, that they'd attack. Indians rarely fought at night, believing that if they lost their life, their spirit would wander the night endlessly.

He caught the whisper of a sound and listened hard. If anything had been there, it was not there now. He felt sure, but crept cautiously forward, studying the earth. He found nothing.

When he came back he saw her huddled against a flat rock, gun in hand. It startled him for the moment and he wondered if her intent was hostile but, on sight of him, she lowered the gun. Her blue eyes were expectant.

"The Apache," she said.

"I saw nothing."

Her face kept its calmness. "The Apache does not fight at night."

"We must be up and ride before dawn," he said.

She looked at him but said nothing.

He slept, as he often did on the trail, with part of his mind interpreting the sounds of night, which told him there was no threat. He had given himself a wake-up signal, so that his eyes opened before the light of dawn. She slept, but when he moved near her, her eyes opened, and she seemed fully awake.

For a time, he took the trail east then turned south, trying to confound anyone tailing them. The land was pocketed with boulders, thin twisted trees, dusty brush and dry earth. They stopped and ate breakfast, and after coffee he felt better. He climbed a pileup of rocks and studied the land behind him. A lone eagle, high in the sky, was lazily soaring west toward the mountainous cliffs. Otherwise, he could see nothing.

When they reached the outskirts of the town of Grey Rock, he pulled up. "Slocum will go into town and find out about Sean O'Brien, where his ranch is. It should take an hour or two. This is a good place for White Flower to wait."

She nodded calmly. "White Flower will be near."

A lot of dignity in that girl, he thought as he rode toward town.

3

The town of Grey Rock baked in the hot Arizona sun, and Tom Stryker's saloon baked on its Main street.

Slocum tied the roan to the railing and pushed open the batwing doors. Some hard-looking men stood drinking at the bar, some played poker at the tables, and three women in slinky dresses sat talking.

The bartender, Stryker, a burly man with a bald head and stony gray eyes, came over.

"Whiskey," Slocum said.

Stryker put the bottle and glass on the wood in front of Slocum. "Where you ridin' in from, mister?"

"Name's Slocum. Northwest."

17

Stryker put his elbows on the counter. "Run into something, Slocum?"

"Like what?"

"Like Apache," drawled a hard-faced cowboy standing nearby.

Another nearby said, "Coupla bucks picked off some hosses at the Harris homestead. Rode in, nice as you please, shot the Mex and took the horses."

Slocum emptied his glass. Felt good going down. "Ran into one," he said, thinking it could be dangerous for cowboys not to know two Apaches were close by.

The men at the bar stopped drinking.

"Took care of him," Slocum said.

The drinking at the bar began again.

A big red-headed man stared at Slocum. "The only good redskin is a dead one," he said coldly and swaggered toward a woman at a table alone, playing solitaire.

She was pretty, with auburn hair, deep cleavage, and big breasts pushing against her filmy dress. She looked up from the cards as big Red approached, then looked past him to Slocum and she smiled.

Big Red didn't like it, and scowled as he sat down and talked to her.

A square-faced man with blond hair, looking at him with smiling blue eyes. "Say, would yuh be the Slocum fought with the Georgia Regulars?"

"That's me," Slocum said.

"I'm Bill Dykes." He stuck his hand out. "Glad to meet yuh. I was in the Regulars, not your out-fit, but we heard about John Slocum. 'Bout your sharpshootin'." He turned to the cowboy next to him. "This man was the shootingest rifleman in the company. Pickin' off the Union brass."

The men looked at him curiously. Slocum poured another drink. He didn't care to think much about the war; the memories were not good. It never was a neat job, just shooting the faceless enemy. You saw them clean and whole one moment, then busted and bleeding the next. And it happened around him, too. Men partly destroyed, groaning, wanting the peace of death.

"It was a bad war," he said, "brother fightin' brother."

"The bad part was how it ended," Dykes said.

Slocum looked thoughtful. A different world if the South had won. He had gone home afterward and, on the land that belonged for generations to his family, he found the arrogant carpetbagger who claimed title.

Slocum remembered the red rage that shook him, as if the holy earth of his forefathers cried out for vengeance. So that the carpetbagger did get title to the land, six foot deep. He had to run after that, and it had meant years of drifting in a territory where the wrong word or look could bring instant death.

Slocum's mind came back to Stryker's saloon where Bill Dykes was watching him with a friendly eye. Slocum leaned toward him. "Say, Dykes, know anything about a rancher named O'Brien?"

Dykes frowned. "Sean O'Brien?"

"That's the one."

Dykes nodded. "Big rancher, lots of cattle and horses."

The cowboy next to Dykes spoke up. "He's got a rotten drunk of a son, too, Chet O'Brien."

"There are two sons," Dykes said, "Mike O'Brien, a square shooter, and Chet. I hate a man who can't hold his liquor, and Chet's like that. When he stops here, he makes a stinking ruckus. If his old man wasn't O'Brien, he'd get the heave-ho."

Slocum lit a Havana. So there were two sons and one a bad drunk. "Where's the ranch?"

"Southwest, near the border. One of O'Brien's men just went through here yesterday—another miserable polecat. Same stripe as Chet, a killer. Quick-Draw Brady."

Slocum smoked, thinking that Quick-Draw Brady just recently lost that skill. He looked at the poker players, then the pretty, fine-breasted girl sitting with the husky redhead. He had pale blue eyes and a flushed, roughly seamed face. The woman caught Slocum's look and smiled, an inviting glint in in her eye. Slocum lifted his glass, thinking women like her somehow sensed a man with loaded loins. He was aware of Red, staring with his pale blue eyes. She spoke softly to him, then stood and, swiveling her hips, came to the bar, and stood next to Slocum. She was real female, with sleek skin, heavy breasts. She had soft brown eyes in her pretty face and they studied him.

"Want to offer a thirsty gal a drink, mister?"

"Offer you more than that, if you want," he said, as Stryker poured a drink for her.

She had a full pair of red lips that smiled. "I'll take whatever you offer." She sipped the whiskey, then said, "Ruby's the name, and pleasure's the game."

He laughed. She was original. "Slocum. Be happy to play any game with the likes of you."

She pursed her lips, and damned if he didn't get a jump in his loins. "Slocum, I like two things —a strong man and strong liquor."

He glanced at the bulky red-headed man, drinking and watching them sullenly. "Your friend seems unhappy."

She didn't look. "Red thinks if he rents a woman, he owns her."

Slocum shrugged. He'd known plenty of lonely cowboys to fall for women of easy virtue. They did desperate things. Well, right now he had other things in mind.

He gazed at Ruby's breasts, her nipples were pushing the dress. She picked up his glance. "Are you just for talk or can I interest you in pleasures of the flesh?"

"Lead the way," he said.

She started and he followed, watching the moving rhythm of her buttocks. They had to pass Big Red on the way to the stairs, and Slocum's concentration on a fine pair of buttocks made him miss Red, who quietly stuck his leg out causing Slocum to stumble.

The men at the bar turned with hopeful appreciation of some amusement. They knew how Red felt about Ruby, but Red had picked on this hard, lean stranger who looked plenty tough.

Slocum came up slowly, brushed himself. Big

Red's seamed broad face was fixed in an innocent grin. "Sho' hope you didn't hurt yourself, mister. Gotta be careful *where* you go."

Slocum studied the grinning face. "Gonna sit there or stand up?" he asked.

Red frowned. "What d'ya mean?"

"D'ya want me to hit you sittin' or standin'?"

Red stared, then the seamed face broke in a broad grin. "Well, mister, you sure got a piece of nerve, wantin' to mix it with Battlin' Red Jones." He sat there, rolling his sleeves, showing plenty of bicep. "But don't worry, I'll put you to sleep fast."

He stood up and started a swing, which Slocum blocked, and swung with lightning speed at his jaw, a thundering hard-fisted right, the power of a mule's kick behind it. Red's pale blue eyes went blank, his knees buckled and he fell back.

Slocum waited. The men in the saloon waited. But Battling Red Jones didn't get up, he just lay there, a dead hunk of meat, knocked unconscious.

Slocum shook his head and glanced at Stryker, staring with his stony gray eyes. "A man oughta brag *after* a fight, not before," Slocum said, and started after Ruby, who was standing on the stairs.

The room didn't have much, just a bed, a wooden table and chair, and a window facing Main Street.

She turned to him. "You're a streak o'lightning, Slocum."

He shrugged. The last thing he wanted was a bruising, drag-down fight with someone like Big Red who, if you gave him time enough, could put lumps on you. It was why he swung for the jaw, hoping to stiffen the big ox. It had worked, and now he could concentrate on a roustabout with this filly.

She had peeled her dress, facing away from him, and he was hit by her very female body, fine shoulders, the curve of her back widening to sensual hips, the shapely buttocks. His own flesh responded, and when she looked at him she said, "Every inch a man." She went about her business with hand and lips, showing plenty of skill. He felt her heat, and his desire seethed. He stroked her plump breasts with their thick nipples, her silky buttocks, reaching in the soft warmth between her thighs. She breathed deeply, and fell back on the bed. He bent over her, looking into her dark eyes as he pierced her with his fevered flesh. She squirmed, grabbed his waist tightly, her hips writhing. He stroked her body, her breasts, her buttocks, pushed by rising desire into hard, deep thrusts. She picked up his rhythm, and they did that until she stiffened and grabbed him fiercely, moaning. His surging tension made him drive into a hard, frenzied climax. She writhed and twisted under him. They lay there, breathing fast.

Later, after he had dressed, she still sprawled nakedly on the bed, looking at him.

"That was a lot of pleasure," she said.

He put money on the table and grinned, remembering what she'd said at the bar. "Slocum's the name and pleasure's the game."

He walked down the stairs, wary—no telling what a man like Red would be up to. Might be vindictive; a man who bragged and came to grief was a humiliated man, and Slocum had found such men

could be dangerous. But there was no sight of
Red. At the bar, men were drinking, Dykes, his
eyes heavy-lidded, was talking to the cowboy next
to him. Men still played poker at the tables. Nobody paid attention. Slocum moved easily out of
the saloon to the roan. The sun had slipped a bit
in a sky dotted with cottony clouds. The mountains bulked huge and craggy in the clear air. Slocum swung over the roan and rode west.

He rode out to the boulder, where he expected to
meet White Flower. Her tracks went south, moving into a thicket of brush. He dismounted,
walked to a flat boulder, sat on it, pulled a Havana
and lit up. As he smoked he looked at the thick
cotton clouds, weirdly shaped, drifting in the pale
blue sky. The descending sun threw long shadows
behind the jutting crags of the canyon. A scent of
desert flowers came on a stray fluff of wind. Nice
time of day, just before the sun started its dra-
matic changes on the earth, darker, longer
shadows—a blazing sky, then twilight, then night
and its silver moon.

No sign yet of White Flower, and he wondered
if she headed out on her own. If so, then he'd go
on to his own destination, Plainsville, where he
hoped to find ole Charley Elders, one of the riders
of the Cantrell gang. Then he thought again about
White Flower. He'd ride her trail for a mile, to be
sure she was under her own power. He flipped
the cigar, watched it tumble to the parched earth,
then became aware of her, standing at the edge of
a boulder, looking at him. It bothered him; if
she'd been someone with mean intent, he'd be in

buzzard shit. The quiet craft of the Apache. Again he was struck by the clear beauty of her face, the womanly lines of her body.

"White Flower is slow to appear," he said.

"As is Slocum." Her blue eyes stared coldly into his. He wondered if she had sensed his activities, which might annoy her, since he was pursuing his pleasures at the cost of her time. Well, he owed her nothing and could rightfully find his pleasures, and if she didn't like it, she was always free to ride on her own. But the idea of this beautiful girl riding alone through a territory crawling with danger hit him wrong. He walked toward her.

"Slocum has found out about Sean O'Brien."

Her eyes gleamed and she waited.

"He has a big ranch—down south, near Vista, down at the border. Two moons of riding."

Her face was impassive. "Perhaps Slocum cares not to ride further with White Flower. If that is so, I will go on alone."

He stared. Ready to ride, by herself, into a nest of snakes—brave but foolish. Why? Was she gracious, not wanting to put him at risk, or was there some darker reason?

He smiled broadly. "Slocum goes south and wishes to ride with you." He paused. "Unless *you* do not wish it."

Her blue eyes were piercing; it seemed by some intuitive trick she picked up what he had done at the saloon.

"White Flower offers thanks for the kindness of Slocum." She walked toward the thicket, toward her horse, probably. He watched her, then went to the roan, stroked the horse's nose. With a movement of affection, the roan pushed against Slocum's chest.

"Mebbe, old pal, you can figure the mind of the woman," he muttered in the roan's ear.

They took the trail south and rode uneventfully until the sun reached the horizon. The tall peaks collected purple clouds, and the sky glowed with primrose edged with dark green and orange, and they found a nice nook for camp by the time the North Star gleamed brightly in the sky. They made a fire, ate beef jerky, and later, after coffee, Slocum, feeling mellow said, "Sean O'Brien is a man with much land, many horses and cattle. Does White Flower know this?"

She shook her head. It didn't seem to matter.

"And O'Brien has two sons."

Though her face stayed impassive, her eyes glittered. Perhaps that meant something.

"Is Sean O'Brien a friend to your mother?"

She stared at him, not liking his question, but finally, in a low voice. "I go to find Sean O'Brien."

A mystery, he thought. Wasn't his business, though a mighty interesting situation. White Flower had no intention of telling him about her connection with O'Brien, and he wouldn't push it.

He slept deeply but woke once, aware of movement, and listened, half-asleep, until he heard the coyote growl and scrabble through bush in pursuit of prey. He drifted back to restless sleep. Then prodded by instinct that something was not right, his hand stole to his holster, but it was too late.

"Don't do that, mister."

His eyes shot open and, to his amazement, he saw in the clear moonlight the bulky form of Red, half-hidden by the boulder twenty feet away, gun pointing. He moved forward surprisingly catlike for so big a man.

"Now mister, pull your gun by the handle, with your fingers, and toss it here. One wrong move, I'll blow your head off."

Slocum did it and cursed his stupidity. White Flower, twenty feet away, was leaning on her elbow, her face pale in the moonlight. Red threw a sharp glance at her, then bent for the gun, flung it into the bushes, his eyes on Slocum. He came close, his pale blue eyes glaring in his broad-boned face.

"Turn," he said harshly, pulling a piece of rope from his pocket. He tied Slocum's wrists tightly.

He stared into Slocum's eyes. "I should bust you one, but don't like to hit a helpless man. *Usually.*" He grinned broadly, then walked to the roan, reached into the saddlebag for Slocum's whiskey bottle, took a long swallow, then came back, glancing at White Flower, still watching.

Relaxed, he sat on a nearby flat rock, guzzled more whiskey, wiped his mouth with the sleeve of his blue shirt.

"Been following your trail, Slocum, since you left town. Always outa sight. Couldn't wait for you to settle down."

"What's eatin' you, Red? You lost in a fair fight."

Red glared. "So you don't know what's eatin' me? You gotta be plenty dumb, mister. You ruined me in front of the boys—and worse, in front of *my woman*. That's what yuh did, you dog."

"Your woman? She's the woman for any man with the price."

Red's teeth gritted, and he swung the pistol, hitting Slocum on the jaw. "I oughta cut your tongue out for that, you low-down buzzard. She's doin' it 'cause she's hard up. I aim to take her outa that." He looked at White Flower. "Nice-lookin' breed you travelin' with. *Your* woman, I reckon?"

Slocum's jaw felt bruised. He could see the movements of Red's thought. "No. Just givin' her escort south."

"Givin' her escort." Red grinned. "That's real nice. How come you're screwing Ruby when you got this breed filly?"

Slocum's mouth tightened. How'd you get through the thick head of a man like Red? And what was in his slimy mind? The last thing Slocum figured would be a buzzard like Red to trail him for revenge. But Red was that kind of man, couldn't stand to be knocked down in front of his girl and his bar buddies. Couldn't live with that. Craving revenge, he craftily trailed Slocum, happy to discover the woman. Again Slocum cursed himself for underestimating this mulehead. Now he had winning cards, and Slocum with his hands tied, felt powerless.

Red swilled from the bottle again, wiped his mouth, looked at White Flower, and motioned her to come. Slocum looked at his brutal, leering face —he didn't know she understood English. But his gesture was clear. She ignored him. His eyes narrowed, and he threw a shot inches from her. She didn't jump, just calmly looked at him. "C'mere, you half-breed bitch," he growled, "or I'll fill ya fulla holes."

She came forward, standing in front of him. Red stared in the bright moonlight, astonished.

"Dammit, you got a real beauty here." He stroked his chin, grinning. "Well, mister, reckon it's only fair that since you took my woman, I take yours. Only difference, I'm gonna let you watch— see you go through the misery."

He made a sudden grab at White Flower. She fought like a tiger, but he held her with greater strength, pulling at her buckskins.

Slocum, in frustrated fury, tugged at the cords holding his wrists until they bit his flesh. He stared with hate at the bulking Red who, by this time, had stripped White Flower down to her boots.

In the moonlight, she looked like the sculpture of Diana.

"Looka this, mister," Red crowed, his eyes glittering. "Better than Ruby. Let's find out if she does it as good." He grinned, sat down to pull off his Levi's and, in that moment White Flower moved, her hand swept past her boot and came up. Slocum heard the grunt as Red's eyes went open in shock, staring at the knife buried in his chest.

His hand went up trying to pull it; he stood, stumbled toward her, then fell on his back, his hand closing around the handle. Then, as his body heaved convulsively, his eyes locked on Slocum, and the light of his life slipped away.

Slocum looked at her, still nude, at her curved woman's body. She calmly slipped into the buckskins, leaned forward, pulled the knife from the lifeless body, releasing a spurt of blood. She wiped the knife on his Levi's, came to Slocum and cut the ropes.

Slocum rubbed his raw wrists, moved into the bushes, scrounging until he found his gun, and slipped it into his holster.

They silently looked at Red, at the stain of blood spreading slowly over his blue shirt.

"Well," he said, "couldn't have happened to a nicer guy."

She frowned but got his drift, and as she put the knife back into her boot, spoke calmly. "Not the first time that White Flower has struck down the wolf."

The sky was streaking pink with the light of dawn by the time Slocum dug a grave, pulled Red into it. Later when they ate breakfast, White Flower seemed remote. He lit up during coffee, and as he smoked wondered what was eating her because she scarcely looked at him. Suddenly she stood up.

"White Flower will go on alone."

He stared. "Alone. Why?"

She shrugged. "It is enough that I wish to."

"But it will not be safe."

Her lovely mouth was pressed in a stern line. "Was it safe to ride with Slocum?"

He scowled; it was true that, just because she rode with him, she had almost caught hell. He rubbed his chin, looking at her lovely serious face.

She said, "What did Slocum do to bring this paleface on his trail, to make him want to kill?"

How could he answer? That while she waited here, alone, he had played games with a saloon lady whom, for some idiotic reason, Red considered his woman. Slocum stroked his chin—because he had wrestled in a hot bed with Ruby, it had pitched Red to a jealous fury, and in revenge, he attacked White Flower. A pity, Slocum thought—she had saved his life and he felt beholden, but an Indian maid had her own ideas of the right, and felt no need to lean on a paleface for safety.

He shrugged. "It is not wise for a beautiful girl to ride alone where the danger is great."

She gazed at him with piercing blue eyes, then climbed her powerful pony and sitting straight as a ramrod, rode off at an easy pace.

He watched until she was lost to sight behind a rise of rocks.

Yellow light from the rising sun spread over the gray sky while he drank another coffee. Then he put the utensils into his saddlebag, mounted up, and followed her trail south.

As he rode, the sun washed the sky of gray, casting new clean light on the peaks and crags of the canyon.

He rode easy, his eyes picking the tracks left by White Flower, and thought about her. Beautiful half-breed. Why was she heading for O'Brien? Was he in some strange way connected with her? What did O'Brien have to do with her? That document in her wampum, which Red Thunder seemed fascinated by, did it have meaning? Well, he'd never solve the mystery. The girl had gone, probably out of his life forever.

Then he saw the object flying toward him and ducked, but not enough, for the blunt edge of the tomahawk hit the side of his head a glancing blow, enough to explode a hundred lights in his brain. Then all went dark.

When his eyes opened, his head ached, and he found himself looking at a bright blue sky. He tried to move his hands but couldn't. He was tied to stakes driven into the ground. He looked up and saw two Apaches squatted near him, broad faces, slitted brown eyes, long black hair tied with red headbands. The two braves who White Flower had warned would discover the death of Red Thunder and come in pursuit of the paleface killer. Nice, and he'd walked into their trap. His hands were tied with leather thongs to the stakes.

The Apache nearest had eyes that glinted like brown marbles. He grunted, spoke to his broad-shouldered comrade, then pulled his knife and, staring into Slocum's eyes, slowly cut a six-inch slash on his chest. Blood surged to the surface and, to the astonishment of the Apache, the pale-face made no sound. The Apache stared at him, grinned, and pointed to the sun, and to a buzzard flying over them. They were going to leave him to the frying sun and the greedy buzzards, he was saying, to pay him off for killing Red Thunder. The Apache leaned close and Slocum could smell his sweat as his knife crisscrossed the lines left by the other cut. While he did this, he stared into Slocum's eyes, looking for fear or pain, and to his disappointment found none. The Apache turned to his broad-chested comrade, and they spoke for a few minutes. One of them went to Slocum's roan, grazing about thirty feet away, near a pileup of rocks. The Apache searched the saddlebag and pulled the whiskey bottle, threw his head back, and took a long drink. A thin, double-bladed throwing knife swished through the air and struck his throat, severing his vocal cords, and he stumbled back, unable to make a sound as he went down slowly on the grass-carpeted earth.

The other Apache, fascinated by Slocum's courage, and the blood creeping from his wounds, grinned ferociously, holding up the red edge of the knife to let the sun glitter on it. He leaned forward to cut again on the paleface's chest, when the thin-bladed knife flashed through the air and thunked, burying itself deep in his back. The Apache grunted, sprung up in anguish, and twisting to look behind, tried to reach for the sticking knife. His eyes shocked wide open as he saw White Flower coming toward him, and his face grimaced horribly as he tried, with all his strength to throw his own knife at her, but he fell to the ground, then crawled toward her, his face menacing. She walked slowly to him, her face impassive, and stopped a foot away. He looked up, his eyes ferocious with hate and the expression froze on his face.

Her face emotionless, she took the knife from the Apache's lifeless fingers and came to Slocum, bit her lip at the sight of his bloody chest, then cut the thongs. Slocum, who had been thinking desperate thoughts, looked at her as he came to his feet, rubbing his wrists. The second time she'd saved his life. And he had thought she needed *his* protection. He walked to the roan, looked at the

Apache crumpled on the ground, his throat red
with blood.

Bloody mess 'round here, he thought, pulling a
cloth from his bag, and lifting the bottle from the
ground. It still had whiskey; he poured some on
the cloth and bound it against his chest which
leaked blood. He put on his shirt, pulled his gun
from the belt of the Apache, and stuck it in his
holster.

He turned back to White Flower who'd been
watching.

The girl was a jewel. "Slocum gives great
thanks to White Flower." He pointed to the dead
Indians. "How did you know about them?"

A small smile twisted her lips. "I knew. They
let me pass to take you first. They would come for
me, later. I came back—to stop them."

So, she understood the Apache mind. They
would get to her, time for that, after they did their
dirty work on the paleface. But she hit the first
blow. So, it was twice she'd delivered him from
death. He'd be a strong right arm for her.

He pulled out a Havana and lit it. "Slocum
would care greatly to ride with White Flower to
find O'Brien, if she wishes."

She looked piercingly at him, then gazed at the
distant peaks. "The Apache had come to kill Slocum because of Red Thunder. Slocum had no
quarrel with Red Thunder—he gave help to
White Flower." She smiled. "It is right for me to
help Slocum. Slocum owes nothing for this."

He looked at her lovely face. What did it matter? She had put her life at risk coming back,
using a throwing knife against two powerful

Apaches. He would have been buzzard bait, frying in the sun. He owed her plenty.

"Come," he said, "we will ride together to O'Brien."

Again she smiled, and he was damned if she didn't look happy about it.

4

The Arizona sun broiled down on the strong, square face of Sean O'Brien and he mopped his brow as he watched Chet, his younger son, start toward Hellfire, the stallion. A shout went up from the men hanging on the fence of the corral. The kind of shout, O'Brien judged, that recognized it took guts to try and break this killer bronc. He'd already thrown Younger, Herb, and Amos. Thrown them mean and kicking up a storm afterward. That devil-hearted stallion could easily brain a fallen rider with one of those kicks. Any smart cowboy would give Hellfire plenty of space. But not Chet, he took the challenge. Out to show the boys they couldn't do it, but he could. O'Brien felt he'd been cursed with a blasted fool for a younger son. Where in hell was Mike—his smart son? Riding the range, keeping an eye on things, as he should.

Chet strutted toward the black-nosed, four-legged murderer who stared at him with malicious black eyes. O'Brien could read hate in those eyes, hate for the vicious, two-legged creature who put a burden on his back, who cut his haunches with spike heels.

O'Brien watched Chet wave at the cowboys hanging on the corral fence, eager for the fun, to see a confrontation between two mean critters, the stallion and the rider. O'Brien wondered how many of the cowboys wanted Chet to break the bronc or break his neck. His younger son was not exactly popular with the men. The lad was a spoiler; it seemed to happen after the death of Millie, his mother.

Yes, after she died, he went bad. Why? A mystery. What the hell, O'Brien never figured that out.

He took a deep breath, mopped his sweating brow with his neckerchief. He had a powerful body, a square-jawed handsome face, with fine blue eyes and a long Irish lip. He had come out to the territory as a yearling, and gone through plenty of hell. Started from scratch and, with hard sweat, he carved a great ranch, a thousand head of cattle. Done it for Millie, the kids, Mike, his first-born, and Chet. Now Millie was gone, dead from the bite of a rattler; he had put six bullets in that snake. She left Mike, a fine son, a square shooter, and Chet, a blister of a boy. Always in scrapes; look what he did to poor Addie Baker. Took plenty to fix that up, and what about the time he shot the butt off that Mexican kid just for bumping him. It was the drinking. That was the misery. He'd go haywire, like now. Plenty of hooch in him, that's what put his devil up, pushed him to try Hellfire.

Chet reached the bronc, held tightly by Sonny Evans, and turned to the men cheering him on. "Watch it, men," he called. "Show you how to turn this heller into a pussy cat."

He laughed. He had the bright blue eyes of his father, but the facial contours of his mother, delicate, and a soft, spoiled mouth that twisted in a mocking smile. That was his smile as he looked at Hellfire.

The stallion quivered with rage when Chet came close; this was one of those queer, two-footed animals who tried to dominate him. In the sun he could see the cruel spikes glittering on the boots of the rider, the hurtful whip in hand. Hellfire stared at the laughing face, and pulled against the iron bit that tore his mouth, holding him tight so that this hated man could climb over his body. The rider pulled viciously on the bit, and dug the steel into his haunches. An unbearable insult to the stallion's pride; he lifted on two legs, pawed at the sky to shake the hated human burden from his back. But it clung; and the iron teeth bit against his sides. In fury he came down, humped his body violently, keeping his legs stiff. He felt the rider loosen but still hang on. The bronc again pawed at the sky, and when he came down rushed headlong at the fence, as if he'd drive through, scattering the sitting cowboys, yelling in harsh voices. The bronc stopped suddenly and heaved, felt the rider slip forward, but somehow hang on. Now, in a paroxysm of rage, he stomped the ground, frenziedly lashed his body and, feeling the rider slip, suddenly heaved and threw the man into a crazy somersault. He hit the ground with a thud and lay there. The bronc, in a fury of triumph, kicked wildly, blissful to be free. He saw the grounded two-footed creature, his face distorted with rage, reach for the iron at his side, point it at him. The bronc never heard the roar of the gun, for the bullets had riddled his brain, and his body slipped slowly to the ground. *The bronc died like all earth creatures who choose death rather than servitude*.

O'Brien stared at Chet, feeling white-hot anger that he didn't want to show. Not to humiliate Chet in front of the men. *But he'd shot that fine stallion because it had beat him*. That was the truth of it. There was no manhood in Chet O'Brien—*his* son.

Most of the men hanging on the corral fence didn't like it but said nothing; Chet was the honcho's son. But Wilbur and Lonnie Smith were grinning, sidekicks of Chet—cut from the same cloth, O'Brien thought—miserable.

"That's how to tame him, Chet," yelled Wilbur, hanging on the fence just a few feet from O'Brien.

"Yeah, nice shootin', slugger," said Lonnie, still grinning.

O'Brien stared coldly at him. "What the hell's so funny?"

Lonnie looked astonished. "Sorry, Mr. O'Brien, but Chet said he'd tame the killer. Reckon he did."

"Is that what you'd do—if you couldn't ride a hoss—kill him?"

Lonnie bit his lip. "Sorry boss, but I'm thinking that Hellfire wasn't a hoss. More a devil, lookin' like a hoss."

Chet brushed at his Levi's, looked impassively at the dead Hellfire, and called to the men watching him. "Coupla of you drag this carcass off." His face hard, he said, "Feed the buzzards." He picked up his fallen Stetson, dusted it, and stuck it over his honey-colored hair. As he walked toward his father, his eyes narrowed, knowing instantly the old man wanted to fry him, but mightn't do it there. Didn't like the men to know there was family friction.

O'Brien looked into the depths of Chet's blue eyes, trying to find the secret that made this boy, flesh of his flesh, do such a rotten trick. From whom did he learn it? Mike never did it, nor did he.

Chet knew the look and hated it, but he wasn't taking any crap from the old man.

"Why'd you do that, Chet?" O'Brien's voice was low.

Chet's face was hard. "It was a killer hoss, that's why."

"You did it because you couldn't ride him, that it?"

"Nobody could."

"Maybe Mike could."

Chet's face clouded. "Always Mike—is that it, Dad? Well, he's been dumped, too."

"But he didn't shoot the hoss because he got dumped." O'Brien's voice was cold.

Chet ground his teeth, looked at Lonnie, a friendly face. "If I couldn't break that devil, Mike couldn't."

"But you don't kill a fine-spirited animal like Hellfire because he dumps you. There comes a time when you just might break through. Then you've got a special hoss. You gotta see that, Chet."

Chet wiped the sweat of his brow with his kerchief, watching two men put heavy rope around the neck of the dead horse. "That special hoss could easily have kicked me in the head."

"That might help."

Chet glanced at the men; though out of earshot, they had to know the old man was hammering him. A flush stained his cheek.

O'Brien took a chew on a plug; he didn't want to break Chet's spirit. He did rotten things, he was wild, but he might make the right turn, maybe. Shouldn't bear down too hard.

"Look, Chet." He smiled. "I don't want to beat on you. I know you've got good stuff." He grinned broadly. "You come outa good blood. It's just that you go off half-cocked. I figger you got dumped in front of the men, didn't like to look bad and in a fit, shot the hoss. Okay. All I'm sayin' is you gotta control that temper." He waved his hand. "All this will be yours and Mike's someday. And you'll need a wise head to run it. I don't get tired of telling you, it took a lot of sweat to build all this. I did it for you boys and for Ma." His eyes clouded at the memory. She'd been bit by a rattler and died in his arms after he emptied his gun at that slick, squirming bastard. He cleared his throat. "I hate to think all my work will go into mighty careless hands."

Chet flushed. He hated to be criticized, felt his

father sniped at him and favored Mike. But the O'Brien ranch was a jewel in the territory, and the idea that his father, out of spite, might bypass his lawful rights, was a most aggravating thought.

"Tell yuh, Dad, I figgered that hoss a killer—that a wild kick might brain me. So I shot him. I'll take your word that I did wrong. Don't want to set you against me."

O'Brien smiled. "I understand, boy. No more of this." He glanced at the men who seemed happy the old man was smiling again. "Where the hell is Brady?"

Chet grinned, glad that he'd put the old man back into a good mood. He could handle him; all he had to do was eat crow. That's what the old man wanted. He lit up a cigarillo. "Brady's gone to Tombstone, to pay off Doc Holliday."

O'Brien shook his head. "Brady, I fear is gotten too big for his britches. Doc's one dangerous critter; wouldn't like to hear bad news about Brady."

"Brady can take care o' himself, Dad. I seen him do it."

Two riders, straining their horses, dragged the dead Hellfire out of the corral. O'Brien watched the magnificent animal on its side pulled through the dust. A dirty end to a beautiful animal, he thought and looked at Chet.

Chet started toward the red bunkhouse. He wasn't going to hang on and take more of the old man's preaching bullshit. If Mike had shot the damned bronc, the old man would not beat on him. But Mike wouldn't have pulled his gun, Mike was like the old man—"you don't kill a hoss

'cause it dumps you." Chet rubbed his cheek.
They thought him wild. Maybe he was wild, yes,
and it started after Ma died. She stumbled into
that snake pit, when the old man was near. *He
shoulda stopped her*. Chet gritted his teeth. God,
how he loved Ma, and she cared, too, standing by
him against the old man. Chet never got over the
way she died, and the sight of any rattler brought
out his rage and his gun.

As he passed the hillock near the bunkhouse,
he saw Brady riding. He smiled, ole Quick-Draw,
his one real friend at the ranch. But Brady was not
smiling, in fact, looked downright mean. As he
came near, Chet shocked, saw his bandaged hand.
His shootin' hand. Damned, what in hell happened in Tombstone? Brady had gone up there
with Doc Holliday as a target. After all his brag-
gin' that Doc Holliday had more rep than speed,
he turns up with a bad shootin' hand.

Brady slipped off his saddle.

"Doc get you, Brady?"

Brady flushed and looked away, at the peaks of
the mountain glowing pastel pink in the sun.

Chet waited, but Brady said nothing.

"Mebbe a mule kicked your hand, Brady. Can't
believe you got beat in a draw."

Brady's face hardened. "A polecat drew on me,
afore I knew he was goin' to. That's how I got
beat, Chet."

Chet stared at him; was he lying? It was a matter of pride. Never goin' to admit someone pulled
a faster gun than Quick-Draw Brady.

Brady took a cigarillo from his shirt pocket, and
Chet lit it with a lucifer. Brady looked at his ban-

daged hand in disgust. "Someday I'm goin' to run up against that polecat and hope you're with me. So we can pulverize his carcass."

Chet shook his head. "You ain't gonna be much good with that hand. Be glad to help, Brady. Who was the man?"

"Called himself Slocum."

Chet shook his head. "Shot before you drew? He's gotta be a low-down buzzard. I'll remember the name. Slocum."

5

Early in the day Slocum's green eyes clouded when he saw the swirl of smoke, three miles south, on the trail used by settlers headed west. White Flower had seen it, too, and didn't like it. *Apache attack*. They were riding this trail and to avoid it would mean a long circle north and lots of rock climbing. The idea didn't discourage White Flower because she pointed north.

"Too much travel time lost that way," he said.

She studied the smoke. "Burning wagons."

His face hardened. It was, as he thought, settlers under attack. He had to move forward and help, if possible. He had seen Apache fury against the intruding whites who tried to usurp the land.

"We must try to help," he said.

Her eyes shone with feelings. "Best not to go."

47

He looked at her lovely face; he had to remember that she was part Apache, and that it
would be a harsh thing for her to confront the fight
between White and Apache. But it was every
white man's duty, to help the settler under Indian
attack.

"Come—we must go this way," he said deci-
sively, starting the roan.

She held her pony, her face strained, aware
that he would not stop, but press on whatever she
did. She eased her pony forward.

Slocum could hear the hoofbeats of her horse,
and it pleased him. The smoke was darkening, and
he pushed the roan harder through a trail that
thickened with bushes and rocks, and descended
into a valley. The sort of ground easy to trap
wagons. The cracks of rifles reverberated off the
cliffs, and Slocum's jaw clenched. When he felt it
right, he swung off the roan, rifle in hand, and
moved quick and silent behind brush and boulder.
Only once did he glance back to look at her.

From a boulder that gave a view to flat ground,
he saw two wagons burning, and white bodies
sprawled around the wagons. A man lay flat on the
ground, behind the wheel of the front wagon, firing at two Apaches with rifles, crouched behind
the shelter of rocks. They didn't seem aware of
Slocum, but he didn't have much of a shot until
one Apache stuck his head out to aim at the
settler. Slocum fired instantly, his bullet ripping a
piece of the Apache's skull, and he went down.
After firing, Slocum ran, crouching low, to a
nearby boulder for a different position. The other
Apache, long-haired, with a red headband, aware

someone other than the settler had fired, went into hiding until he could discover what happened. The settler looked in Slocum's direction, puzzled. He figured it had to be a friend and waved. A bullet from the hidden Apache almost hit him, and he went flat again.

Slocum signaled for White Flower to stay put and began a careful movement to encircle the Apache's rocky position. He crawled on his stomach until he reached a solid formation of rocks, slipping silently behind them. The firing had stopped, since gunfire could clue the Apache's position. After slow, crafty movement, Slocum reached the spot he wanted and peered, his rifle ready, but all he saw behind the rock was empty space, and the dead Apache, blood flowing from the wound in his skull.

Slocum, with a jolt, realized his move had been cunningly anticipated by the Apache, who made his own. It meant sudden danger. He listened hard but heard only the crackle of burning wagons.

Peering out, he could see the settler, down flat, his rifle pointed, puzzled about what was happening. Then Slocum heard the faint sound of hoofbeats, and moving quickly he caught a glimpse of the Apache, crouched low on his pony, racing into a rock cluster, beyond Slocum's fire. He waited, then came toward the settler who, alarmed to see him emerge from the position of the Apache, raised his rifle, staring hard at the big, lean, white stranger holding his hand up in warning.

Slocum came forward, and the settler, believing the danger past, rushed to the woman sprawled on the ground and, overcome by grief, he threw himself on her. She was young and the swell of her abdomen revealed her pregnant, and she was dead, her eyes stark and staring. So the man had not only lost his wife, but also his unborn child. An older man and woman who could be the father and mother, lay near the other wagon; they were bloody from rifle fire, and also dead. Slocum watched the settler, a stubble-bearded, brown-eyed, raw-boned man in his grief. A farmer, who'd probably come west with his family to grab a piece of land and start again, got an ending instead. Wiped out—family and possessions. Again and again, Slocum had seen it—men hungry for a new life, in the promised land of the west, finding instead a violent end. The Apache was in a rage at these pale-faced despoilers who killed his food, the buffalo, carelessly for their skin, and grabbed the land of his forefathers. The Apache believed the paleface must be destroyed, viciously, to discourage this assault on his land.

Slocum came forward and the man, his eyes moist with grief, looked up, still in shock from the sudden loss of everything dear.

"Those bastards," he cursed wildly, "those red-skinned bastards." And he rushed to where the dead Apache lay and emptied his rifle, pumping bullets into the body, making it jump.

Slocum bit his lip. The man had to do that to get the hate out. "I'm sorry," he said simply.

"Why do they do it?" the settler demanded. "Why?"

Slocum's face was impassive. "Trying to hang on to their land, I reckon."

"But they've damn well lost it!"

"Makes them mad all the more," Slocum said.

The settler stared evely at Slocum; he wanted sympathy, not explanation. "They're animals—hitting women and children—scalping. They're less than human." His voice softened. "Thanks for your help, mister. You saved my scalp. Figgered myself a goner till you showed up. I came out with my woman and folks from Ohio. Foster's my name."

"Slocum."

Foster stared out at the land. "There's still one out there."

Then his eyes grew rigid, and he brought up his rifle and triggered it, but it was empty. Slocum, with a sudden movement, grabbed the barrel and tore the rifle from his hand.

"That's one of them, mister," Foster snarled as White Flower came toward them. And he tried to grab Slocum's gun from its holster, but Slocum caught his wrist and pinned his arm behind his back. "Go easy, Foster. She's not your enemy."

They watched White Flower, in her buckskins, her face impassive, walk slowly toward them.

Foster, by this time, had seen her face and it made him aware of her white blood. He chewed his underlip ferociously, baffled about what his response should be. She wore the buckskins of the Apache, but she seemed white. Then he looked again at the dead body of his wife, and dazed, walked toward her, dropping to his knees and covering his face with his hands.

Later, Slocum helped him bury his family,

placing stones at the head of the graves. Foster kneeled again and prayed. Afterward, he burdened the horses with the remnants of his possessions, thanked Slocum, hoped to see him someday in Tucson, and rode west. He never looked at White Flower.

They watched him ride, a small figure against the vast, towering mountains. Then White Flower turned to him.

"Slocum?" Her face was thoughtful, her small white teeth pressed against her lip.

He looked at her.

"I ask this. Would White Flower find such anger against her when she goes to Sean O'Brien?"

The afternoon sun hit the fine bones of her face, intensified the glowing blue of her eyes, the curved lips. Beautiful with something indefinable from the Indian. What man could fail to respond to her?

"For an answer, one must know *why* White Flower goes to Sean O'Brien."

Her face was solemn. "That is something I cannot tell."

She tightened the belt around her waist, and started toward her pony. He walked to his roan, wondering if the answer lay in the pocket of that belt, the dried parchment that Red Thunder had lifted and seemingly the reason he came after her so violently. What in hell was it? Though mystified and sure it held the answer, he wouldn't ask her.

They rode silently toward the O'Brien ranch, now a few miles southeast. A dazzling sun burned in a luminous light blue sky clear of clouds.

It was sultry hot.

After an hour of riding, they reached a slow, flowing stream and made camp. They let the horses drink, and Slocum washed his head and face. He looked at the thick brush around them. "I'll mosey back there, see if I can hunt us some fresh meat. In that time, White Flower might want to swim."

She watched him, a green-eyed paleface who rode straight and strong on his horse. She thought of Red Thunder who held a knife inches from her heart, and how this man, a stranger, had with a quick, accurate bullet, saved her life. She, an Apache, a race that desired only to destroy the paleface. But she, too, was partly a paleface. She had repaid Slocum, twice saving his life. She liked his manliness, his warmth. A great white warrior who offered protection. Her mission was to reach O'Brien, and Slocum vowed to bring her there safely.

She peeled her buckskins and walked stately and beautiful to the stream, plunged in, feeling the cool freshness of the water. She swam, looked at her reflected body, smoothed her hands over her sleek skin, her full breasts, her slender waist, the billowing hips. Her head turned sharply as she picked up two riders. She moved quickly to the shore, snatching her buckskins, and within minutes was at the fire, preparing coffee. She had gauged their distance, hoping by the time they reached her that Slocum would be back.

The men rode at a brisk canter, obviously interested in the stream toward which they'd been heading. Horses need water on a hot day.

When the riders reached the stream, they brought their horses to the water, filled their canteens, and stared at her. They were brawny palefaces, in blue Levi's and broad Stetsons. One had a bandaged hand and, with a start, White Flower recognized the one who called himself Brady—whose shooting hand Slocum had spoiled. Her skin prickled as he stared at her, his face darkly sullen.

"This is the bitch half-breed I tole you about." Brady's eyes slitted; they were bloodshot from drinking.

Chet's face, also whiskey red, looked hard at her. "Mighty good-lookin' breed."

Brady's lips twisted in an ugly sneer as a couple of thoughts skittered through his head. But he had seen the hoofprints of a horse. "Slocum—where is he?"

"Not with me now," she said.

"He run out on you?" A boozy smile as he came closer to her. "He left the pretty squaw alone in the badlands?"

She stared coldly into his eyes and said nothing.

"Not too chatty, hey." He turned to Chet. "She's why I got no shootin' hand. That low-down skunk with her pulled his gun when I wasn't lookin'."

Chet stared at her.

"Paleface has lying tongue," she said calmly.

Brady slapped her face and brought his left hand to his holster, the red mark of his fingers was on her cheek; her face stayed emotionless.

Brady scowled. "Waitin' for her to throw a knife so I can put a bullet up her butt."

Chet was looking at the coffee.

Brady had seen her voluptuous body in the stream and licked his lips. "You did me a great hurt, bitch squaw, and I figger you owe me something."

Chet laughed, "And yore goin' to collect, you dirty-minded buzzard. He pointed to the coffee. Got any whiskey for this coffee, squaw lady?"

"Coffee." She nodded, a gleam in her eyes.

Brady, close to her, put his hand on her breast, grinning into her face. "Yeah, first we'll have the coffee, *then we'll have the half-breed squaw.*"

Chet laughed as she started for the coffee pot, to pour the cups. But a slithering on the ground in the nearby thicket made him go rigid—he slowly pulled his gun and moved softly toward the sound. Brady watched, grinning, aware that Chet, if he could, would kill all the snakes in the world.

White Flower, at the fire, her back to them, slipped her fingers into her belt, and passed them over the cups. She poured the coffee, brought one to Brady, which he sipped absently as he watched Chet crouching in the thicket. Suddenly he fired, and the snake jumped and squirmed in its death throes. Chet's eyes glittered vindictively. In his mind, he had once again avenged the death of his mother.

He holstered his gun and turned. Brady was pale and holding his throat. He coughed violently, then stared at White Flower, and his eyes, rigid, were frozen with terror as he slipped slowly to the earth.

Chet was astounded. He leaned down, shook him roughly. "Is this a joke, Brady? Brady! Get up, man."

Brady just lay there, his mouth open, his eyes lifeless.

Chet stared, aware that Brady was as dead as a doorknob. he looked at White Flower, at her calm face, then picked up the coffee cup and saw the powdered herb in the bottom of the cup.

"You poisoned him, didn't you?"

She said nothing, her blue eyes gleaming.

"You killed him, you rotten bitch squaw. Now I'm going to tear the hell outa your body, and leave you for the coyotes." He put out his arm and pulled at her buckskins, tearing them from her body. She stood there, her full figure naked in the sun.

He put his left arm out to grab her when the sound of gunshot bounced off the nearby rocks. Chet looked at his arm; the bullet had passed through the flesh and was spurting blood. He wheeled and on the rock nearby a lean, green-eyed man smiled at him.

"Not nice to treat a lady like that."

Furious at the tear in his arm, Chet glared at Slocum. He couldn't pull with his right because the polecat had his gun pointing.

"Drop it," Slocum said.

Through gritted teeth, Chet said, "That half-breed bitch poisoned Brady."

Slocum nodded. "Not a nice fella, that Brady. Chances were, he needed killing. Drop it."

Chet didn't move.

Slocum fired, and the bullet nipped the front of

Chet's boot. He hopped clumsily, and glared in humiliation. "Mister, you don't know who I am."

"Don't care much," Slocum said, and he fired at the other boot, nipping it. Again Chet danced, feeling ridiculous.

"The gun," Slocum said.

Chet slowly pulled his gun and dropped it.

Slocum came forward. "Now if I were you, I'd get on that hoss and make fast tracks. While the rest of you is still working."

Chet glared. "You're Slocum."

"That's the name."

"You'll be sorry you were born, mister," Chet said.

Slocum casually raised his pistol, pointed it, and Chet turned pale. "Kill an unarmed man?"

Slocum's trigger finger slowly pulled, the gun fired, and Chet's hat flew off. "Get movin', little cowboy, before I aim lower." He fired again at the hat, and it skittered up a few yards.

Chet glared at the girl and at him, and Slocum had rarely seen such hate blaze in a man's eyes.

Chet O'Brien dismounted near a flat boulder to put a fresh cloth on his wound. His arm wasn't bleeding heavily; it actually was a light wound, but he was seething with rage. He felt for Slocum the same hatred that he had for the rattler. And the feeling couldn't be eased just by a bullet. Too easy. Humiliate him first, then feed him to the coyotes. He thought of how Slocum, shooting at his boots, had made him dance, feel like a clown. He could taste the rage. And for the squaw, he wanted something special. He'd felt the contempt in those eyes, a blue-eyed half-breed, how'd she get to look like that? Who the hell was she? Something about her set him off. He felt attracted and furious at her. She'd poisoned Brady, his sidekick. But she hadn't offered *him* coffee. Why? Because Brady had roughed her up, promised her mean times.

Well, he'd make them pay. His left arm wasn't too bad, and he still had his shootin' right, and that's what counted.

The sun blistered and he gulped from his canteen. He had to get up a story; couldn't say that Brady was going to stick the squaw, so she killed him. That squaw bitch had been responsible for Brady's busted shootin' hand. He had a grievance. As for the polecat, Slocum, he'd go through a lotta pain first.

No, he wouldn't tell Dad; he'd clear this up himself, with Wilbur and Lonnie. He could do it himself, on a one-on-one, but it was smart to have backup.

He reached the ranch just before sundown, and worst luck, ran into Mike, his brother, talking to a ranch hand. Mike spotted him, waved his hand, walked to the corral fence, and waited. Chet could tell Mike was going to rack him.

Mike stared at his bandaged arm. "What happened?"

"A scratch. I'll take care of it," he said coldly.

Mike stared at him grimly. His kid brother, always a pain in the butt, a screwup, a drunk, a deadbeat—and making a mess that someone else had to clean up.

His sharp eyes went down to Chet's boots,

nicked by bullets. Trouble for the wild young rooster again, somebody pushing him.

Chet's brown eyes burned hard. "Something on your mind, Mike? Or you wastin' my time?"

Mike scowled, he was powerful, broad-shoul-dered, with light blue eyes in a square, strong face. "Yeah, something, you sawed-off squirt. What the hell did you do to Hellfire?"

"Shot him—that's what I did."

"Yeah, you knucklehead. And you knew I wanted him. The fastest horseflesh in the terri-tory. I wanted that horse. And you shot him."

Chet glowered. "Don't hand me that. You couldn't break him, Mike. You tried."

"Yeah, I tried. And aimed to try again. Takes patience to break a fine-spirited breed. Patience, something you know nothing about."

"When you goin' to stop preachin' to me?"

Mike stared. "How in hell did someone like you ever get into this family?"

"Same way you did." Chet grinned diabolically.

"The old man musta found you in a junk heap. *Shootin' a horse 'cause you can't ride him.* The lowest thing I ever heard."

Chet showed his teeth. "That damned hoss was kickin' wild. Coulda brained me. That's why I shot him."

Mike's lip curled. "I heard about it. That damned hoss would need legs a mile long to brain you where you got thrown. And Lord knows, a kick in the head might bring you some sense."

Chet gritted his teeth. "Always faultin' me, Mike. You, doin' everything right for Pa, and me, the black devil, doin' it wrong. All right, Mike. Just remember, every dog has its day."

Mike's lip curled. "Yeah—sometimes you act like a yellow dog." He took a long deep breath, got hold of his anger. "Look, Chet, you're my blood. I don't want to be against you. Gimme half a chance—be a man, that's all I'm askin'."

Chet's eyes slitted and he hissed. "I am a man, and don't you forget it. Don't force me to prove it—*against you*." He stalked away, and Mike's blue eyes watched him, troubled.

Chet walked past the ranchhouse carefully, trying to avoid his father. The last thing he wanted was to justify his hurt arm and the dead Brady.

At the bunkhouse, he ran into big Curly Jack, who was smiling, always in good humor. "Hi, Chet, did a hard day's work on the range with the boys? Where the hell's Brady? Your pa's payin' good wages, and he ain't earnin' it."

Chet stared. "Where's Lonnie and Wilbur?"

Curly got serious. "In town, belting a few by now." He looked at Chet's arm. "Something wrong?"

"Brady's dead, I'm gonna take care of it. Don't say anything, especially to my father. I'll tell him. Lend me your gun."

Curly frowned, and reached for his holster. "Need me?"

"No. Just want you to keep your mouth shut." He took Curly's gun. "Stay mum. Don't want Mike to know." He went back to his horse, and rode toward town.

* * *

As he rode toward Rusty Hills, Chet thought about Slocum and the half-breed. To trap them, he would have to get on their tracks fast, not knowing where they were heading. He'd grab a few drinks, to feel easy, then ride out with Wilbur and Lonnie.

The town was lit up and rowdy. It had been a hot day on the range and, after sundown, the cowboys came to the saloon for drinking, gambling, and girls.

Chet saw Lonnie and Wilbur at one of the poker tables, their faces flushed from boozing. They were big and bulky cowboys, Lonnie older by two years than Wilbur. Chet had used them in dirty deals, and they were always ready; they liked the excitement, and they liked the favors Chet could do for them. He himself had a terrific thirst. His arm ached, and his thoughts were bad. He stood at the planked bar where Albie, the thick-necked, rotund barman, put a whiskey glass and bottle in front of him.

"What's in the wind, Chet?" Albie asked.

"Death and destruction, Albie."

"Same ole thing, eh, Chet," Albie said dryly. "What's Mike doin'?"

"Polishin' his wings, Albie. Tryin' to be an angel."

Albie shook his head. "He's square-shootin', that brother of your'n. Never saw a man so well liked."

Chet, not crazy about hearing Mike touted, threw him a poisonous look.

Albie moved to serve a cowboy, thinking that

Chet was one of his best guzzling customers, and there was no need to spoil it.

Chet drank three fast whiskies, and liked the burn in his gut. He glanced at Lonnie and Wilbur playing poker. Okay, let them. Nothing wrong with relaxing. He had this hard, vicious knot inside him and needed loosening.

He saw Flora, her dark shining hair falling sideways over her doll-like face. She wore a filmy black dress, which showed her breasts trying to bust through the seams. He looked at her, drank two more whiskies, and felt the buzz start. He clamped his teeth; a pretty beastie like Flora could get the poisons out of a man's system. Chet took the bottle to her corner table. She gazed at him with smart black eyes, which could con you outa your skin.

"What's eatin' you, Chet?"

"Eatin' me? How in hell did you know that?" His face was puzzled. He poured another whiskey and swilled it.

"Written all over you."

"The world's full of mangy coyotes," he said, staying on the booze.

"Just find that out, Chet?" She had full lips, smooth skin, and dark eyes in a doll's face, everything petite but her breasts—they were queensized.

"You find it out, over and over."

"What's it this time?"

He felt boozy. "Me and Brady ran into a coupla mangy drifters on the train..." He stopped and his rheumy eyes looked far off, as his mind replayed it at the stream, him asking the squaw for coffee, she fixin' it, but giving it to Brady while he was shooting the rattler. And that damned Slocum, making him dance like a clown, shooting at his boots! Rage snaked through him.

Flora was watching, waiting for him to finish his sentence.

"Lost Brady to a sneakin' half-breed and an ornery polecat," Chet said finally.

She said nothing. Flora knew Brady and, in her mind, he was a loudmouth and a bastard, faking to be all man, but she knew better.

"Brady was my sidekick for years. He's gone now," Chet said dolefully.

"Hard to believe that anyone could beat Brady's draw."

"They got him on a trick. That's how. Lost the best friend I ever had." Chet sounded maudlin; the booze made him believe Brady was his true-blue friend, though most everyone knew Brady as a first-class bastard, who killed pushovers to build his rep.

Flora lifted her drink, so she wouldn't say there was just one less asshole walking the territory.

Chet had enough booze now to lie easy. Held up his arm. "Shot at me, when I was lookin' the other way. That's how they did poor Brady. Behind his back. Ornery polecat."

Chet looked at her breasts, and felt a perk in his loins.

"Let's go upstairs, Flora. Need a bit of consolin'."

Flora shrugged. He could be dead when he was drunk—all lust and no action. As she went up, Chet stopped at the card table, and leaned down to whisper in Lonnie's ear. "Stand by, you and Wilbur, I gotta job for you boys. *Fun job*," he added, with a wicked leer.

Lonnie grinned at Wilbur. Chet's fun job meant a hot party. Just then Lonnie drew a second ace and to his superstitious mind, it meant good times ahead with Chet on the trail.

He watched Chet climb the stairs; he could carry plenty of liquor, but he sure labored going up.

Chet opened the door and saw Flora on the bed, slipping her silky dress over her head. His eyes glittered at the big breasts. She had fine white skin, and her body, while petite, was graceful. But Chet was no connoisseur of grace; all he wanted was to get something bad out of his system, and Flora was the way.

She lay on the bed, resting her head on her elbow, her dark eyes on him. "Put the money out, Chet, before you forget."

He dug dollars out of his pocket, then clumsily slipped out of his clothes.

She frowned. "Don't see any great excitement here, Chet."

He growled. "Don't hafta tell me—with all I'm feelin', it's a wonder I'm here. Get on it—see what you can do."

She shrugged and with professional skill, brought him alive. He looked at her on her back, thighs apart, the pink of the flesh gleaming beneath the dark hair. He slid over her, his palms on the silk of her breasts, and lowered his big body over her, piercing her and feeling the velvet. The anger in his mind for what happened to him that day and his lust for her body came to a focus. His body moved hard almost violently against her, as again and again, he pounded, until his body jerked, giving him a sharp, powerful release. He sunk against her breast, breathing hard, then fell asleep.

Flora lay still, her mind and feeling absent from what had just happened to her body. When she moved, it wakened him.

Chet got up, foggy-brained and spun around. He put his hand to his head, as if dizzy, then saw Flora. To his sodden mind, she looked like the bitch half-breed he'd seen nude at the stream. He didn't know where he was or how in hell she got there, but there she was—real as life. He growled drunkenly, "What the hell," and stumbled toward her, holding his fist up to swing. Flora, who had experience with drunks and their fantasies, ducked, so that when he swung wildly, he fell on the bed.

Flora caught her dress on the way to the door. "You stupid drunk," she muttered. Out the door she caught the eye of Bronc Kelly, the bouncer, who came upstairs fast. "It's Chet, drunk out of his mind, threw a punch at me."

Bronc showed his teeth. "Should I throw him out the window?"

She considered. "I wouldn't mind it, but O'Brien might. And there's Mike."

Bronc looked disappointed. "A pity. Been wanting to do that. Okay, I'll ease him downstairs."

He went into the room, and ten minutes later, Chet came out, dressed, but boozy-eyed. He

walked the stairs unsteadily, and when he saw
Flora sitting alone, he stopped at her table and
smiled genially. "Hey, Flora, le's have a party."

She gave him the gimlet eye. "What?"

He grinned foolishly, his eyes spinning in his
head. "A party, a bit o' screwin'."

She sighed. "I'm feelin' poorly, Chet. Some
other time. Besides, you might have a party and
not know it."

He scowled drunkenly. "What the hell's that
mean?"

"Means I aim to sit here and mind my business."

Then he caught sight of Lonnie, and ideas
burned in his boozy brain. He made an unsteady
way to the table and leaned down breathing whiskey fumes.

"Lonnie—gotta job. Need you boys. Le's go."

Lonnie stared at Chet's boozy brown eyes. The
man was loaded, but he still could operate. He'd
seen him worse.

He glanced at Wilbur, and dropped his cards.
"I'm out, and so are you, Wilbur."

Chet already was weaving drunkenly toward
the door, ready in his sodden mind to destroy that
polecat, Slocum.

He got outside the saloon, where to his surprise, it was night, the moon coming up big and
silver. What the hell happened? Well, they'd start
on the trail and pick up the breed and the polecat
tomorrow. He reached into his pocket, pulled out
a cigar. It took a few matches to get it lit and he
cussed plenty. Then he saw the Smith boys come
out, stop, and look at him.

"Okay, Chet, where we headed?"

Chet pointed with a quaky hand. "Goin' north-west, we got a polecat and a bitch half-breed squaw. Beautiful." He grinned. "You boys gonna like this." He tried to get his foot in the stirrup, and Lonnie moved under him, shouldered him up.

When Chet got on the saddle, he took a deep breath, and threw away the cigar. "We'll ride till the moon gets high, then bed down. In the morn, we'll nail 'em—the polecat and the squaw. Tomor-row." His eyes were almost shut.

Lonnie looked at Wilbur.

"Tie him so he don't fall, and we'll ride some. He'll sleep it off and, tomorrow, make some sense."

They tied him, with tight rope to the saddle, and rode northeast, Wilbur holding the reins of his sorrel while Chet snored.

They rode until the moon swung high, big, and clear, lighting the stony soaring peaks, then Lon-nie found a sheltered nook of rocks. They eased Chet from the saddle, still snoring. They made camp, spread the bedrolls, and lay under the great silver moon, shining with calm mystery on a seemingly quiet earth.

6

Chet, after a night's sleep woke up bleary-eyed and remembered only part of last night, until he drank coffee. His wounded arm brought back his memories and his rage.

Lonnie rubbed his stubbled chin. "Well, I s'pose, Chet, you'll tell us now what the hell we're doin' out here."

Chet looked at the baked land, the saw-toothed ridges, the copper sky. Going to be a fierce sun; they'd head for the Yellow River, where he had run into Slocum and the squaw.

"Brady's dead," he said, sipping his coffee.

The brothers looked at him silently in wonder.

"Poisoned by an Apache half-breed squaw. The polecat with her, name of Slocum, shot when I wasn't lookin'." He held up his arm. "We're goin' to nail his carcass to a tree stump for the buzzards before sundown." He sipped more coffee. "And we'll pleasure ourselves with the half-breed—a beautiful filly. All easy as eatin' apple pie."

Lonnie jerked his elbow into Wilbur's ribs, because he was just staring.

"Who is this blasted Slocum?" Wilbur asked.

"Just a driftin' hardheaded rebel. Didn't know who he was tangling with, boys. We're goin' to smear him over the territory. Show him the breed o' men round here."

Lonnie smiled carefully. He wasn't crazy about the way Chet told it, and wondered if this Slocum might *not* be a pushover. He'd noticed the bullet nicks in Chet's boots, and figured this Slocum had made Chet look like a chump—that's why he was roarin' for the man's hide. But that didn't matter to Lonnie. He liked excitement. A beautiful half-breed for fun, and a rebel for shootin'. Could be a lotta laughs. And after they did him a good turn, Chet always gave favors.

So Lonnie hefted his Levi's, straightened his holster, and said to Wilbur. "What are we waitin' for? Let's go for this polecat's tracks."

"After we get his tracks, we'll figure how to hit him," said Chet, and he started for his sorrel.

The sun hammered down hard from a scalding bright sky, as Slocum pulled the roan to a halt at the small swirling stream. The heat had driven the animals to shelter where they could find it. No chirping of crickets, no slithering of snakes, and the bushes looked parched in the broil of the sun.

The horses were coated with sweat and before

reaching the stream, Slocum had stopped often to rest them and give them water poured into his hat from his canteen. Now he eased the horses into the stream, where they drank gratefully. White Flower managed to look cool but he could see beads of perspiration on her upper lip.

She moved into the water, and ran some over her face and neck.

Suddenly she straightened and looked into the distance.

Slocum turned sharply, scanning the horizon behind him, until he saw the small figure of a rider come out of a fine dust swirl.

"Another follows," she said.

Slocum, too, picked up the second dust swirl from which a horseman emerged. Two riders headed for water, as anyone would be on this scorcher. Slocum refilled the canteens, ran water over his sweat-streaked face and hair.

He pulled some biscuits and a can of peaches from his saddlebag. And they had it finished by the time the first horseman made it to the stream. He was a hulking, stubblebearded cowboy in a blue shirt and a flat hat, with the florid face of a hard drinker. He looked sharply at Slocum, then shifted his gaze to White Flower, and his gray eyes gleamed. He looked again at Slocum and managed a smile. "Howdy, mister. A rotten hot day. Need to wet down."

Slocum nodded pleasantly, his piercing green eyes fixed on the cowboy. He slipped off his horse, led it to the water, then bent to drink from his cupped hands.

He slowly turned to Slocum. "I'm headed for Tombstone. Reckon the trail is right."

"You're doin' fine ," Slocum said.

The cowboy glanced at White Flower, but spoke to Slocum. "Picked up on the trail of a lone Apache back there. Got a bit nervy, but he didn't bother me."

Slocum nodded. "There's one prowlin' the neighborhood. Reckon he's more interested in me."

The cowboy's thick-featured face became alert. "Yeah, why's that?"

Slocum jerked his thumb at White Flower. "Maybe she's the reason."

The cowboy nodded, "Half-breed, huh. Lonnie Smith's the handle."

"John Slocum."

The cowboy took it in stride, not surprised. "Good-looking filly, hardly looks Apache." He stared at her body, licked his lips, then caught himself. "Tell yuh what, Slocum. I was lookin' for a polecat named Brady, movin' in these parts."

Slocum studied him. "Say you *was* lookin' for him? Not lookin' anymore?"

Lonnie rubbed his stubble-bearded face. "Did I say *was?* I mean I am. Know anything that might help?"

Slocum smiled. "Well, Lonnie, he's in a *was* condition. Had to bury the poor fella."

Lonnie stared hard, from Slocum to White Flower, who was kneeling at the stream, washing her pony. He rubbed his stubbled chin, then glanced in the distance, at the second horseman coming nearer. "Well, I'll be damned. Brady dead.

Mighty hard to believe, 'cause he was one of the fastest guns round here. Wasn't you who beat him, was it, Slocum?"

"No, not me, the little lady there, she put him under. He tried to get funny, and she didn't share his sense of humor." Slocum smiled.

Lonnie stared at her, with slitted eyes. "Mighty dangerous filly. But she don't look it."

Slocum had to grin. "Name's White Flower, but she's got a thorn, when you try to pick her."

By this time the second rider was approaching in a slow jog, and they stopped to watch him. His nod was cool, when he reached them, and he looked more at White Flower than Slocum, whose green sharp eyes studied him. He was built like Lonnie, burly and broad-shouldered, stubble-bearded, with gray eyes. He swung off his saddle, went straight for the water, ignoring his horse, which anyway, followed him.

Then the man turned, gazed at Lonnie, a curious look, then stared at White Flower, and finally at Slocum.

"Howdy. Parched with thirst." He walked toward Lonnie. "What's goin' on?"

Lonnie bit his lip. "This is Slocum. Tells me that Brady, who we're lookin' for is dead and buried. And that he tried to get fresh with the Injun filly there, and she put him away."

Wilbur showed his teeth in a weird grin. "So she took care o' Brady. Ole Quick-Draw. Always figured only a woman would get him in the end, 'cause no man was fast enough." He grinned wickedly. "Of course, I expected him to croak in some filly's bed."

Slocum pulled out a cigarillo. These two men were the same breed of men—brothers? Why did they travel separately?

"Brady a friend of yours, gents?" Slocum asked.

Lonnie laughed. "This here is Wilbur. To tell the truth, Brady wasn't even a friend to himself. More a gunman. He cut a mark every time he gunned a man." He turned to Slocum. "I know that Injun filly met him and put him away, but I was wonderin' if *you* ever met up with Brady?"

"Yeah, I did. Told me he was goin' to Tombstone to take care of Doc Holliday."

"But he never got there," said Lonnie.

"No."

"Wouldn't be surprised if someone sidetracked him. They say he got shot when he wasn't lookin'."

Slocum's eyes glittered. "Who says it?"

Lonnie shrugged. "It's said down at the O'B corral."

"What corral?"

"Why, the O'Brien place."

Slocum glanced at White Flower. She was sitting on the edge of the stream and, he wondered if from that distance she could hear them. "Did Brady work there?"

"Sure—for old man O'Brien." Lonnie wiped his brow. "Well, 'nuff of this chitchat. I'm goin' on to Tombstone. What d'ya aim to do, Wilbur?"

"I'm goin' back to Rusty Hills since ole Brady is daid and buried." They looked at each other, smiling, then went for their horses and swung up. With a long look at White Flower who had sat apart, they started to ride, one north, the other south.

Slocum watched, wondering if and how they'd try for the hit. The look they gave White Flower convinced him they had rough ideas for her. He had been waiting for their move, but they made none. As long as they were together, he might have handled it, but boxing him like this was smart strategy. If he fired at one, the other could clip him.

He glanced about—no cover, no boulder, bush or rock nearby—a bad spot. But what if he was wrong, and they were peaceful? No, he had felt from the beginning hostile intent under their smiles. He'd have been smart to drop one right off. But you couldn't shoot a man because your instinct told you he *intended* harm.

Now they had him in a nutcracker. Lonnie riding north, Wilbur south. Nerve-racking. Slocum's eyes flicked from one to the other, realizing that if they intended to fire, it would be prearranged, and he'd be caught in crossfire. He dared not look at White Flower, unwilling to take his eyes off Lonnie, who he guessed the better shot. Their riding pace was slow, as if they they didn't want to move too far from target.

If they pulled their guns, all he could hope was to hit the one who turned first—but who?

His gaze flicked from one rider to the other, his hand hear his holster, then it happened. Lonnie swung in his saddle, gun in hand and, as Slocum fired, he heard the shot from Wilbur's position, and expected the bullet to rip his body, but it didn't and he swung back, ready to fire but, to his astonishment, saw Wilbur falling, head down from his horse, blood bursting on his forehead. *Someone* had fired and Slocum went flat to the earth, expecting more gunfire, and it happened—the sound of another shot, and he heard White Flower cry out, grab at her arm, and fall.

Slocum, gritting his teeth, crawled forward, looking for the gunman who might be concealed in the rock cluster not far from Wilbur's body. He focused on it, saw the rifle inch out from behind rock, and then a slight part of the face and Slocum fired, his bullet hitting stone, which chipped, and the face went back fast—the man hit only by chipped rock.

He waited, but nothing happened, and he put his head against the ground to listen and soon heard the sound of hooves getting fainter. Whoever had done the shooting was now racing off.

Slocum crawled toward White Flower. She was holding her arm, nipped by the bullet and bleeding. Her fine face was impassive, her blue eyes gleaming; if she was feeling pain, she didn't show it. Instead, she rose to her feet, pointing to Wilbur sprawled on the earth.

"Apache did it," she said. Then she pointed beyond to a distant high rocky ledge, beyond rifle range. "Paleface watches us," she said.

And Slocum saw the glitter of glass in the sun. Damn, someone out there, watching with field glasses what had happened here. Perhaps directing it. All except for the unexpected action of the revengeful Apache.

* * *

Chet O'Brien on the high rocky ledge, stared in shock, through his field glasses, at Lonnie and Wilbur sprawled in death on the earth below.

It had gone wrong!

Figuring that Slocum would not recognize them, he had sent Lonnie and Wilbur ahead. He had thought up the crossfire trick, telling Lonnie to wing Slocum, not kill him. Then he'd join them and they'd do a job on the Apache filly and have vicious fun with Slocum before setting him up for buzzard meat. But the scheme went blotto because of the Apache who came out of nowhere and shot Wilbur from ambush, while Slocum outdrew Lonnie.

Blast Slocum, for a lucky bastard.

Chet lifted the field glasses again, and damned if Slocum and the girl weren't looking up to his position. He jerked behind the rock, cursing as he stalked back to his sorrel, hitched to a bush.

All right, the polecat Slocum had won the second round, by luck, but he'd never win the third. Chet rubbed his chin thoughtfully. He'd go back to the ranch, tell his father that a half-breed Apache and a cursed yellow-livered rebel had ambushed *Brady, Lonnie, and Wilbur*. He'd show his bad arm. If his dad hated one thing, it was sneaky shooters and Apaches; didn't care much for rebels, either.

Yes, he'd set up a hollar, get a posse of the roughnecks, even Mike—it was a matter of blood now. And they'd hunt down his rotten rebel and devil of a half-breed.

Chet reached into his saddlebag, pulled his whiskey bottle and took a long haul. Damn, he couldn't taste the booze because of hate for Slocum. He started to ride, thinking of ways of revenge. As for Lonnie and Wilbur, lying dead back there, he didn't give them a second thought.

7

White Flower seemed calm enough; he examined her arm, not bad, a superficial wound. Did the damned Apache miss or did he mean to wing her—a sharpshooter? He was gone now, and there was no sign of the cowboy on the high ledge. Quiet for the time being. Slocum moved to his saddlebag, washed her wound with whiskey, and patched her arm with cloth.

She watched him, smiling. There was something new in her expression and it pleased him. He moved behind a big boulder, poured whiskey for her, and took a long slug himself. He was thinking about the Apache who'd shot Wilbur. Why? Well, first, Apaches shoot palefaces. Second, if Slocum was up for killing, this Apache probably wanted the pleasure, and he didn't want the paleface to go out easy. It was not the Apache way. This was the same buck whose tracks Lonnie had seen. He was the same comrade to the warrior Slocum had shot in the ambush of the settler's wagons. So, for the Apache buck, this was a blood feud. He'd been hanging on Slocum's trail and learned about the half-breed girl.

She spiced it up. He had glimpsed the Apache's face before firing. Long-haired, with a red band, strong nose, high cheekbones, a powerful head. He had run away, to fight another day. And done the same this time, knocking out Wilbur, sharpshooting the filly's arm, then making his quick run. A smart polecat. It was not wise to let this warrior pick his time to shoot. Better to head him off now.

From Slocum's angle, the river was behind him, and the trail in front of him, taken by the Apache, was rocky and thick with brush, not good for tracking. But better do that than wait until the sly devil threw lead from ambush.

He looked at White Flower.

"Slocum must stop the Apache warrior," he said. "White Flower should stay here, safe."

She shook her head. "I go with you."

He thought about it. She'd spoil his concentration, and God knows, to track an Apache, the slightest distraction could be fatal, especially this one.

"No, best for Slocum to hunt alone." He glanced at the nearby rock clusters, climbing against the side of the mountain to a ledge with crevices. "You could stay there, hidden in the rocks. By sundown, I should be back. If not, White Flower must go her way."

Her lips tightened. "White Flower will wait. And Slocum must come back."

Her voice had a fine edge, which surprised him, and he felt a powerful desire to put his arm around her womanly body. She stood still, as if waiting for his embrace, but he couldn't do it, not then. He led her to what looked like a comfortable nook, sheltered from sun, looked back at her as he rode off. Her gaze was steady, and damn if he didn't see the glow of affection in those beautiful blue eyes.

It was hot, with a hard beating sun. Slocum climbed and searched the rocks, where he'd seen the Apache stick his rifle out. Mocassin tracks moving to his pony. Slocum followed the tracks, heading south at first, through land pockmarked with boulders and sprawling brush, hollows, and hills, where a clever Apache could hide and shoot. Slocum moved slowly, trying for cover.

The sun was slipping toward the horizon, but heat hung over the earth like a blanket.

Slocum worked slowly, following the tracks, until he realized he was moving in a big circle. Once he examined the prints behind a big boulder, and figured the buck had been observing him. Was the Apache bringing him along, deliberately? He gritted his teeth. The Injun had a shot but didn't fire. Why?

Slocum glanced at the sun moving to the horizon. He had told White Flower, if he didn't get back by sundown, to leave. The tracks continuing in the big circle would bring him back toward Yellow River, toward White Flower's hideaway. Slocum stopped and cursed softly. This was one smart buck. He had hit White Flower on the arm, nothing fatal. Meant he wanted her alive, and expected to get her. Slocum figured the consequence and froze. Why had the Apache taken this trail, leaving his prints clear, making no effort to evade? Was he out to lure the paleface away from White Flower, then trap the girl?

Slocum wiped his wet brow; he had spent precious time sweating out a false scent. The redskin was not in these rocks; he had snaked out—and gone where—back to White Flower? She was no pushover, but this clever bastard... Slocum turned the roan and raced for Yellow River, but long before he reached the rock cluster, her hiding place, he pulled sharply on the reins.

He had to think. He swung off the roan. As he remembered, the rocks were piled in a stiff ascent, crags topping each other against the side of the mountain. Midway up there was the flat ledge where White Flower waited and now, maybe, the Apache waited, too. Slocum took a deep breath; if he moved straight on, he was set up for a bullet.

Should he wait for dusk? But that might be too late. Should he try for the side of the mountain, come down, behind the redskin? Would he still be there? Yes, he'd wait, the Apache had patience— they knew how to wait for prey.

Slocum jumped on the roan, raced to the east side of the mountain. When he reached it, he put the roan under a sheltering rock and started to climb. It was hard going, and he had to move slowly, until he reached a horizontal ledge that led to the front of the mountain. The stone was still hot from a baking sun, rough cut and sharp-edged at times. He felt the sweat on his neck and brow and stopped to get his wind. He had climbed, it seemed to him, halfway round the mountain. The sun had slipped over the horizon now, and the sky was streaked with brilliant orange and red. He moved silently from rock to rock, down the front side, taking care with each step. Soon, very soon, he'd see her ledge.

The sky was flaming orange. His shirt stuck to his body, wet with sweat, his hands were chipped from gripping the serrated rocks; he leaned out to look down.

There she was!

She was sitting on the ledge, her hands and legs tied, a cloth wrapped around her mouth. Gun in hand, Slocum stared as his eyes scoured the rocks for the Apache. *Not there*. Where in hell was he? Would he leave her like that? Had he lost patience and gone to search out the paleface? Again, Slocum stared at the crevices behind and near White Flower, but saw nothing, heard nothing. Yes, the damned redskin got restless and was gone in search of the paleface, leaving her. Slocum moved forward. She heard him, and turned to look, eyes glowing. Was it pleasure at seeing him or something else? His instinct shrieked at a whisper of sound that seemed to come from the side rocks, which materialized into the Apache, huge and muscular. He flung himself on the paleface, crashing him to the stony ledge, jarring the gun from his hand, and Slocum found himself staring into the black, fiery eyes as the Apache brought his tomahawk back with a thick, muscled arm to swing at Slocum's head.

Slocum's own powerful arm went up, and his hand grasped the wrist of the Apache, holding it in a vise. The Apache, astounded that he couldn't bring his right hand down, reached with his left into his holster and pulled his long knife, and brought it up to strike Slocum. He was heavily muscled, and held death in either hand. And Slocum, who knew it, grabbed the wrist of his knife hand, and gripped tightly. They stood like figures, carved out of stone, two massive men, one red, the other white, like symbols of their race, struggling for survival.

There was the threat of instant death from the weapons in the redskin's hands, and Slocum suddenly kicked the man's right leg, which hit a protruding sharp rock as he went down and the bone cracked. He groaned. Slocum on top, pounded the wrist of his knife hand against stone, twisting the delicate bones, until the knife slipped out of the broken hand. Then with all his strength, Slocum turned the right hand, trying to break it, to loosen the tomahawk, but the Apache's forearm held like iron. The sweat and smell of the Indian was strong in his nostrils. Slocum twisted and turned, but the Apache held, his black eyes glowing with hate. Straining with all his might, Slocum reached out for the Apache's fallen knife nearby, grasped it and, pulling back, suddenly plunged it into the heart of the Apache. His body went limp, and a long slow sigh breathed from his lips, his

coal-dark eyes stayed in hate on Slocum until they
went empty.

Slocum looked at the Apache, bronze and muscular, his neck in a bizarre twist, the humiliating way
that death leaves the body. He had put up a desperate fight, and Slocum's chest still heaved. He
drew deep breaths, then walked to White Flower,
leaned down to cut her bonds. He was startled by
the glow in her eyes, as if her entire being had
been fired by what she had just seen. It gave him
a lift, and jolted him that, after her hands were
free, she raised her arms and pulled him down on
her body. The curving womanly flesh sent a fierce
charge through him. She held tight, and his body
was suffused with a fiery excitement. The hunger
of his flesh, the tension of his fight, the feeling of
triumph over an enemy, his escape from death—
exploded together.

They embraced and kissed, and suddenly her
buckskins were off, and his clothing, too. Her
body lay in the rays of the sunken sun, curved and
voluptuous, her finely shaped breasts, flat stomach, the pink lips between her well-formed thighs.
His own excitement was visible, and her eyes glittered at the sight. His hands went to her breasts,
and as he stroked the velvet-soft skin, he could
hear her quickened breathing. She was ready, if
ever woman was—no need to play; the passion
seethed, and her thighs went apart instantly to receive him. He slipped into her moist smoothness
and began full strokes, holding her silky buttocks,
and her body lifted to meet his. His rhythm
quickened, his thrusts sharpened, and his tension

escalated as he reached an agonizing pitch and exploded. Her body stiffened, and she made soft sighing sounds.

They lay on the ledge, with the world darkening, a big silver moon rising for its eternal night gaze on the earth.

Slocum, when he came to himself, looked at the climbing moon silhouetting the sawtooth ridges of the Sierras. He was baffled by his sexual frenzy after his death struggle with the Apache, lying thirty feet away. There had to be something primitive, he thought, in the feelings that rushed over a man after he defeated his enemy. He'd once seen two giant stags fighting ferociously, while the doe watched, stimulated by the battle, ready to reward the victor with her body. In this case, if the victor had been the Apache, it would have been rape and death for White Flower.

She shifted her body, let her finger trace his rib. "Slocum is all fire as a lover."

He smiled. "You're not so bad."

Later, he buried the Apache in a patch of soft earth, near bushes, smoothed the ground as best he could. He brought the horses together, tied them to a stunted tree trunk near a thicket, where they ate. Slocum poured whiskey afterward.

She looked delicately feminine, as the fine bones of her face caught the gleam of moonbeams —she was a beautiful girl, he thought.

"Did you know him?" He jerked his thumb in the direction of the Apache's grave.

She nodded. "Another who hated me."

"Why?"

She shrugged. "I have told you of the hate the Apache had for my mother and me."

He sipped the whiskey. "Because she has gone out of the tribe for her lover?"

She smiled. "Yes. I am the fruit of that love, as you see."

"Fruit ripe for plucking." He was grinning.

She looked at his body. "I have said it—Slocum is a fine lover."

She was as straight as an arrow, honest, no flirting. "This Apache—who shot at you, did he want to kill you?"

"No." Her eyes glittered. "Some things are worse than killing. He wanted the body of White Flower."

He looked up at a hawk flying top speed across the moon-splashed sky in pursuit of prey. It suddenly dived, and in the silence he heard the cry of the doomed animal.

"I am outsider," she said. "Not all Apache." Her blue eyes narrowed. "Not the paleface either. The *outsider*."

His lips tightened. She was neither fish nor fowl; where did she belong? A mystery, yet given the clothing of a white woman, would anyone know her Apache blood?

"Why do you go to O'Brien?"

Her gaze was reproachful. "You asked this before, and I did not answer. Why does Slocum ask again?"

She had a stubborn streak. He shrugged. "There may be bad things for you there."

"Why say that?" she asked sharply. "Do you know the place of O'Brien?"

"No." He hesitated. "Just hate to see you hurt."

"Why should White Flower be hurt?"

"You speak of yourself as an 'outsider.' That is one reason." He paused.

"Is there other reasons?" Her lovely lips were smiling, but her dark blue eyes were serious.

"The man, Brady," he said, "the one you gave *bad* coffee. He came from the O'Brien ranch."

She was startled. "Brady. How do you know that?"

"The cowboy, Lonnie, said it. They came looking for him. They, too, might be from the O'Brien place."

She thought about it. "What did Brady do for O'Brien?" She leaned to him, as if the answer meant a great deal.

He shrugged. "Don't know. Worked as a gunman, maybe. Men like O'Brien need gunmen to drive off men who steal. Steal the cattle, steal the land."

She thought about it and a grim smile twisted her lips. "Steal the land? For the Apache, land belongs to everybody. Then the paleface came and put up wire and made it his land."

Slocum sipped more whiskey. It was true. For the Indian, land belonged to the Great Spirit, until the evil paleface came who pushed them, killed their buffalo, drove them ever west. Slocum shook his head. That's how it was—just so much of anything—and men had to fight to get a piece of it. The strong took it. O'Brien had to be one of the strong—he had the land—and he was smart enough to hire guns to keep his land.

She stared at him. "Do you know about O'Brien? Is he a bad man?"

He looked away, at the peaks of the Sierras thrusting upward, a hopeless yearning for the heavens. "I don't know that," he said. "There may be bad things for you there."

Her eyes clouded. "I must go anyway."

The sudden rustle of sound from the roan, then a sharp neigh brought Slocum up and running, his gun out. In the glitter of moonlight, he saw the glowing eyes of the cougar as it came in a violent run toward the horse. Slocum's gun barked, over and over, and the cougar let out an inhuman sound as the bullets hit its body, one finding his brain, and he fell in flight as if turned suddenly into lead. He was only four feet from the roan that still strained frantically at its reins.

8

"Where the hell's Chet?" O'Brien asked his son, Mike.

"Dunno, Dad. And he's not the only one. We've got other men missing."

"Like who?"

"Brady. And the Smith boys, Wilbur and Lonnie."

Sean O'Brien, astride his black gelding, was riding his range alongside his son, Mike, who rode the black stallion. O'Brien's blue eyes swept the landscape, his land, miles of rich grass, fed by a fine swirling stream. Land wrestled with toil and stained with blood—of red and white men. His lips tightened as he thought of it. He had a square, ruddy face, from which jutted a strong nose. His body was still powerful, and he had become a wealthy rancher by being ruthless and smart. He was a strong family man, and he had built all this for Millie, his wife, who he lost when she was bitten by a rattler.

Chet—from the beginning Chet was trouble. Chet had grown up wild, and it was hard to know if it had been the lack of a mother or if he had just been born with cursed spite. He drank too much, went off half-cocked, always found trouble.

O'Brien wondered if he had caused the problem. He tried to get Mike, a true-blue son, to help Chet. Go easy on him when he screwed up. But that was hard for Mike—doing it right was always easy for him.

O'Brien's face stayed hard. "All them are Chet's cronies. What the hell is goin' on?" He turned to stare at Mike. O'Brien hadn't reached the stage yet when he was ready to sit back and let his sons take over, but it wasn't far off. He was thinking about his younger son.

Chet needed to be tamed. O'Brien stroked his chin. If only he could find the right button, he felt sure, Chet would straighten out. He felt guilty about the boy. In the early days, he'd been harsh and he wondered if his rough treatment had spooked the boy. The lad was bitter, hard, vengeful, and self-destructive.

O'Brien pulled his horse, and they stopped near the river that sparkled brightly in the glint of the sun. He lifted his Stetson, mopped his brow, and looked up. The sky was burnished blue and a few cotton clouds hung still, as if painted there. A beautiful country. O'Brien wanted to start a dynasty; he had the land, the money, and he could visualize the O'Briens as a dominant family in the territory. It was why he backed off, why he didn't come down heavy on Chet when he screwed up.

He suddenly thought of the Gibson girl, Lulabelle. Both his boys were courting her, and if Chet came through, that might be his salvation. A good woman could do plenty to straighten out a man. Lulabelle Gibson might do the job. And that Gibson land, set alongside his, would turn every ranch owner in the valley green with envy. They had the Big Barn dance coming up, a good time for Chet to stake his claim to Lulabelle. Though hard to imagine, it seemed like she favored him a bit over Mike, but maybe Lulabelle liked her men a bit on the wild side.

Mike's voice broke through his reveries. "Yes Dad, not only Chet, but Brady, Wilbur, and Lonnie are all missin'."

O'Brien thought of the missing men. "Where'd they go—this gruesome foursome?" he asked.

Mike laughed. "Hard to say. Curly Jack knows something, but he's not talking. Just says that Chet was looking for Wilbur and Lonnie. Then went to town after them yesterday, 'fore sundown."

O'Brien's lips tightened. "I told you, Mike, to keep a lead on that boy. And not to ride him hard."

"Ride him. That brat shot Hellfire, the finest

piece of horseflesh in the territory. I was working to break him. And he shot him."

"I was there," O'Brien said dryly. "A bad thing. That's how he is. If he can't master something, he wants to kill it. Where the hell did he learn that? Not from me or you. He's gotta lot of devil in him. But he's still our blood. We gotta straighten him out. It can be done. You tame a wild horse, don't you? Think of him like that."

Mike bit his lip. "I try, Dad." His brown eyes squinted as he stared over the land to the massive crags of the great Sierras sweeping eternally west. "Some wild horses can't be tamed—never. Something to think of."

O'Brien scowled. He didn't like to think that anything descended from his loins could be hopeless. "A man's not a horse, Mike. And he's your brother. Give him loyalty."

They rode back toward the ranch buildings, and Mike spotted Curly Jack, honcho, talking to Charley Turk, Lefty Leon, and Deadeye Dunay, three heavyweight hands, bunched around the corral. Mike caught Curly's eye and waved, and he came over, while the others idly watched.

O'Brien studied his foreman. "Mike tells me you saw Chet yesterday."

Curly Jack nodded. He was a tall cowboy with gray eyes and a humorous smile in a round face, a man who tried not to take seriously the worries of the world. But he could run a tight crew, and the hands liked working for him.

"I saw him, boss."

"What'd he say?" Mike asked.

Curly Jack's honest eyes looked grave. "Wanted to know where he could find Lonnie and Wilbur."

"Did he find them?"

"They'd gone to town, for a bit of boozin'."

"Did he say *why* he wanted them?" O'Brien asked.

Curly looked troubled. Chet didn't want his movements revealed, but this was his boss asking —Chet might be in trouble.

"He said Brady was dead—that he was goin' to take care of it."

O'Brien scowled and looked away. Mike's face hardened as he thought of Chet's boots, the way they'd been nicked by some sharpshooter's eye. With Brady dead—could be Chet got tangled with a sharp gunman.

"Brady dead? In a shootout?" O'Brien asked.

"Chet didn't say."

"What did he want with the Smith boys?" Mike asked.

"I reckon he wanted their help."

"Is that *all* you got from him, Curly?" O'Brien asked.

"Told me he'd take care of it, not to worry you."

There was silence, then O'Brien spoke curtly. "If you had worried us, Chet might not be in trouble. Better pick up some men for a search party."

Mike had been looking to the north range, and saw the dim figure of a rider. He recognized the familiar outlines.

"It's Chet—*alone*," Mike said.

O'Brien pulled out a chaw and bit into it savagely. *Trouble followed Chet around like a hound dog.* He'd gone out with Brady and lost not only Brady, but also maybe two more men.

They watched the dusty figure materialize clearly into Chet who, after spotting them, put the spurs to his sorrel and came up in a rush. O'Brien saw the bandage on his arm, the nicks on his boots, and scowled.

Chet read his father's face and did some fast thinking. "All right, Dad. I made a mistake. Shoulda come to you first."

O'Brien, ready to put the boy into the grinder, softened. The kid admitted a mistake; he might be learning something.

"Where's the Smith boys?"

Chet's eyes shifted and he flushed.

They stared at him.

"Shot in cold blood, Dad."

"What d'ya mean?" asked Mike. He tended to be skeptical of Chet's explanations, finding through experience they were mostly fantasy, meant to protect his pride.

"I'm tellin' yuh," he said angrily. "We were ambushed. Look." He shoved his bandaged arm in their faces.

"What happened?" O'Brien asked quietly.

"Brady and me ran into this rebel polecat, name of Slocum, and his half-breed bitch. Stopped at their camp for coffee. Slocum didn't like a remark made 'bout the half-breed. Had a few words with Brady, and when he was drinkin' coffee, Slocum shot him. Then he turned on me, got my gun, told me to make tracks."

Chet grimaced, stopped to pull a cigarillo and light it. They watched him silently.

"I went off, in a burn, wanted to put a bullet up that polecat's tail. Didn't want to bother you, Dad. So when I ran into Curly, I got his gun, told Lonnie and Wilbur to help me trail those dogs." He puffed his cigarillo, then flipped it.

"Reckoned I underestimated Slocum 'cause he knocked off Lonnie and Wilbur with his rifle. I ducked under cover, waited till dark. Next day I was goin' after him, felt poorly about losing the boys. Decided it would be smarter to get our top guns in a lynch party." Chet stared defiantly at his brother.

Mike felt Chet was playing with the truth; those shifty eyes: he couldn't tell the truth if his life depended on it. But his father, eager to get Chet back in the family, bought his story.

"You did it smart, coming back, Chet. We'll make a real party for this polecat."

Chet looked alarmed. "No, Dad, not you. We can handle it. The man's a sharpshooter, deadly with a rifle. Bad if he got you in his sights. Lemme take a couple of the good guns and get this polecat."

O'Brien smiled. He liked the boy's concern. "No, Chet, this is a family fight. Anyone hit an O'Brien catches hell from the rest of us. Right, Mike?"

Mike, who figured Chet's story had ten percent truth, felt he should give him the benefit of the doubt. You might tame a wild horse with kindness.

"Sure, Chet, we'll go with you on this one. We'll nail this polecat to a tree. Who was with him—an Apache half-breed bitch? We'll have a look at her."

O'Brien's face hardened when he heard that. *Apache bitch*. He'd heard a phrase like that years ago. But for now he put it out of his mind. He lifted his Stetson, mopped his brow.

"Now, listen. I know you boys, for some time, been aimin' for the Town Dance this afternoon. Been achin' to see Lulabelle, both of you. No reason to miss it 'cause of this polecat. Just as easy to lynch him tomorrow as tonight. So mosey on home, and get cleaned up for that party."

He turned to Curly Jack. "You get Johnson and Charley Turk. Tomorrow, at sunup we start on a lynch party."

9

Lulabelle Gibson, one of the belles of the southern Arizona territory, looked in the mirror and liked what she saw. She was as pretty as a doll, they all said it, especially Mike and Chet O'Brien. She had an oval face, high cheekbones, sleek skin, a lovely neck. She was going to the Annual Town Dance this afternoon, and her mind was full of it. And she had her eye on the two O'Brien beaux. She liked the cut of them, both handsome, manly looking. And she liked the size of the O'Brien ranch, which, like the Gibson spread, stretched for miles. Folks said that if the Gibsons and O'Briens were ever, through marriage, to come together, it would team up the best grassland in the territory.

Anyway, she liked the O'Brien boys, who

courted her passionately, and it sometimes made bad blood between them. She couldn't make up her mind but felt that at the dance, she might make a choice. Mike was a square-shootin', red-blooded man, and any woman would be delighted with him. Chet was a maverick, a little wild, but he made her laugh. You never knew what deviltry he'd be up to, and for some dumb reason, she found that fascinating.

Well, later, at the big dance, maybe she'd find out once and for all who she liked best.

She combed her long red hair, burnished in the sun striking the window and suddenly stood in front of the mirror, lifting off her nightdress and looking at her body. Well, mercy, she said to herself, *Nature has surely been kind to me*. She gazed at her well-formed abundant breasts, at the long curve of her slender torso, widening hips, her fine-shaped thighs and legs. She smiled happily and couldn't help feel she was lucky.

She looked out the window at the cottonwood tree, at the bluebird on a branch shaking its tail and chirping, at the diamond blue sky, glittering behind the peaks and massive shoulders of the bronze mountains. A glorious day, she thought. But she yearned for the dance that surely would be great fun and frolic.

In the sun's fierce heat, Slocum mopped his sweating brow and looked at the sky. Still clear, but a few clouds were collecting over the peaks in the north. They were camped near the side of a cliff and they had eaten the last of his beef jerky.

He thought it wise to replenish his supplies with a visit to the nearby town of Rusty Hills, and, thinking of this, he stared at her.

She was drinking coffee. "Why does Slocum look at White Flower?"

"Well," he drawled, "I was trying to imagine you in clothes worn by a paleface woman."

She frowned, but said nothing.

"If you're going to the O'Brien's, it might be smart if you wore such clothes."

"Why do you think that?"

"If you want to talk to O'Brien, it will be easier if you don't look Apache."

She flushed and glanced at her buckskin dress, which showed her strong legs. She didn't think much of the clothing of paleface women, but felt Slocum would like her to wear them.

He was stroking his chin. "With such clothing you could move around better. Go into towns and nobody would ask questions."

She thought about it, intrigued at the idea of such clothing, curious, in a feminine way, what she'd look like.

"Maybe," she said.

"Tell you what. I've got to go into town to get supplies. I could pick up a coupla things for you."

She scowled. "Does Slocum know the clothes of a woman?"

He studied her size. "I'll find something." He looked at the side of the cliff that had a couple of crevices.

"There are some nice nooks up there, for hideaway, if you want them. Be back before sundown."

* * *

Slocum rode into town and found it bustling with cowboys, men loading wagons with supplies, getting haircuts, drinking whiskey. He went into Levinson's General Store and bought canned goods and sundries, and then picked out a woman's riding pants and boots, a blue shirt. He put all in his saddle pack. Then feeling a craving for homemade food, he went into Ada's Restaurant, ordered bacon and eggs, potatoes, biscuits, and coffee. On his second coffee cup, he noticed the sign: *Annual Dance at the Big Barn*.

Ada, a motherly looking woman with a nice face, saw him looking at the poster.

"Might enjoy yourself at the dance," she said. "We've got good-lookin' ladies in this part of the territory."

"Sure wish I had the time." He was thinking it might be nice to see how White Flower, in these new clothes, would handle herself in a social situation.

From his window seat, he had a clear view of Main Street, the riders, and the livery, the hotel, the bank, the general store. A prosperous town, with plenty of cattle money, Slocum thought. He tackled his bacon, eggs and biscuits with pleasure.

Two muscular cowboys with flushed faces, wearing hard-worn Levi's came into the restaurant and took seats at the window table next to Slocum's.

"What'll it be, gents?" Ada asked. She was built with womanly lines, fine breasts and hips, and the cowboys looked at her.

"I'd like it to be some huggin' and kissin', but reckon it's too early for that. Right, Willie?"

Slocum glanced at him. He was a dark man with a hawk nose, a hard mouth, and a compact, muscled body. The butt of his Colt looked shiny, and Slocum figured him a gunslinger.

Willie was staring with pale yellow eyes at Ada. He had a snouty nose, loose lips in a thickly boned face. "Right, Chuck," he drawled. "'Cept I figure she rates more than just huggin'." His face twisted with such an evil smile that Slocum felt instant dislike. He turned to his coffee, wondering if the taste was spoiled. But a man could look like a wolf and be a rabbit. Slocum dug into his food, thinking that, after a time, you got the face you deserved.

Ada, who handled all sorts of customers, didn't pick up on the remark. "You interested in food or flirtin', mister?"

"Why not both, Ada?" Chuck asked.

"'Cause this is a restaurant. If it's flirtin' you want, there's a dance just up the street."

"Yeah—we heard," said Chuck, glancing at Slocum's plate. "That looks mighty good. Reckon we'll have the bacon and eggs."

Ada, stone-faced, went back to give the order to her Chinese cook. The cowboys watched the movement of her buttocks.

"Nice bedtime filly," said Willie, his voice slurred from drinking.

"Bit over the hill."

"I like 'em that way," said Willie.

"You like 'em every way," said Chuck, and

stared out the window down the street. "But we got better things in mind."

"Nothin' better than a hot little filly who knows the right moves," said Willie, his pale yellow eyes gleaming.

"Yeah, yeah, but let's keep our mind on the main thing. You start thinkin' of fillies now, you're askin' for trouble."

Chuck turned suddenly, as if he sensed the presence of the big cowboy at the next table. He looked into Slocum's cool green eyes and ironic smile, and felt irritated. "Whatcha looking at?" Chuck asked rudely.

Slocum smiled slowly. "A hawk-nosed cowboy weighing 'bout 180 pounds of muscle and bone, wearing a black Stetson, worn-out Levi's, a smooth-lookin' Colt, just about to eat some bacon and eggs."

Chuck listened, amazed at this cool appraisal, and studied the lean, big, green-eyed man, and decided that nothing said had been insulting. Chuck's scowl turned into a grim smile.

"Reckon you're a bit of a clown, and don't mean any harm."

Willie, more combatively drunk, twisted his nose and spoke coldly. "Not sure about that, Chuck. He sounds like a smart aleck."

Slocum's eyes glittered and Chuck, who more than once had to keep reins on his buckaroo mate, spoke soothingly to Slocum. "Don't mind him, mister, he's off his feed. Been givin' me trouble, too." But his smile was yellow, as if, at another time, he'd gladly throw cow dung at this smart-talking polecat.

Willie glared. "That's the trouble, too many cowboys stomping around bein' smart aleck. Oughta be a way to shut them off."

Chuck glared at him, then turned to Slocum whose jaw had hardened.

"Mister, I'm goin' to apologize for my friend's bad manners. Been drinkin' and sorta talks rubbish. I ask you to let it go by."

Willie stared, opened his mouth, but Chuck said quickly, "You goin' off half-cocked about the wrong things, Willie. Get clear in your head what we're here for. I ain't gonna tell you again, just gonna walk off and let you go down on your own."

The threat seemed to get through Willie's alcoholic brain, and he shut his eyes, tightened his jaw. When he opened his eyes, he looked different. He gazed at Slocum and shrugged his shoulders.

Slocum nodded, aware that whiskey could bring out the devil in a man.

Then Ada brought their food and they wolfed it down. They talked to each other in low tones, occasionally looking out the window at passing wagons and riding cowboys. When they finished eating, they paid up and went out of the store without a backward look.

When Ada came to refill Slocum's coffee cup, he asked if she'd seen them in town before.

"No. They're low-down hombres and I hope not to see 'em again," she said smiling. "While it's always a pleasure to serve a customer like you."

He grinned and couldn't help look at her feminine gifts with appreciation. A seasoned woman like her could give a man a lot of pleasure. And, from the signals she was throwing, she seemed ready to offer them. He watched her go to another customer, the moves of her nicely packaged body a bit provocative, and his mind did a few tricks.

His eyes idly followed the cowboys on the street as they trekked up to the saloon, some in their Sunday best, headed for the dance. A couple of young women in fine calico, laughing, rode up in a buckboard, excited about the dance. Slocum lit up his Havana, smoked, and watched the action from the window. Then he saw this beautiful girl in a fine carriage, pulled by a high-stepping, spirited white horse, stop near the bank. She was one beauty, her red hair glowing in the sun, a cute doll's face, and she was smiling with all the joy of being young and beautiful. Then Slocum heard the sound of shots.

He looked sharply and saw two men in hardworn Levi's come out of the bank, guns drawn, holding moneybags. Chuck and Willie! They headed for their horses, hitched in front of the bank. When a man appeared at the doorway, Chuck shot him dead. A cowboy in the middle of the street started for his holster, and Willie shot him. Then, Willie, seeing the redhead, grabbed her, held a gun on her head, and everyone in the street froze as he and Chuck got to their horses. Willie forced her over his horse, got behind her, still holding his gun on her, while Chuck went up on his horse, and they started to race up Main Street.

Slocum was standing at the doorway of the restaurant, hugging its side, watching the outlaws thundering up the street.

Willie and Chuck saw him, and swung their guns to fire, but Slocum's gun fired twice, so quick, it sounded like one shot, and two bloody holes appeared in the foreheads of the outlaws. They bounced like sawdust dolls in their saddles, then fell into the street, their bodies somersaulting, the moneybags rolling and laying there. It was over so fast, the townfolks just stared. The redhead, her face crimson with fear and excitement, grabbed the reins and brought the horse to a halt. She looked at Slocum and her beautiful face broke into a brilliant smile.

Slocum smiled at her, went back into the restaurant, paid Ada who said, "Please, this is on the house, mister. Never saw anything like it."

When he walked into the street, the redhead was waiting. "I sure do thank you, mister. You saved me from a lot of grief."

He looked coldly at Chuck and Willie, dead on the ground, townfolk gathering around. Then he smiled at the girl. "Always a pleasure to rid the world of a stinkin' hyena."

Lulabelle Gibson watched the powerful, green-eyed stranger on his roan ride west. Her heart skipped a beat, and she couldn't help feel sudden regret to see him go. She had no idea who he was. She wondered if he knew about the dance in town, and yearned for him to come to it later.

Folks crowded round, talking at her excitedly, asking about the tall stranger who came like the angel of death to destroy those evil outlaws.

She remembered her feelings when that yellow-eyed, ugly mongrel had roughly grabbed her, and put his gun to her head. She could smell the awful sweat of him. She'd seen him shoot Josh Ellis stone-dead as he rushed to the bank doorway. Then he shot Tom Healy, who was reaching for his gun in the street. She recalled the outlaw's dead, yellow eyes; a man like that would do anything, she had no doubt of it, and it amazed her that, for one moment, he had been alive holding her in the threat of rape and death. And in the next, because of the powerful green-eyed stranger, who seemed to come out of nowhere, that horrible outlaw was dead.

She shivered at her narrow escape and walked with some of the other girls to the dance hall.

A thought struck Slocum as he rode west toward White Flower's hideout. What would it be like to take her to that dance in town? She could dress in the clothes that he'd bought, and learn what it was like to socialize with palefaces. She seemed interested in the ways of paleface girls. Here was an opportunity. She seemed to want to impress O'Brien, and if she went to the dance, she'd become more used to the ways of paleface girls.

It was still early, and plenty of time to get to town—spend an hour or so, looking on, even trying to dance. Afterward, they could pick up the trail to O'Brien's ranch.

It was a warm June day, with few clouds in the burnished blue sky. The light of sun sharply sculpted the serrated rocks of the mountains. The scent of June flowers drifted on a stray breeze to his nostrils. Fine day to go to a dance.

When he reached the side of the cliff, she came

out of a crevice, somewhat surprised to see him before sundown.

He pulled the clothing from his saddlebag; the riding pants, shoes, and the blue dress. Her eyes shone as she handled it, looking with wonder at its fine fabric. Then she looked at the shoes and the boots.

She laughed. "Though I find it most beautiful," she said, "one can hardly ride with such clothing."

"The pants are for riding, but this—" he pointed to the dress, "is for the paleface dance." He was smiling broadly.

She stared at him and frowned. "Dance?"

"They have a dance in town. What do you think of this—we ride in and go to it?"

Her brows were knitted. "Why should I go to this dance?"

He grinned. It was his belief that her meeting with O'Brien was important, and she wanted to be right for it. "It is a way for you to learn the ways of the white women."

She studied him. "You think I should learn their ways?"

"It won't hurt to know them."

She hesitated and looked at the dress in her hand. It fascinated her.

"You will learn how white men feel about you. You may discover that White Flower is beautiful. Much admired by paleface men."

She looked off, her dark blue eyes thoughtful. Why should she take on this challenge? But he was right, it might be worthwhile to spend time, observing the ways of the paleface. Part of her dreaded such an encounter, but because of that, she decided to do it and get rid of her fear. She felt Slocum's curiosity to see her in such clothes. She, too, was curious. After all, what could she lose? She would go to this paleface dance. Let whatever happen. Afterward, she would go to O'Brien's place.

"You think White Flower should go?"

He nodded. "Yes."

"Then White Flower will go."

He stroked his chin. "We can't call you White Flower. Better to call you 'Daisy.' It is like a white flower."

"Daisy." She sounded the word and smiled. "It has a nice sound."

They rode toward town, and Slocum felt good about it. Nature around them bloomed, the grass was green and lustrous, the June flowers were red and purple, rabbits were jumping, little white puffs, until a coyote appeared and they scrambled frantically.

On the outskirts of town Slocum saw an abandoned wooden hut. He pulled up, and suggested it might be best if she changed from her buckskins into the dress before they reached town. She shrugged and went in, and when she came out her face was clouded, as if she felt ridiculous in the paleface dress. But to Slocum she was dazzling, the blue dress playing off her dark lustrous eyes and falling with feline grace over her breasts and hips.

She gazed at him, almost embarrassed. "What does Slocum think?"

"He thinks you're gonna knock those cowboys on their tails."

She looked puzzled at his expression.

He laughed. "You look beautiful."

A small, pleased expression twisted her lips, and she looked at the lean, broad-shouldered, strong-faced man. "Slocum, too, looks beautiful."

He laughed.

When they reached town the sun was still high, and the street was cleared, the bank closed. You wouldn't think outlaws had hit the town. But in front of the dance hall, there were horses and carriages hitched to the post, and festive-looking girls and cowboys out on the porch, chatting and laughing.

White Flower had stiffened at the sight, but Slocum's easy smile and his hand on her elbow seemed to calm her. And she looked easy as they walked to the porch, a couple of cowboys making a point to look at her. They went through the door into a huge room decorated with ribboned paper and red tissue over the oil lamps, which threw soft, cheerful light on the cowboys and the ladies, some of whom clustered near the punch bowl, some sitting on benches, chatting. Others danced to a fiddler and pianist who at the moment were playing "Dixie."

Slocum smiled broadly as the tune brought back a lot of marvelous memories of his youth in Georgia. Then he thought of the war, and gloom hit him, the way it always did when he remembered it, the wounded and the dying.

Some girls turned at the sight of him, their eyes widening a bit, and Mady Evans, an older woman, who had been in the street during the ruckus with the outlaws, recognized him. She went to the red-headed girl sitting in the corner with a hefty cowboy.

"Lulabelle," Mady said, "you won't believe this, but the cowboy who shot the outlaws is over there."

Lulabelle stiffened and turned sharply to look.

Mady then said, "He's brought a lady with him, a very lovely one, too." Lulabelle studied the young woman Slocum had brought and had to admit this was a very pretty girl, with a fine figure. But she looked just a bit uncomfortable, as if she wanted suddenly to wriggle.

Lulabelle turned to Eddie Fowler, one of her beaux. "Eddie, the cowboy who saved me from those rotten outlaws is just come. I think it right for me to give him thanks."

"Thought you had already done that, Lulabelle," growled Eddie, quick to jealousy.

She smiled coquettishly. "Eddie, you can't thank a man too much for saving you from something worse than death." And she moved, cool as a cucumber, toward Slocum who had managed to get White Flower to the punch bowl, which was touched a bit with whiskey. Sipping it, White Flower felt more relaxed. She studied the women around her, talking and flirting, and found them ordinary, nothing too strange.

"Well, mister," said Lulabelle, "I'm lucky to have the pleasure of thanking you again for saving my life early today."

He grinned, figured it'd be a good time to get White Flower socializing. "A pleasure. This is Daisy."

Lulabelle stared at her. Too good looking, but

something a bit odd about her. She didn't look easy. "Wanna tell you, Miss Daisy, that your friend here took me out of the hands of hell itself."

White Flower looked at Slocum curiously. "What do you mean?"

"Hasn't he told you? Well, he's one modest man."

Mady spoke up. "He shot two outlaws who were about to run off with our Lulabelle and the bank's money. Shot so fast, they didn't know what hit them. Deadeye, right smack in the forehead, both of them."

Eddie had dragged after Lulabelle but stood apart, looking sourly at Slocum. He didn't like to hear Lulabelle gush over any man.

Slocum glanced at White Flower who had been studying Lulabelle, her face, her clothes, her hair. When the women looked at White Flower, expecting her to speak, Slocum took a breath, thinking she might say, 'Slocum is a great warrior,' but she didn't. "He is a deadeye," she said, repeating Mady.

Just then a stocky, gray-haired man in a vested black suit and shoelace tie came through the door with an older woman. They walked to the punch bowl.

Mady Evans smiled broadly at the man. "Mr. Johnson, you might be interested in meeting the cowboy who shot those outlaws. Saved the bank money. This is the man."

Johnson's mouth fell open as he stared at Slocum. He came forward with a grin on his broad, beefy face and grabbed Slocum's hand.

"Mister, you disappeared so fast, I can't tell you

how disappointed I was." His face turned grave. "They shot Josh, my teller, down in cold blood. Terrible thing to see. But it sure did my heart good to see them dead in the street." He stepped back to look admiringly at Slocum. "Both shot— right in the forehead. Amazin'." He stroked his chin thoughtfully. "You saved the bank some money. And the bank would like to show its gratitude, if you just drop by the bank tomorrow."

Slocum shrugged. "I figure men like them are better off dead. Nobody owes thanks for that. Now, this is a dance. Why don't you girls do what you came for?"

Eddie came forward. "You got the right idea, mister." And he turned to Lulabelle. "Let's get some dancin' in, honey, before your two hot-blooded cowboys come in and take over."

Lulabelle looked a bit long at Slocum, then went out to the dance floor with Eddie, where they picked up the rhythm of the music.

White Flower watched Lulabelle's flirtatious smiles, her moves on the dance floor. Then she turned to watch the other couples as they danced.

Slocum refilled their glasses from the punch bowl, which they took to the benches that lined the side of the hall. She was smiling. "Slocum seems to have a habit of saving the ladies."

He looked sharply at her. Was she teasing or mocking? Hard to know.

"Are you making fun?"

She shook her head. "It is true."

But he was thinking differently. "It is true that you saved me twice."

She turned to watch Lulabelle dancing. "Do you like this girl?"

Slocum watched Lulabelle move gracefully on the floor, flashing her dark eyes and her flirtatious smiles, a girl coming out of Nature's cocoon, like a radiant butterfly meant to throw a spell on the male. He turned to White Flower, looked at her finely boned, high-cheeked face, her calm expression.

"She's a cute filly, but nothing like you."

Her eyes radiated feeling and she turned away.

"How'd you like to dance?" he asked.

She frowned. "I can't do that, Slocum."

"Dancing comes naturally to women. Look out there, how they move."

She bit her lip, but watched the dancers. She had danced in tribal ceremonies, and was fleet of foot. This dancing did not seem that hard.

The women followed the men and the steps were simple and clear.

After a time, White Flower smiled, especially when the musicians played a slow country tune. Slocum took her hand and led her to the floor. Though her hand felt soft, her body was stiff. Still she moved as light as a feather, following him like his shadow. She had good rhythm and, as she became aware of the repeated steps, her confidence grew and her body loosened. She moved with fine grace, so that several of the men began to watch her.

One of the men was Sean O'Brien. He had come with Curly Jack, ahead of Chet and Mike, who were left to take care of some unavoidable chores. O'Brien had come to the dance with plea-

sure, hoping for headway in the courtship of Lulabelle by Mike or Chet.

He walked to the punch bowl, and watched
Lulabelle dancing with Eddie. Didn't bother him,
since he knew Lulabelle liked lots of beaux, but
thought seriously only of the O'Brien boys.

As he quaffed the punch, his eye strayed to the
other dancers, then he saw the tall, lean stranger
and the girl.

His eyes at first skimmed over them, to the
other dancers, then he came back to the couple
and frowned. Something about the girl caught
him, and he stared. She had hit some memories of
long ago, and he scowled, as if they were painful.
He drained his glass and refilled it.

Then Curly Jack said, "Hey, boss, whyn't I cut
Eddie away from her, then you pick her up. She's
gonna come into your family, ain't she?"

O'Brien's eye went back to Lulabelle. Might be
a good idea to uncouple that low-life cowboy,
Eddie Fowler from Lulabelle. Kick out any hope
he might be cherishing.

"Do that, Curly. We don't want Eddie reaching
out and getting his fingers burned."

He watched Curly sidle up to Lulabelle and
Eddie, give them an ingratiating smile. "Hey
Eddie, you cain't go hoggin' this beauty. Gotta
give other coyotes a chance."

Eddie grimaced. He'd seen O'Brien come in
and figured his time was running out. But he
hated goin' down without a fight.

"Wait a minute, Curly. Let's hear what Lulabelle has to say."

Lulabelle laughed, for she loved men to squabble over her. "Reckon Curly likes to dance, too, Eddie." And her eyes strayed to White Flower.

She had been feeling the strain of the new experiences. "Let's leave now, Slocum. It's enough —the first time."

He nodded. She'd done well, nothing disagreeable had happened. It worked fine.

"We slip out, nice and quiet," he said.

And within minutes they were out of the hall, on their horses, riding west as the sun started toward the horizon. They were three miles out of town when the two riders came into town from the east—Mike and Chet O'Brien. They reached the dance hall, dismounted, and fixed their horses to the hitch rack. Then they went up into the dance.

10

O'Brien, in the corner, thought of the girl who walked out the door, the look of her, so like someone he once knew. Then the memories came up, hard and sharp. He shut his eyes, and in his mind he saw vividly the way it was that day years ago. He had gone into the thickets tracking the deer, when he heard the piercing neigh of a horse in agony. He ran forward, his rifle out, and saw the lion. A massive male, it had grabbed the mustang by its throat and brought him down. The pony was kicking violently, the lion's claws were hooked into its neck. Then O'Brien saw the Apache girl, only fifteen feet away, looking horrified at the death struggle of her pony. O'Brien shot at the lion, trying for its brain. He missed but hit the lion, which took the bullet, jolted, but still clutched the mare.

His third shot hit a crucial piece of the head, and the lion shut its eyes in pain, then turned his broad face toward O'Brien, its dark brown eyes in a dull rage. Slowly he released his clutch of the pony as its nervous system began to die; he lay down curled in death.

The Apache girl looked gratefully at O'Brien and ran toward her mare, caressing its head in her lap. O'Brien walked to the pony when the girl turned sharply and screamed, pointing behind him. By then he had heard the rush of the soft padded claws and turned to see the dead lion's mate almost on him, ready to leap. O'Brien fired point-blank, his three remaining bullets. The lion was mortally hit, but the jump brought her up to O'Brien and she clawed him as she fell.

As if hit by a hammer, O'Brien stumbled back, dropped, and went out cold.

It was almost dusk when he opened his eyes, and it took a full minute for him to get his mind clear. He felt a vicious burn on the side of his forehead where the lioness had hit. There was plenty of blood on his shirt. He remembered that she had dropped in front of him, but he couldn't see her. Then he realized *he* had been moved. He sensed someone nearby and through slitted eyes picked up the Apache girl who was wetting a cloth with whiskey. She had found them in his saddle-bag, and as she came forward, he shut his eyes. With a gentle hand she put the whiskey cloth over his brow, where he felt the harsh claw marks. There was a sharp burn, and he opened his eyes.

She bit her lips, partly in fear. She had soft glowing eyes, fine bones in a lovely face, and dark long hair, held by a red headband. He smiled and it had a calming effect on her. He sat up, felt dizzy. That damned lion had knocked him upside down. And the Apache girl had stayed to show her gratitude for what he'd done. A good girl, and fine looking, too. She was watching him, as if she expected him to bowl over.

When he didn't, she pointed to herself. "Sunbird," she said.

Sunbird! She was something like that. He pointed to himself. "O'Brien."

Her face twisted as if the word were difficult. "O'Brien?"

He nodded and put his hand to his brow. A bad cut, and she had done the right thing to try and clear it with alcohol. A tear from such wicked claws could put poison in a man's blood. He felt lousy.

"O'Brien should rest," she said softly.

"Why?" He smiled and tried to sit up and found his head spinning. Might be the loss of blood.

She bit her lip, realizing he was in bad shape. Only because he had come to help her. She would have to stay with him, until he was able to ride.

She managed, somehow, to get him to a line hut set back in a cut of land, far from the trail of men. It had a floor mattress, and a bench table and chair. She got the bedroll from his gelding and used it for herself, put him on the mattress because he caught the fever. At first she used the water and whiskey and jerky in his saddlebag.

Then he went into wild dreams and delirium, and he'd wake up bathed in sweat and find her there, with a wet cloth and some medical herbs she put on the clawed wound. She went out and trapped rabbit, made a nourishing stew, and fed him. It was a tough nursing job, and she brought him back from the edge of disaster. Her herbs quieted the rage in his blood, and the fever finally left him. One day he awoke calm and looked up and saw her sitting near him, her eyes shut, as if in a dream. He studied her face, its fine bones, lovely profile, and damned if he didn't fall in love. As if his life belonged to her, because she had saved it.

His strength came back slowly, which made her smile. She knew a lot of words, but mostly they communicated beyond language. She, too, felt their destiny was entangled because of what they had gone through together.

The hut was so far from the trespass of men that it seemed to him they were the only two people on earth. Her touch was tender, and he responded. One night he reached up and pulled her down, kissing her. Then he pulled her buckskins off. She had big round breasts, with dark nipples, and she was flat in the stomach and powerful in the thighs and legs. He never before had felt such passion for a woman, and they made love countless times; buried in her, he felt the fires of heaven.

When he became strong and healthy again, he wanted her to go with him to his world, the world of the paleface. She shook her head. "My place is not with your people."

He pleaded, but she would not come. Finally, he had to face the separation. "If ever you have need of me. Whatever it is. Come to Vista, near the border. Ask for me, for Sean O'Brien. They will know me. Remember, Sean O'Brien."

It took many months for the pain of the separation to ease, if it ever did. All that happened was it went underground, buried itself deep in his mind. But he was scarcely free of it. Look how it had spiraled up from the lower depths at the sight of that girl. That girl! He wondered who she was. Where she'd come from. She had put him in mind of Sunbird. It was the look of her, the walk of her, the way she carried her head.

O'Brien opened his eyes, and the music of the fiddler and the piano came in full volume to his ears, pushing him rudely into the present. He saw the dancers, and Lulabelle smiling at Chet. Some others were there.

O'Brien shook his head. It was a waste to go over the past, the memories of unfinished love. All they did was awaken old wounds. He sighed; it was a mystery the way the mind worked—the sight of a girl had thrown him back into a precious part of his past. But here was the real world again —his sons, Mike and Chet. And that adorable filly Lulabelle, who might well become his daughter-in-law before long.

He started toward the group.

They were standing together, Mady Evans, Lulabelle, and her three beaux, Chet, Mike, and Eddie. What struck O'Brien was the wild look in Chet's eyes, like he was ready to go off half-cocked. When O'Brien reached them, Chet turned, his face red. "Did you hear this, Dad? Coupla goddam outlaws grabbed Lulabelle."

O'Brien scowled. He had come to town from the range, and had heard nothing. He looked at Lulabelle.

Mady Evans spoke up. "That outlaw put a gun to her head. So they could ride outa town with the bank money. And nobody was to bother them."

Mike turned to his father. "Some cowboy shot both their brains out."

O'Brien's eyes narrowed, then he smiled. "Who was he?"

"A stranger," said Mike, "who stopped for a meal at Ada's Place. Just passin' through, I suppose."

O'Brien looked at Lulabelle, then at Chet. What the hell was he in a sweat about? "Man deserves a medal."

Mady said, "He was here, dancing, just a while ago."

O'Brien remembered the lean stranger, a strong face. And the girl was with him! Who the hell was she?

"Did you know the girl?"

"Name of Daisy," Lulabelle said. "Not a town girl."

Mady was staring at Lulabelle. "Must have been terrible for you, Lulabelle. That stinkin' outlaw, holding you, holding his gun at your head."

Lulabelle nodded slowly. "Oh, he was rotten. I was feared plenty, and that's the truth. I know he'da put a bullet in me, if anyone tried to stop him. And he stunk, all right."

She took a deep breath. "Thought I'd be dead, one way or another, and the easier would be a bullet."

Mady said, "I feared for you, Lulabelle. Terrible thing to see. Then that stranger, shooting from Ada's Place. He was the answer to a prayer."

Chet glared at her, hating the stranger for doing something he would have yearned to do.

"Don't know about that," he said harshly.

Eddie frowned. "What d'ya mean, Chet? The man saved her."

"That polecat took one helluva chance, shootin' when the outlaw had a gun on Lulabelle. What if the stranger missed. What then?"

In the silence they thought about it.

Chet felt a lift, that he had scored. "The right thing would have been to trail those damned outlaws. Then nail 'em. When Lulabelle didn't have a gun barrel against her head."

Eddie nodded. "Yeah. Sounds right. That damned stranger took a long-shot bet. On Lulabelle's life. Not his."

"You got it," Chet said with satisfaction. He had pulverized the stranger, though they had raved about him.

He looked at his brother and scowled. "You don't see it?"

"Dunno. What if we caught up too late for Lulabelle? Men like that are not gonna hang on too long with someone who slows them down."

"We woulda come down on them hot and heavy," Chet bragged. "Woulda caught them in time."

"Woulda," said Mike scornfully.

Eddie stayed with Chet. "That fool of a stranger took one helluva chance. He wasn't bettin' his life, but Lulabelle's. No, not an ace in my book."

They turned to Lulabelle.

"What do you think, Lulabelle?" asked Mady.

She smiled slowly. "All I know is that I'm here. And those outlaws are dead. And it was done by a man with a sharp eye and a steady hand."

Mike smiled. "That's how I see it, Lulabelle. Now, let's just take a take a turn round the floor and celebrate."

They went out to the floor, and Mike held her close, while Chet watched, his face red.

He turned to Eddie. "Who the hell was this stranger? You got a look at him."

"Big, lean, green-eyed. Looks tough, but could be cut down to size."

Chet's eyes glittered. Could this be the polecat who had shot Brady, made him feel like a fool, gave him all his miseries? And now, this, with Lulabelle, making her starry-eyed about him. The rage seethed in him.

"Hey, Eddie. We O'Briens are goin' on a manhunt tomorrow. Some damned dog back-shot Brady, in cold blood, also got Wilbur and Lonnie. Might be some fun for you."

Eddie Fowler figured it was a good idea to be on the right side of the O'Briens. Could mean work on their trail drives. And the excitement of a manhunt appealed to him. The odds sounded good.

"Count me in, Chet."

Lulabelle felt the strong arms of Mike, and it made her feel good. She looked at his craggy face, and liked it, he was four-square, and she liked him. Mike had made it mighty plain already that he wanted them to hitch up. She found him real, and felt he could be a man to lean on.

Then, there was Chet, who also wanted to get hitched. He had always been interested in her, even when she was a pigtailed kid. Of course, Chet was a touch wild, and a bit of a showoff, but that didn't bother her much. He still had a lot of the boy in him.

And jealous? Because she had admired the stranger, Chet tried to tell her that the man had put her in danger by shooting the outlaws dead. He couldn't stand for her to favor anyone—even Mike, his own brother! Why was he like that? Yet, she liked it. He had strong feelings.

She was thinking this when Mike pulled her into a quiet corner. He looked at her full breasts and well-developed body. He remembered when she was a kid, he had thrown a rope around her, as if she were a young calf for branding.

"Lulabelle," he said, "it's hard to believe you were once the freckle-faced, pigtailed filly I once roped like a steer."

"I remember that, Mike O'Brien, and that's the worst memory I have 'bout you."

"Well, I have better memories of you, Lulabelle. Never thought you'd grow into this beautiful, desirable woman." He leaned forward, his light blue eyes gleaming with admiration. "It's time you put aside your flirtatious ways and settle down with me."

She looked at him—stalwart, broad-shouldered, handsome—and felt his appeal.

"Mike, I can't tell you how much I favor you." She sighed. "But I also favor Chet. I like Eddie.

Reckon I just like the man I am with." She bit her lip. "I'm gonna tell you the truth, Mike. When that big, green-eyed cowboy came up to me, after shooting the outlaw, and said, 'It's all right now, miss,' I felt palpitations in the heart for him. You see, I'm sorta confused, Mike. Need a little extra time. I reckon I'm gonna sit down, in the next few days, and just make up my mind who it's gonna be."

Mike's lips were tight. "You're like a humming-bird, sippin' at each flower in the garden. Well, you've gotta settle sometime. One thing—are you goin' to tell this to Chet, too?"

"Bet I am, Mike. Right now." She had seen Chet coming up with a big scowl.

"All right," Chet said, "you've been hoggin' her long enough."

Mike said nothing, just walked to the side of the floor.

From his bench seat, O'Brien could tell that Lulabelle still wasn't clear in her mind who or what she wanted. Though her body looked plenty mature, he wondered if she needed more growing up. Well, there was no hurry. In a way, it might be good she didn't commit herself. The boys were goin' out tomorrow on a man huntdown, and it was best in affairs like that for them not to be thinking about a woman.

He got up, and again the image of Sunbird, the Apache maiden, came to his mind. Remarkable how the sight of that girl at the dance revived such deeply buried memories.

* * *

They were riding toward the ranch under a blue star-studded sky with a big silver moon that sharply silhouetted the mountain peaks. After an hour's riding, they stopped near a patch of scrub pine to rest the horses and have a smoke.

Chet had been surly, and he pulled a whiskey bottle from his saddlebag and took a long haul.

O'Brien scowled. "Do you have to do that now?"

"Yeah—I have to," Chet growled. "It's the only way I can stand *him*."

Mike bristled—he knew the way Chet's mind worked. "Stand what?"

Chet turned on him. "Tell me this, Mike. All those years Lulabelle was growing up, you paid no mind. Never noticed her, till you noticed *I* liked her. Then you got interested. Why was that?"

Mike smiled. "Wasn't interested because she wasn't interesting. But she growed up suddenly. Became interesting as a woman. That's what happened, Chet."

"Yeah, well, we were doin' all right, Lulabelle and me. Then you barged in and started courtin'. Why?" He turned to his father. "Just to block me. Won't let me get out in front of him in anything. Is it any wonder I drink sometimes."

Mike grimaced. "All's fair in love and war, Chet. Why should I step out—so you can get her. It don't work that way. Gotta fight for what you want. If you beat me, and she wants you, I won't like it, but I'll take it. But I'm goin' to be trying for her. And I'm not goin' to make it easy for you."

They turned to O'Brien, wanting the weight of his favor.

"I s'pose it's true that all's fair in love and war. But what I want is for *one* of you to get her. Put the Gibson and the O'Brien ranches side by side, and we've got a powerful hunk of land. Something to hand down to the O'Briens for generations to come. So stop growling at each other. Just make sure *one* of you gets Lulabelle."

He walked to his gelding. "Reckon we ought to ride. We've got a hard day tomorrow, tracking down the killer polecat who shot Brady and our boys."

Chet looked at his bottle, then as if defiant, took another haul out of it, then grumbled, "Yeah, let's get that dog in the worst way. Maybe I won't feel so bad."

11

Miles southeast of the O'Briens, under the same full moon, Slocum, in a thoughtful mood, lay on his bedroll, hands behind his head. He had camped in a shelter of boulders, near a gulch on the trail to Vista. He could hear the horses, the hushed sounds of night, and the movements of White Flower.

Wouldn't be long before they'd reach the O'Brien ranch, and the mystery about White Flower's trip would finally be cleared.

She was lying nearby in the extra bedroll he had got in town. Her eyes were open, her hair fluffed about her head; she didn't seem to be sleepy.

Slocum was thinking of the dance, of Lulabelle and her flirty eyes—the sort of girl who wanted all the men, even him. Well, maybe it was gratitude, for shaking her free from the outlaw's clutch.

In his mind he saw ugly Willie, the look on his face when he got Lulabelle on his horse, the gun to her head. His look said, 'Well, we got the money, a juicy filly, and now we got a getaway.'

Poor Willie—a bullet crashed his dreams. Lucky, Slocum thought, that they rode west, passing Ada's Place; they might have rode east and made it.

Then he heard White Flower. "Slocum is awake?"

"Yes."

"The dancing. I liked it."

"Good."

"That girl, Lulabelle. Did you . . . You liked her, didn't you, Slocum? She was pretty."

Slocum turned toward her. "Yes—pretty."

"The men looked at her. They wanted her."

"They looked at you, too," he said.

"I did not see that."

"Reckon you were too busy looking at her."

She was silent.

"Tomorrow, we may reach O'Brien's ranch. Your ride will be finished."

"How do you know that? Finished?" she asked.

There was a long silence. Could he say what he suspected? But it seemed farfetched. Yet it was possible. He raised on his elbow to look at her. The moon outlined the fine bones of her face, a beautiful face.

"You do not look Apache."

She said nothing.

"Perhaps the Apache took you as a child from

white folks?" He leaned forward to see her expression. "Is that what happened?"

Her face was impassive. "My mother did not say this."

Another thought lurked at the edge of his mind, but he couldn't bring it forward.

"What *did* your mother say?"

She looked toward the tall peaks for a long time, and at first he thought she was tired of this question; then he felt a tinge of tension, aware that she was about to say something important.

She said, "Sean O'Brien is my father."

The words hung in the air.

A thought like that had come to him once, but it seemed so grotesque that he dropped it. Now he tried to believe it.

"Your father?"

"She met him long ago. O'Brien was hurt, he saved her horse from the lion. She stayed to nurse him. They became lovers. I am the child of that love."

He shook his head. So that was how it happened. Fate was a joker who played games. So the child lived among the Apaches, an outsider—spawn of the hated paleface. No wonder they gave her and her mother a hard time. But what the hell was ahead for her at the O'Brien ranch? What would he do? The girl rides in and announces, 'Hiya, Dad, I decided to leave the Apache and live with you.'

O'Brien would probably turn the dogs on her. Depended on what kind of an hombre he was. He might feel shamed for folks to know what he'd done one dark night to an Indian maid. Slocum thought of Brady, who he'd been forced to shoot. What kind of a man would hire a nasty gun like Brady? O'Brien owned a lot of land and, in Slocum's experience, such landowners were hard, ruthless men. He glanced at White Flower. She might find hard times ahead.

He spoke gently. "Slocum believes O'Brien will be happy to find such a beautiful daughter."

"We shall see." Then she looked away, thoughtful. "That girl, Lulabelle—did Slocum find her beautiful, too?"

Slocum grinned. "She is pretty, like many—but not like you."

Her eyes glowed. "Why is Slocum so far away?"

It was a good question. She was lying on her bedroll. And he moved close to her; her lips were as soft as velvet, her breath sweet. The womanly curves of her body delighted him. She put her arms tightly about him and he felt the fire in his loins. When her thighs widened to receive him, he felt marvelous pleasure. The movements of their bodies had fiery passion in it. And the climax was poignant. Afterward, he looked at the sky and the stars, and felt the night was beautiful.

The sky was bloated with dark threatening clouds, as Chet led the six-man posse toward the stream where Slocum had beat Brady to the draw.

Chet pointed to the burial mound nearby. "That's Brady—back-shot, just like I told you." The men looked at it silently. Then he pointed to the prints. "By that polecat, Slocum. He's riding a roan. He also shot Lonnie and Wilbur. He's out there now." He pointed to a long sweep of land set between the steep sides of the valley.

O'Brien looked at the prints. "We lost three men to this polecat. And he shot Chet. Reckon we owe him a rope." He scanned the sky and grunted. "Let's close in on him before that sky breaks loose."

Slocum and the girl had been riding toward Vista, open country, that rolled in long smooth swells. Slocum examined the sky, heavy with thunderclouds. Now the land was changing, rising steeply with gigantic rock formations.

They were riding toward a high slope when Slocum saw the six riders off about five hundred yards. They had come suddenly on each other, and it was a jolt. The six pulled their horses and stared. Then a cowboy, who looked familiar to Slocum, pointed and yelled, and the riders started forward, whipping their horses. The man who yelled jerked his gun.

Slocum recognized the spoiled brat polecat who, with Brady, tried to get rough with White Flower. After she had given Brady a dose of bad herbs in his coffee, the polecat had wanted to do her violence. Slocum had to put a nick in his arm to stop him.

Now, the polecat was leading a bunch of guns —he'd brought his friends.

White Flower, startled by the hostile move of the riders, turned to Slocum who spoke sharply. They wheeled their horses and began a run for cover of brush and boulders. Not far off, Slocum could see a steep trail that led to tangled thickets and crags.

As Slocum rode, he remembered Lonnie and Wilbur, the two dogs, who had tried to ambush him. This polecat was the reason; he had to be the one watching the action with field glasses from the cliff.

Who the hell was he? He had said, "You don't know who you're messin' with," and made hard threats. An unforgiving fella, a pesky coyote, who kept coming back for mischief. And now he had brought five tough hombres.

And they were out for no good. He put the roan into a hard gallop toward a steep rise of land, bordered by rocks on one side, and rough brush and boulders on the other. Good place to make a stand, if he had to. He glanced behind and, to his surprise, the riders split, two riding south, four sticking to his tracks.

Then a cowboy in a short brim hat pulled his rifle and fired, and White Flower's pony stumbled and went down. She jumped clear, rolled, and stood looking at her horse, gutted and kicking in pain. Slocum, in cold fury, grabbed his rifle, sighted and fired, and the cowboy, in the short brim hat, jerked hard in his saddle and fell from his horse. Slocum fast-fired a couple of shots, and his near hits impressed the riders, for they pulled up and went for boulder cover.

It gave Slocum time; White Flower was staring in horror at her gutted horse, whinnying in pain. Slocum pointed his gun at its head and fired. The horse jumped convulsively then lay still. Slocum grabbed White Flower, pale with shock, pulled her behind him onto the roan, and galloped toward the nearby cover of rocks. He barely reached them when he heard bullets singing close and echoing off the cliffs.

He raced behind cover out of the line of fire to high ground and climbed. Finally the stony ground leveled and, by looking north, he could see a long valley, a winding stream and weird rock formations. To his south was thickly tangled brush and trees and rocks. He had a good perch, not one to attack easily. Maybe he could hold out, if he kept alert. No question of running—they had only one horse.

He'd wait for dark and try for a border town, to get an extra horse. But that sky looked bad.

To rest the roan, he stopped and lifted White Flower off. Dusk was coming fast.

"Those devils killed my horse," she said, her face in pain.

Slocum's face hardened as he remembered the man going down. "He paid for it."

She closed her eyes. "I loved that horse."

Slocum gritted his teeth. If he hated anyone, it was a man who would shoot a horse. Brave, loyal animals who ran their hearts out for their riders. He was glad he shot the mangy dog.

"Who are these men?" she asked.

"You remember the spoiled brat cowboy, who came with Brady? Brady wanted to hurt you?"

She nodded. "Brady, a bad one. I remember the other, too, with blue eyes. Bad, too."

"Well, this one with blue eyes has brought his friends."

"Why does he want to shoot?"

"I made him look foolish. He lost his friend, Brady. His kind can't forgive that."

She looked out at the dark sky. "So he will come until the end."

Slocum lit up a Havana, thinking of the five men out there. "Till his end or ours."

White Flower looked at him. "Let it not be our end."

He nodded. "That's how to think."

"But we have one horse. They will catch us."

"Maybe the rains will come. We'll try for the border and get a horse."

Slocum puffed his cigarillo. "Wonder why they split? Looked tricky."

"It *was* tricky, cowboy," said a voice. "Don't move."

Slocum froze, and to his astonishment, there, coming out of the dense brush, was a cowboy he had seen at the dance, pointing his Colt. Somehow, this dog had managed to find a trail up the steep rise. A secret path? Was that why they split, because he knew about it?

"Mighty clever of you, cowboy. How'd you do that?"

"First your gun, Slocum. By the handle, throw it."

Slocum pulled his gun and threw it. The cowboy leaned down, never taking his eyes off Slocum, and stuck the gun in his belt.

"You know my name, mister. Who the hell are you?"

"Eddie Fowler is the handle."

"Well, Eddie, how in hell did you get here?"

He smirked. "The reason we split and pushed

you toward this pocket is I knew the secret Injun trail. It cuts a lot of ridin'. Not bad, was it?"

Slocum nodded, glad the man was talking and not shooting.

"Hafta admit it. But tell me, Eddie, *why* are you chasing us? Don't remember doin' you any mischief."

Eddie stared, recognizing Slocum as the cowboy who had shot the outlaws in town. He had saved Lulabelle, which made her go all gooey. Given Eddie a jealous bad time at the dance.

"You didn't do mischief to me, but you did plenty to the O'Briens. *Killed three of their men*." Eddie took out a cigar, lit it nonchalantly then puffed the smoke up. "You shot a piece out of Chet, too. So we're gonna give you fast justice. My job is not to put a bullet in you. The boys want to make a party of it. *Rope* party." He grinned and waved his gun. "Now, s'pose you get to your horse, with the girl. We'll meet our friends."

Slocum looked at the gun and shrugged. He motioned to White Flower whose face was pale, lifted her to the saddle, patted her. Then reached for his saddlebag. "Got some whiskey here, and I could use a drink." He smiled. "Condemned man, you know."

"Throw the bottle here," Eddie said grimly. "I'll drink for both of us. You don't have much of a future." Suddenly he said, "Wait, lemme have a look. Never know." He glanced in the bag, saw no weapon. "Okay."

Slocum threw the bottle, then out of the special secret pocket of his saddlebag, he pulled a second gun. Eddie wide-eyed, caught the bottle with one hand and, with the other, brought up his Colt. Slocum fired, and the gun jumped from Eddie's hand, which he shook as if it had been scorched.

Eddie scowled deeply. "That was a lousy trick, mister."

"We're all playing tricks," Slocum agreed lightly. He motioned Eddie toward the thicket. "Where's your horse?"

Eddie's face darkened. "Not thinkin' of takin' it?"

"'Fraid so, Eddie. Simple justice, since one of your friends shot the lady's."

They were out of earshot of White Flower, who was still sitting on the roan, waiting.

Eddie scowled. "Well, you got the upper hand. There's a trail through this thicket that snakes down to the bottom of this hill. The hoss is down there." He smiled grimly. "But you can't hope to escape. We've got five men out here. They're gonna string you up for what you did to Brady."

"What the hell did I do to Brady? I shot his shootin' hand. But he came back and tried to rape this lady."

"You back-shot Brady, we heard about it."

"Who told you that?"

"Chet did."

"Chet? Who the hell is he?"

"You nicked his arm."

So Chet was the name of the pesky polecat, the one who kept bringing gunmen for revenge. Damn! Where had he heard the name. He had a terrible suspicion.

"Well, Chet is a helluva liar. What does Chet do on the O'Brien place anyway?"

"He's the boss's son, that's what he does."

The boss's son! Slocum scowled. That would make him *Chet O'Brien*. Slocum was stunned. All this time Chet had been locked in a revenge vendetta—not only against him, but *his own half sister*. And if anyone had a hate on a woman, and a desire to do her violence, it was Chet for White Flower.

Slocum thought about it hard. There had been a moment when he almost shot that mongrel dead, when he was manhandling White Flower, threatening her with rape and death. *His own half sister*. But would it make any difference to someone like Chet, if he knew, especially believing she was also Apache?

Eddie's eyes, like a hawk, were fixed on Slocum. There was a gun on the ground, but the man's gun was still in Eddie's belt, and he believed Slocum had forgot about it. Slocum looked mind-wandering. Now he was turning to White Flower, as if to tell her something important. The perfect moment for Eddie, and his hand swept to his belt and he had the gun coming up, feeling a surge of confidence, because the polecat was still looking at White Flower, when it happened, *a blur of movement*, a gun spurting flame, and Eddie's body hurtled back and he stumbled to the earth, a bullet in his heart.

Dead.

Slocum grimaced—that was the last thing he had wanted. He didn't want to kill the man, but his shot had been hurried. He had wanted Eddie to go back to O'Brien and tell them about White Flower.

But would it make a difference?

A bad situation

That posse was coming to string him up—they believed he had back-shot Brady. Chet had to be the first cousin to a rattler—and a liar. What if he knew that he had been ready to violate or kill his half sister? What then?

And that she was half Apache.

Well, the acorn never fell far from the tree, and the father, Sean O'Brien, could well be the same breed as his son. If that was so, then White Flower had bad prospects.

Well, first things first. He had to get Eddie's horse, so she'd have something to ride. He picked his gun off the ground, slipped it into his holster, and put the backup gun in his saddlebag.

There had been six men, and now there were five. They were on his trail. They had split like this because Eddie Fowler knew of this secret Indian path up the side of the rise.

He'd better steer clear of the posse because they were interested in fast, harsh justice. And he had to find some way to get a message to O'Brien. But what did you tell the rancher? "We got a woman here who claims you're her father. By the way, she's part Apache."

How do you get such an idea to him? O'Brien might pull his gun and shoot on sight. Not the sort of thing he'd want to hear.

He turned to White Flower. "His horse is down there. But we don't know what else. I'll go first— stay far behind. We must go quiet."

He went into the thicket, following Eddie's tracks as they sloped down a narrow, twisting trail.

He moved silently until he came to level ground where there were boulders, thick brush and trees, and far away the sight of humpbacked mountains. But nearby, roped to a tree, Eddie's chestnut gelding grazed peacefully.

Because of Slocum's natural caution, he waited but heard and saw nothing. He slipped silently forward and drew a sharp breath. Just beyond the cluster of rocks lay a cowboy staked out, his body scarred by Apache knives. Slocum pulled his gun and heard the swish of an arrow; it missed his neck by an inch. He flung himself to the ground, fired blindly toward the boulders, elbowed his way behind a protection of rocks. His eyes searched the area, but he saw nothing move. As he glanced at the dead cowboy, Slocum's jaw clenched. Such stakeouts left him with overpowering rage. They were done by hostile young braves, lusting for revenge. This was Apache country, and the Apache, most warlike of tribes, made war their way of life.

Slocum stayed low behind his boulder, knowing that White Flower, who must have heard the shot, would not move until she felt it right.

He listened intently but heard nothing. The Apache was a crafty warrior.

Again Slocum looked at the cowboy sprawled out. He had a broad face, thick mustache, long sideburns, one of the posse. He had found a bitter end at this godforsaken place.

His upper body had fine knife slices—not a pretty sight. Devilish work. The Apache admired courage—and was fascinated by how much a man could endure. He had contempt for the paleface believing he could not match the heroic endurance of the Indian.

Though Slocum's mind worked, he never stopped scanning the terrain, ready to fire at the smallest movement. But there was nothing, just dead quiet.

He glanced at the sky where black clouds were boiling and headed this way. Looked like a monster of a storm.

Then he heard the horses start up from behind a thick rise of rocks. He had no target for shooting. They had taken a smart fall-back position so that if discovered they'd be safe from attack. The pounding of the hooves grew fainter.

He came out cautiously, glanced at the horse. He had interrupted these Apaches, otherwise they would have taken the gelding.

A strong moist wind hit his face.

Slocum studied the moccasin tracks, two pair. These were braves on a tear, out to hit the paleface, do damage, and run. There were such warriors who searched out the unwary rider or settler. Bloodthirsty.

He looked at the sky, darkening, with thunderheads. The clouds stretched far past the mountains, far as he could see. They had to get shelter, but where?

"The rains will come. Very strong," White Flower said.

He turned, surprised. She had come silently behind him, seen the dead cowboy. Her face was pale, her lips firm. She had seen plenty in her time. She was a tough lady.

"Not a bad idea, the rain," he said.

"Why?"

"It will wipe out tracks. Bad for those who follow us."

"Bad for us, too," she said, glancing back at the dead cowboy. "We will not know where the Apache is."

He shrugged. "They won't know where we are, either." He glanced at her. *She still didn't know it was the O'Briens who were hunting them.*

He looked at the sawtoothed Sierras to the south. He should aim for a border town. He had to take evasive action until he could get close to O'Brien and give him the message. He sighed. Even that didn't guarantee a friendly reception. O'Brien had lost two more men, and now probably his orders would be shoot on sight.

Slocum clenched his jaw. A dangerous situation —pursuit by the O'Brien riders, down to four now. Two vicious Apache raiders, ready to strike at any paleface. More especially at White Flower who they would have a particular grudge against.

The O'Brien posse was north, the Apache west —he'd head south to the border. He looked at the chestnut gelding; it looked fit, didn't have the muscular chest of the roan, but it looked like a stout heart. He would go back, get the roan. And he couldn't leave these dead men out for the coyotes. Give 'em quick burial. And race like hell for shelter because there would be one hell of a downpour.

12

From the open mouth of the cave, Slocum looked out at the far blue mountains, the slopes, the bulky crags, and the darkness swirling over them from huge black clouds in the sky.

The storm would be on them in minutes, but he had found a notch in the side of the mountain, which offered shelter. It started as a narrow passage but widened into a spacious cave. Chances were that ages past, it had offered generations of men shelter from the storm.

He had brought in the gear, to keep dry, and tethered the horses between two towering crags that would protect them from rain driven from the west.

Behind him in the cave, White Flower lay on her bedroll, resting on one elbow, also looking out. They had enough comfort, and could stay till after the storm, while he'd figure what to do about O'Brien.

He bit into a biscuit, and looked out, listening to the wind as it started to howl, picking up volume, until it sounded like the screeching of a giant witch. Then suddenly the sky cracked open and lightning flashed wildly, followed by a deafening rumble of thunder that bounced crazily off the mountains. The sky turned black, and the rain came down in torrents, striking stone. The wind howled, an unearthly, throbbing sound, and to Slocum, it seemed like a replay of Noah's flood. The rain lashed with fury against the rocks as if it was trying to tear them apart.

White Flower came alongside, and stared out in fascination. She moved close to him for comfort, and he put his arm around her, and from the shelter, he looked out at Nature gone mad.

They huddled together for warmth, and he felt like an early man in a primitive world, when things were beginning.

The excitement of the storm seemed to touch something elemental in White Flower, for her lovely breast heaved. She stared at him with brooding eyes, pulled him gently to the bedroll, down to her. Her hands were all over him, pulling at his clothing, and before long their flesh touched. He was again aware of the beauty of her body. He stroked her breasts and nipples, the curve of her long waist. They kissed, and her firm body pushed hard against him, with its urgent wanting. He felt overpowering arousal, and she spread to receive him. The rhythm of their movements responded to the sounds of the storm and he seemed to reach his climax at the height of its fury.

Next morning a dazzling sun climbed in a sky of orange and red to start the dry-up of a besotted earth.

After breakfast, which they ate in the cave, White Flower sipped her coffee and watched Slocum with knitted eyebrows.

She's got something in mind, he figured as he looked out from the mouth of the cave at a different world. Last night, all creatures cowered in holes, hiding from the assault of the storm. Today, against the sky, he saw the fierce hawk, the high-soaring eagle, and the ugly buzzard flying low in search of gruesome breakfast.

Small earth animals also scurried around, one eye out for a quick meal, another for the marauder with the same intent toward them. A lot of hungry critters, Slocum thought, had come out of their holes.

"Slocum."

He turned. Her eyes were brooding, something on her mind.

"This cowboy you shot yesterday."

He thought of Eddie Fowler who tried to sneak-shoot him. "Yes. He had a good horse."

"What did he *tell* you—this cowboy?"

Slocum stopped to light a Havana. She watched him with tight lips. As he remembered, she was sitting on the roan, too far to hear what Eddie had said.

When Slocum didn't answer, she asked, "Why did you kill him?"

He shrugged. "Didn't mean that. A hurried shot. He was about to hit me. With my gun. Remember?"

"I remember. But he said something. It upset you. What was that?"

She was asking, and he couldn't lie to her.

"I asked him who were the men hunting us."

She waited, but he said nothing. He looked out at the warming earth.

Her eyes narrowed. "And who are they?"

"He told me it's the O'Briens."

She didn't seem to understand, for her face screwed up. "The O'Briens?"

"You remember the one with the blue eyes—who was with Brady, and who wanted to kill you? He is Chet O'Brien, *the son of Sean O'Brien*, the man you want to meet."

As the idea pierced her understanding, she put her hand to her breast, as if in pain.

The man she wanted to meet, and reveal to him that he was her father. *This man and his sons were hunting her and her friend—like animals*. Why? She thought of Chet, a handsome, spoiled brat who had put rough hands on her. He had meant to do bad things. *And he was her half brother!* What *kind* of father would raise such a son? Her heart sank.

She flung the coffee in her cup at the cooking fire, where it sizzled.

But it would be wrong to blame the father because his son was bad. She would have to meet Sean O'Brien, make up her mind about him.

Gloom swept over White Flower. She had been looking forward with excitement to meeting O'Brien, believing he would welcome her. She was beautiful, all the men said it, and he had loved her mother. Surely he would welcome her warmly. Too warmly—for these men with him rode with killing in their minds. Her lips tightened. Slocum had shot four men from the O'Brien ranch. These men had wanted to destroy him and abuse her. Slocum killed to protect her. And she had killed Brady because of his evil intentions.

Suddenly she made up her mind.

"It is useless to try and meet O'Brien," she said. "He is a man who wishes us dead."

Slocum was able to read her misery, and smiled. "Maybe we can, somehow, let O'Brien know who you are."

"But he is coming to kill."

"Not if he knows you are the daughter of Sunbird. He's supposed to have loved her. We must find a way to let him know."

"But his guns may kill us before that."

He looked out at the freshly washed land. All signs were wiped out.

"He'll have to find us first, there are no tracks," Slocum said grimly. "And it is not easy to kill such as we are."

Her eyes were brooding. "Slocum is a fine warrior. But they are many. It will be best for me to leave all this."

Slocum was startled. "Does White Flower think to go back to the tribe?"

"There is no going back." Her face was stony.

He dropped the Havana and put his boot to it.

"We don't know what kind of a man O'Brien is. He may be different from Chet. Even Chet may be different, when he discovers you are his blood."

She thought about that and brightened. "Chet does not know this yet. Surely he will be different when he finds this out."

Slocum smiled. "You'd hardly expect he'll try to hurt one who has his blood. The trouble is—he doesn't know." Slocum grinned.

For the first time she smiled.

Slocum looked out of the cave. "They don't know where we are. No tracks. We just keep moving until I figure out a way to tell O'Brien who he is hunting."

13

The three O'Briens and Charley, who rode with them, found a hut where they weathered the storm, staying dry and warm from a fire in the stove. They had been waiting a long time, at the prearranged spot, Rusty Creek, for Eddie and Jim Johnson. These two had raced for the Indian shortcut over Apache Rock, where Eddie would hit Slocum by surprise. Eddie was a canny cowboy who could handle himself. And Johnson, with him, was a brawler, rough and tough. O'Brien expected them to bring this Slocum polecat down without any trouble, especially as Slocum would never expect attack from the backside of the Rock.

But neither boy turned up. It made Mike thoughtful and Chet restless. Chet paced around, muttering to himself. He had wanted to storm the

153

hill, but the idea of climbing a steep rise, in the open, seemed idiotic to O'Brien and he vetoed it.

"This Slocum don't know about the Indian trail. Eddie and Jim Johnson will bring 'em down," O'Brien said.

Mike agreed.

But as time went on, and the skies began to blacken, O'Brien scowled.

"It's not goin' to happen," he said finally. "We better go for the hut before we get washed away."

They made a hard run to the hut, and just beat the storm. In the hut they made a fire in the small stove and sat around, listening to the crackling thunder and the rain pounding on the timbers.

"That damned roof is gonna cave in," Mike said, and he looked at Chet, sitting sullenly in the corner.

O'Brien lit a cigar and shook his head. "Can't understand it. Eddie is smart as a fox. What the hell happened up there?"

"Maybe he got outfoxed," Mike said.

Chet grunted and looked sourly at Mike. "Sometimes I wonder whose side you're on."

"On the side of good sense," Mike said grimly. "Who the hell is this Slocum we're hunting?"

"I tole you."

Mike studied his brother. "You told us he shot Brady when he wasn't looking. That he nicked your arm, when *you* weren't looking. And maybe he shot Wilbur and Lonnie when *they* weren't looking. Seems mighty careless, especially for a man who was riding and shooting at us, from about 500 yards and just about hitting. I figgered he could have hit us, if he wanted. Just warning

us. Now, why would a man who shoots like that
have to back-shoot anybody?"

Chet flushed. It was the damned truth. When
Brady said he had been back-shot, how come it
was only his shootin' hand that had been hit?

Chet remembered thinking about that. His
own arm had been nicked, a warning. And Slocum
shot Lonnie and the Apache had shot Wilbur. The
damned truth was this Slocum was a deadly sharpshooter. And not stupid. Where the hell was
Eddie and Johnson? Had they gone the way of the
others? This Slocum was turning out to be a
cursed devil. And he'd done the unforgivable, not
only made him feel like a clown, but also five good
men from the ranch were gone.

Chet looked up nervously. His father and Mike
were watching him. He couldn't admit he had
been wrong. It would make Mike right, and he
couldn't stand that.

He tried to smile. "That polecat Slocum just
threw a coupla lucky shots at us, that's all. But he's
a rotten dog who's killed five of our men. And he
deserves to be strung up."

Mike knew his brother pretty well, and from
the look on his face, he surmised that Chet had
told a lot of whoppers.

"Is that the girl with him—the one you told us
about?"

"Yeah, though she did look a bit different."

"Thought you said she was Apache." Mike
pulled a cigarillo. "You told us Brady made a remark about Slocum's *Apache* girl friend, and this
Slocum back-shot him."

Chet stared hard at him. "Yeah—so what?"

"So what. The girl don't look Apache, though she rides like one. And the man looks too handy with guns to back-shoot. That's what I'm saying. I figure Chet, you let your imagination get away with you."

Chet ground his teeth in fury. "Damn you. That girl is Apache. Just changed the clothes. I'm tired of talkin' to you. Don't hafta tell you anything." He glowered darkly.

O'Brien, who had made up his own mind about things, spoke to Mike. "Fact remains this critter, Slocum, has caused the death of five of our people. Don't matter what the hell Chet is imagining —he didn't imagine that. And we're gonna pay this Slocum out in rope."

Mike shrugged. "Didn't say not to. Just want the truth." He reflected a bit. "You got to keep in mind that this Slocum was not coming after our people. They were goin' after him. Reckon a man has a right to defend himself."

"See what I mean," Chet said furiously to his father. "It's hard to believe he's got O'Brien blood. He don't think like us. 'The enemy of one O'Brien is the enemy of all O'Briens.' You taught us that, Dad, and I live by it."

"Something to that, Mike," said O'Brien.

Mike grimaced. "S'pose an O'Brien raped and murdered—are we still s'posed to back him up?"

Chet threw his cigarillo into the fire. "That's what Mike thinks of me—a rapist and killer. Damn, I'm sick o' you, and if you weren't my brother..."

Mike shook his head. "What I want to know is

where in hell did you come from? You aren't like Dad or me. Some freak."

Chet's eyes blazed and he threw a right that staggered Mike. He followed with a left, which hit Mike's nose, spouting blood. Mike shook the dizziness off, looked calmly at his brother, holding his fists up, ready to swing again. Mike brushed away the blood of his nose with the back of his hand, and said, "This is gonna hurt me more than you, Chet."

He feinted quickly with his right at Chet's gut, pulling his guard down, then swung a powerful right at Chet's chin, then brought a hard left to Chet's solar plexus. Chet's eyes glazed and he toppled like a tree struck by lightning.

O'Brien watched it all with no visible emotion, as if he knew the foregone finish of a mix between Chet and Mike. He turned to Charley. "Give him some whiskey. I've got a fool for a son. Must be a punishment for something I did."

He turned to Mike.

"We're going after this damned Slocum and his woman, first thing tomorrow."

"There won't be any tracks out there," Mike said, brushing the blood from his nose, not looking down at Chet.

"We'll keep searching till we find his sign. We'll start at the bottom of Apache's Rock."

Slocum's eyes squinted against the blazing afternoon sun as he looked down at the land with its bulking mesas, its scattered growth of prickly pear and dusty gray sage.

They had been riding cautiously, on the lookout

for the O'Briens. Slocum had a plan, hoping to cross their trail, keep them in sight until dark. He had to make the first sighting, for if they made it, again there'd be the game of run and pursuit.

He made a point of working from high ground, which gave the broad view and, just now, he was lying on this perch of rock.

Then he heard the sound of repeated gunfire, and though he scanned the broad horizon for some time he saw nothing. Finally, about half a mile away, where the trail ran alongside the huge bulk of a mesa, a wildly careening stagecoach came into view, with the driver cracking his whip. The man alongside him, riding shotgun, could be seen jouncing on the seat, with an arrow in his body.

Then, behind the stagecoach rounding the turn, raced two Apaches on spotted ponies. They were riding all out and, to Slocum, oddly, nobody in the stagecoach was shooting. A sinister thought hit him that perhaps it was too late for them. The Apaches were big, well-muscled, had rifles and bows. Two braves revenging themselves on the palefaces who had stolen their land and destroyed their people.

They might well be the two raiders who had staked out the cowboy Slocum had buried. Slocum's green eyes had a steely glint. The coach was racing parallel to his position, and Slocum brought up his Sharps. But before he could set up for sighting, one of the Apaches shot the lead horse of the stage. As it fell, the other horses ran into it pell-mell, and in the tangle there was great squealing, neighing, and screaming of horses. The driver of the stage was thrown and when he hit the earth, he lay still. The stage rocked side to side but, miraculously, did not overturn.

Slocum, in a cold rage, watched the Apaches ride up alongside the stage. One, broad-shouldered, slim-hipped, with a feather in his headband, walked to where the driver had been thrown and started to raise his rifle to shoot.

Slocum, who had him in sight, squeezed the trigger. The Apache was a long way off and there was a scary moment when nothing happened, then the Apache jerked and collapsed in slow motion. The rifle sound bounced off the crags. The other Apache, astounded at the sudden death of his comrade, though nobody was in sight, flung himself to the earth, crawling swiftly under the coach.

Slocum had no shot at him, but waited. He would have to come out. The Apache soon figured where the bullet had come from that killed his comrade. He crawled low, keeping the wagon between him and Slocum's firing position.

Then, to Slocum's astonishment, he saw the Apache lift the unconscious driver, swing him on his back, using him as a shield till he rounded a bulky mass of rocks. Then he whistled thinly and his spotted pony trotted around the bulk. Slocum could have shot it, but he had never done such a thing.

And that was it; there was no further sign of the Apache.

Slocum went down, back to where White Flower had been waiting impatiently with the horses. She had heard the gunfire, but didn't know what happened.

"What is it?" she asked.

"It's the stagecoach. We'd better ride up and see."

Slocum approached carefully, making sure the Apache was not lurking. He followed the moccasin tracks around the boulder, and found the driver. His throat was slit. The tracks of the pony went southeast. The shotgun rider hit with the arrow was alive. Not too bad.

When Slocum looked into the stagecoach, he saw three men sprawled in death, and a young woman, still alive. *Pregnant*. Her eyes were wide open and she was struggling, groaning, gasping for breath.

She gazed at him despairingly. "Please," she moaned, "please."

Slocum jerked up. Good God! It hit him that she might be giving birth—that the shock of the attack had started her.

He turned to White Flower who was trying to help the shotgun rider. "Come here, quick," he yelled.

She scowled, ran to him, and he pointed to the woman. "Can you help her? She's goin' to have a baby."

She stared, astonished. Then she turned to him. "Bring water, whiskey, and cloths. Hurry."

Slocum took a deep breath. He'd seen lots of things in his time, but nothing like this. As he went to his saddlebag and pulled what she needed, he was thinking that White Flower had to know the facts of life. Indian women gave natural birth—she'd know what to do. He brought her what she wanted; she looked calm, which seemed to have helped the woman. She was young, about eighteen, with big, dark, anxious eyes, a pretty face, that would distort with sudden pain.

White Flower turned to Slocum and pointed to the men in the coach. "Get them out."

He pulled them out, three businessmen, with mustaches, derbys, in fancy long-jacketed suits, with ties. They had been ambushed, never knew what hit them, shot by rifle fire poured into the coach by the Apaches.

He looked at them, gritted his teeth, and followed the moccasin tracks. He'd go after this Apache if it was his last thing. The prints went toward a dense mass of brush and scrub pine.

Slocum lit a Havana and did some thinking. He had shot the comrade of this Apache and he knew their ways. This one would never stop hunting him. Best to get it clear now, instead of waiting until the redskin picked his time.

Slocum went back to the stagecoach. The woman was groaning, with a rhythm. White Flower talked to her in a calm, low voice.

"I'll be back soon," he said.

White Flower turned sharply. "You can't leave now."

"That Apache could come back—anytime."

"That chance must be taken. After the baby comes, the wagon must go to town quickly."

Slocum bit his lip in frustration. He ached to go after the Apache, aware he'd never give up his desire for revenge. If the Apache knew what was happening, he'd make it a point to strike soon.

Slocum heaved a sigh and studied the land around him.

* * *

The sounds that came from the stagecoach were unnerving to Slocum. He had never before heard a woman giving birth.

He kept himself busy; he disentangled the good horses from the dead one. Behind deep brush, he dug a big pit in which he dumped the bodies—the businessmen, the stage driver, the Apache. All of them, to hell with it. When you were dead, it was too late for hate. When he came out from behind the brush, he scanned the land, aware that the Apache would attack when he felt it right.

He finally talked to the shotgun rider who had been hit by the arrow, a red-haired, rugged man named Egan.

"The Apaches hit when we passed Creek Crossing," Egan said. "Hit me first with an arrow. Then poured lead at the passengers. It was a miracle that Maisie Jones inside wasn't hit. We were done for. But Smitty pushed the horses, they were good horses, and we could have outrun them, except they shot the lead."

Though Egan was hit in the right shoulder, he said he could drive the stage with his left hand.

Slocum blew out his cheeks, feeling restless. Maisie groaned a lot, and he decided women went through plenty to give birth. He lit a Havana, thinking that women created men, and men destroyed them—a crazy cycle.

And hanging around was an Apache, ready to do his bit of destruction. Slocum puffed at his Havana. So, he had to worry about the Apache, about the O'Briens, about Maisie Jones, who

White Flower said must be driven quick to town. Miles away—could he take time for that?

Maisie Jones had a husband waiting for her in town. If lucky, she would bring him a child.

His mind worked restlessly because he was nailed down and had to wait on Nature in that stagecoach. His eyes kept studying the land for a hostile sigh.

Then he heard a piercing cry. It came from the coach.

By God! They had done it. Out here!

After awhile he stuck his head in the coach. White Flower was smiling, wiping off an infant, its mouth open, squawking. The mother, her eyes as big as saucers, was staring, amazed at what she had made.

White Flower held up the baby for Slocum to see—a boy. Then she put him carefully in the arms of the mother.

"We better get goin'," he said.

Egan was ready to drive. He looked into the coach. "You did a fine job, miss. Who shall I say did it?"

"Daisy," said Slocum. "Daisy O'Brien."

Egan looked back sharply. "O'Brien did you say? Kin?"

"Reckon," said Slocum. "You better git. That woman should see Doc when you get to town."

They started to ride, Egan holding the reins, White Flower in the coach with Maisie, White Flower's horse strung behind the stage. Slocum rode the roan, in front and behind the stagecoach, studying the land.

14

It was Mike O'Brien who found the burial site at the foot of the Apache Rock. When he and Charley dug it up, they found Johnson. They stared at him in shock. He was cut plenty—Apache work.

"What d'ya figure happened?" O'Brien asked.

"Johnson ran into the Apaches, that's what happened, Dad," Mike said.

"I know. But who the hell buried him? Not the Apaches."

Mike looked at the prints while the others watched. "Johnson waited here, with the horses, while Eddie went up the old Indian trail. The Apaches came along, gave Johnson a bad time. Then Slocum came down, not Eddie. He's up there, I reckon. The Apaches went off with one of

165

the horses. They shot at Slocum—there's the arrow."

Chet's jaw was set hard. "You say Eddie is up there?"

"He ain't down here," Mike said. "You might dig him up, just to make sure."

Chet cursed. "I'll dig Slocum's grave, if it's the last thing I do."

Mike and O'Brien looked at each other.

"This damned Slocum is a tough one. And he's got himself another horse, for the woman. Makes it tougher," Mike said.

"We'll get him," O'Brien said.

Egan rode the stagecoach gently, White Flower sat inside with Maisie Jones, Slocum stayed with them, riding where the spirit moved him.

They were in thick brush country, with rocky hills and hollows. Not easy to see the enemy. Slocum studied the ambush sites, the high ground from where the Apache liked to strike. There was nothing.

They rode for a couple of hours, then Slocum's skin tingled. He saw the prints of the Apache's pony. They crossed the trail, went up a slope, disappearing into brush. The trail ahead looked clear. He rode to the front of the stage.

"Say, Egan, I've got a lead on the Apache. Can't let him run free. Too dangerous. I'm goin' after him. You ride on, fast, but gentle. Hope to catch up."

He followed the Apache tracks.

The tracks were fresh and he moved carefully toward any boulder or brush that seemed threatening. He rode into hollows, up hills, through stands of thick brush, always wary, his hand near his holster, ready to fire at any suspicious movement. The tracks, which had been headed south to Huachua, now turned north sharply. The pace was *fast*.

Slocum frowned. Far in the distance he could see the Mule mountains, and the glitter of the river. What devil's work was the Apache up to? Slocum realized he'd been following *circular tracks*. A nightmarish idea hit him and he put the roan into a fast run back to the trail. When he saw the stagecoach, he began to breathe easy again. Then he realized the horses of the stage were moving on their own, that Egan, the driver, was dead, shot, though he still held the reins.

Slocum clenched his teeth as he rode forward, gun in hand. He looked into the stage. The girl Maisie was there, nursing her baby. No White Flower.

His eyes searched the terrain, but he saw nothing. He leaped off the roan into the stage.

The girl's eyes were wide with fear.

"Are you all right?" he asked.

"Yes."

He waited.

"The woman . . ." she said, faltering.

"What happened to her?"

Maisie's voice trembled. "I think she saved my life. Mine and his." She looked at her baby. "The Apache came in to kill. He had the knife. She talked to the Apache. In his language. He understood her. And she went with him. I think she bargained herself for me and the baby, that's what she did. Gave herself to him." She shut her eyes wearily. "He killed Egan."

Slocum grimaced against the pain. She had sacrificed herself. His impulse was instantly to go after the Apache, but what about Maisie and her new baby? A hard choice, but he made it. Whatever happened to White Flower, it already had happened. He had to help this one. He tied the roan to the stage, climbed to the driver's seat, next to the dead Egan who he roped to the wagon. His mind was full of murderous thoughts, but he could do nothing but drive the stage. After twenty minutes, he glimpsed two cowboys far in the distance, riding parallel to his trail.

He shot his gun into the air and waved hard. They rode toward him.

They were wranglers, on their way to town; they stared at the dead Egan.

"Howdy," Slocum said. "This stage has been hit by Apaches. We've got a mother and new baby in there."

"Who's the lady?" asked the man with a rugged face and black neckerchief.

"Maisie Jones."

"Damn," said the wrangler. "Maisie!"

"Listen," said Slocum, "I aim to go after the Apache. He's grabbed a friend of mine. Will you take the stage in? Should have a doc look at Maisie."

"Sure we'll do it. Who are you, mister?"

"Slocum's the name. I'm in a rush."

"I'm Kearny. You just go ahead." He stuck his head in the coach and yelled, "Hiya, Maisie. So you're a mom. We're gonna bring you in, right quick."

Slocum didn't wait, but put the roan into a gallop back to where the Apache had grabbed White Flower. He began tracking, which took him to high ground. It was a tortuous trail that went into a dense thicket, backed up against a cliffside. There could be no escape from this, he was thinking, if they were there. No tracks coming out. He crept forward, through brush, sometimes holding his breath, until he came to a small mossy clearing.

Then he saw them.

The Apache was lying there, looking at the sky, crusted blood on his chest, and a knife, where he'd been stabbed.

And, she too, her eyes on the sky, lay motionless.

Dead?

His heart jumped, and he stepped forward. She twisted, bringing up a rifle pointed at him. She frowned, as if disbelieving her senses. But when he grinned, she leapt to her feet and sped to him as quick as an antelope. Flung her arms around him.

"Slocum. I knew you would come."

He held her tight, then looked at the dead Apache and shook his head. "That Indian ran a one-man war. There's no telling how much killing he's done. He was one very bad Apache."

She nodded. "Very bad. He killed Egan. He was going to kill Maisie and the baby. He hated palefaces. He told me they had killed his family—

a massacre. Killed his father, mother, wife, and
son. He swore revenge to the death.

"I talked to him. Told him the baby did no
harm. That I would give myself to him if he let
them go. Give him firewater.

"He nodded. When we came here, he drank,
and when he got drunk he told me that he'd have
me, kill me afterward, because I'd given myself to
the palefaces. That he'd catch up with the stage
and slit the throats of mother and baby. His family
was gone, he said, and no paleface could have a
family. Then he turned to me, to make love, before killing. I had my boot knife ready and stuck it
quick in his heart."

Slocum looked at her in wonder. "In our language, we have a saying—the female is the dead-
lier of the species."

She looked puzzled, but the sense of it came
through, and she shook her head. "No, only in
defense. Slocum is the deadly one."

He sighed, and looked at the sinking sun. "Now
for the O'Briens."

Lying on his belly on the high flat rock, Slocum
watched the four O'Brien men sitting at the fire,
eating and talking. One put his bedroll at a half-
sunk rock, at the outskirts of the camp. Likes his
privacy, Slocum thought with a grin. He'd be the
one.

As the full moon climbed, Slocum came down
from his observation rock to where he had left the
horses. He had brought the gelding, as well as the
roan. Needed both.

He took it easy because he couldn't make his

move until the middle of the night. He thought about what to do and say. Time dragged, but when finally the moon crossed overhead, he started his slow, soundless approach to the O'Brien camp.

Now Slocum could hear the man breathing, he was that near. It had taken almost half an hour to move from the edge of the camp to this bedroll. Slocum had moved Apache-style, holding each position like a rock, before he moved again. He had to be motionless and soundless. His neck and legs ached, but he could handle it.

But the one man he didn't want was Chet. He was the poison kid, the loco kid, the one who had to be stopped. Slocum was inches away from the sleeper when he decided to look at the other men. His skin prickled. He could see only *one* other sleeper. Where in hell were the other two? What in hell happened? When did they go? While he was waiting, half a mile away, killing time, that's when. And where had they gone? Back to the ranch? A mystery.

But he couldn't stop—there were two men here, and any sound could break all hell loose. He took one more silent step and put his hand over the man's mouth, a gun in front of his eyes.

The eyes shot open. Saw the gun, and the eyes grew round. He'd be silent. Slocum looked at him, a good, strong face, straight nose, well-shaped mouth. *Something like White Flower's features*. Slocum smiled, this had to be Mike, the brother.

Mike had been looking grim as if, whatever the cost, he might make a break. But the smile on this gunman's face changed his mind. He lifted himself on his elbow, kept his eyes on Slocum, who put a finger over his lips for silence. Then he reached down, under the blanket to lift Mike's gun. Again Slocum smiled good-humoredly, but Mike took good notice of the steely glint in the green, unblinking eyes.

Mike tried a glance at another bedroll, but Slocum's finger came up in warning, and the gun pointed at his head.

Mike decided the polecat didn't intend violence. Somehow, amazingly, Slocum had got into the camp and, being there, he could have killed them. He hadn't done it; it meant he was not the ruthless killer Chet had been describing. More along the lines that Mike had been saying, a man defending himself.

So what in hell did he want? To palaver. Because if he intended violence, he wouldn't do this.

So he crawled softly to where Slocum pointed, out of the camp to the thick brush. Slocum eyed him and the camp.

They moved beyond the bushes, finally to a hollow where the moon threw dark shadows. Though far from the camp, Slocum still kept his voice low. "You'd be Mike?"

Mike nodded, his teeth clenched. Was the polecat goin' to shoot after all?

"Mike," Slocum said. "I've got no hard feelings, though you men are hunting us like we're dogs. I've got a story to tell. But you won't believe it until I show proof."

Slocum stopped, aware of the burden of trying to tell White Flower's story in a few words. "It's this, Mike—*you're trying to hurt someone who is kin to you."*

Mike looked astounded.

Slocum laughed. "Not me. The lady. We're going to meet her. You'll hear her story, then be free to go. That's all. But I'll ask this, if you believe it—tell your father. And call off this huntdown."

Mike stared. This Slocum talked like a man of sense, but what he was saying was loco. He was hinting that the girl Chet called an Apache bitch was *kin*.

Mike threw a shrewd glance at Slocum, wondering if he had got loco weed mixed in his soup. But the polecat had the gun, and he had said that, after listening to the Apache girl, Mike could go. That made the deal fine.

"Sure, mister," Mike said. "I'll listen. Just you keep your word after."

Slocum gave him the steely eye. "I keep my word, cowboy."

They went to where the horses had been tethered and rode under the full moon, until they came to Slocum's camp in the set-back boulders.

Slocum pulled up the roan, jolted. There was her bedroll, but *White Flower was gone*. Slocum's jaw hardened. He motioned for Mike to stay in front of him. He wanted no sudden attack from behind.

Where in hell did she go? Did she go or was she taken? Who knew they were here? Perhaps she just decided to wash her hands of the palefaces, violent men, and go back to the tribe. Why should she always be on the run, hunted like an animal?

No, it couldn't be that. She would have said good-bye. But she might not want to hurt him. A clean break, maybe?

He came forward to her bedroll, then saw the tracks. *Boots*. Two white men. Who the hell were they? *Chet*.

He turned to Mike who was watching him curiously.

"Did you know we were here?"

Mike nodded. "We had you spotted, and were going to hit you at dawn. Chet did this on his own, he and Charley. He figured we might be soft about the woman. He'd been drinking, and decided to strike on his own."

Slocum's face was grim.

Then Mike said, "He won't kill her. He'll use her for bait, I know my brother. What in hell did you bring me here for?"

Slocum grimaced. "That girl—is your half sister."

Mike looked at him politely, but his eyes were incredulous.

Slocum took a long breath. "I know it sounds crazy. Years ago, your father got hurt helping save an Apache girl from a cougar. She nursed him, they fell for each other. Afterward, your father went home. But he left the Apache maid with a child."

Slocum pulled a cigarillo and lit it. Mike watched him like a hawk.

"She went back to her tribe and got mistreated, because of her paleface lover. Before she died, she told the girl to go for help to her father. *Sean O'Brien* in Vista."

Slocum smiled. "A beautiful girl—wonderful. Your sister. You're lucky."

Mike listened with growing wonder, thinking it was a fantastic story, but true. His father had claw marks on his chest, and he had talked, long ago, of a romance, before meeting Mike's mother.

Slocum went on. "I ran into her when an Apache was trying to kill White Flower. Had to stop him. He threw away the cigarillo. "Now here's where Fate plays a dirty trick. Your brother, Chet, and a gunslinger, Brady, stumbled on White Flower and were ready to do bad things to her. She took care of Brady—a tough lady, and I had to stop Chet who tried to pull his gun. Reckon I hurt his feelings. Because he made a regular feud— bringing one gunman after another—to do us hurt."

Slocum leaned back. "Now you know *why* I brought you here. Get word to your father he's trying to run down *his own daughter*. And the man protecting her."

Mike shook his head. "Mister, that's the damnedest story I ever heard. And has to be true. My father has those claw marks. Let's ride, for God's sake, before my drunken idiot of a brother does something I'll never forgive him for."

15

They rode hard and fast, but Mike pulled his horse near his camp. "Better stay here, Slocum, till I get it clear with my father."

Slocum nodded.

Mike dismounted, hoping to come in quietly. Voices floated out to him, then silence. They had heard him.

"Dad? Chet? It's me, Mike."

Whispered voices.

Then Chet's voice, slurred. He had been drinking. "You alone, Mike?"

"Yes."

"Mike." His father's voice.

"Yes, Dad."

"Come on, boy."

"Wait." Chet's voice. "You in trouble, Mike? The polecat got a gun on you?"

"No."

"You sure?" His voice was slurred and drunken.

"Sure."

"Then come on."

Mike heard whispered voices. They knew Slocum had picked him up, they had found the tracks. Mike came forward slowly. Then he saw the girl. She was sitting erect at the fire, her hands tied, a gag in her mouth.

The bait.

He stared. A beauty—and dammit, her features, nose, mouth were like his own. A sister, all right.

She was looking at him, her eyes despairing. But something in his face seemed to hearten her, for her eyes brightened with hope. He had been out with Slocum. *Maybe Mike knew!*

But where was Slocum?

"Where is he, Mike?" Chet asked from the deep shadows of the cliff.

"Not here. Where's Dad?"

There was a long silence, then Chet and Charley, holding guns, moved from the black shadows to the bright moonlight. Chet's face was flushed from drinking. "How'd you get away from him, Mike?"

"Where's Dad?"

Chet growled. "Why can't you answer? Does he have a gun on you?"

"Talk sense, man. It's night. Where would he be—to have a gun on me?"

Charley said, "It looks clear, Chet."

O'Brien came out of the shadows, too, his gun was in his holster.

Chet moved close. "Why'd he let you go, Mike?"

"We figured he took you to kill you," O'Brien said.

"But he let you go. Why, Mike?" Chet was grinding his teeth in frustration.

Mike hesitated. How could he ever begin to tell it.

"He's out there—isn't he?" Chet said excitedly. "I knew it. That's why we took the girl. We saved your damned life, Mike. He wasn't going to hurt you, long as we had the girl."

Chet turned to his father. "I told you it would work. That polecat has a taste for the breed. Look at her—wearing clothes of a white woman. She's a freak Apache squaw. And she'll pay, too, for all the killin'. All those men, Dad—Brady, Wilbur, Lonnie, Eddie, Johnson—all of them—dead."

Chet suddenly put his gun to her head, and yelled. "Come on, Slocum, come out, you got one minute before I blow her brains."

"Don't do it, Chet," Mike said feverishly.

"What?" Chet stared, then his eyes gleamed. "Hey. I understand. Kinda stupid to blow her brains. A piece like her. Sorta waste. What we want is fun with the Apache bitch." And he jerked at her shirt, ripping it to reveal part of her full breasts.

Chet whistled. "Hey, Charley. Look at them. This little girl is gonna give us a good time. Keep your gun on her, just in case the polecat gets ideas. Comin' out, Slocum?" he yelled.

There was silence.

"I'm comin'," Slocum said.

Chet grinned from ear to ear. He had called it. He had told Charley and his dad the girl would bring them Slocum. And she did.

Slocum appeared in the firelight at the edge of the camp. "Gonna shoot?"

There was profound silence as they looked at him.

"Throw your gun, mister," Chet hissed.

Slocum threw his gun.

Chet picked it up. "We won't shoot, we're gonna hang you," he crowed, grinning devilishly. And he looked at Mike to get a nod for his cleverness. Then he noticed Mike's empty holster. His jaw hardened. "Keep your gun on her, Charley. If the polecat pulls something, shoot."

Mike stared at his father. "Dad, stop this."

But O'Brien wasn't listening. He watched Slocum who came closer to the firelight.

O'Brien came forward. "Let's take a look at this Slocum." He studied the big, lean, rugged face, the steady green eyes, the calm, unfearful look.

O'Brien's lips were tight. "You look tough enough. No wonder my boys had trouble with you, mister. Five dead—because of you. But you've come to the end of the line."

Slocum studied O'Brien's strong, honest face. "I wanted to meet you, too, O'Brien."

"Yeah—well, it ain't gonna be a long acquaintance."

"Right, Dad," said Chet, and he looked at White Flower. "Want to really punish this man before he swings, we take the girl—right in front of him. That's what we do."

O'Brien scowled.

But Chet headed him off. "Five men, dead, Dad. We ain't gonna let him off—just with hanging. Let's give him some pain. *The girl*." And again he tore at her dress, leaving her breasts fully exposed.

"Wait a minute," said Mike.

"Goddammit, Mike," Chet raged. "Don't want you preachy—being good-goody I'm sick of it—d'ya hear. Sick o' you. Now don't get in my way, don't interfere."

"You aimin' to violate your own half sister?" said Slocum. He figured that Mike, without a gun, couldn't talk to this mad kid.

His remark was a bombshell. There was silence. Then Chet went into gales of laughter; he almost doubled over. "The slickest trick I ever heard. My *sister*—this squaw bitch!" He turned to Charley who was also grinning.

"Good try, mister," Charley said.

O'Brien was not smiling.

"Been wantin' to meet you, O'Brien, since I heard about you and *Sunbird*," Slocum said.

At the name, O'Brien was jolted and stared hard at Slocum.

"What did you say?"

"*Sunbird*. You remember her—Apache girl—long ago. How's the claw scars? Still got 'em?"

O'Brien seemed to go into a dream; his eyes grew hazy.

Chet was furious at what he saw was a clever Slocum trick to fog things up.

"That's enough. One more word outa you, Slocum." He raised his gun. "It's your last." Then he sneered. "Trying to pull a fast one. I know your type."

Then Mike said, "It's true, you dumb brat. The girl is our half sister."

Chet glared murderously. "You gone loco. She's Apache. No Apache can be my sister." He stared at his father who was still dreaming, living something that happened long ago.

"He's a waste," Chet said brutally. "Take her, Charley. Screw the squaw. I know you been achin' to."

Mike turned to Chet. "You are the lowest mongrel I ever met. How'd I ever get a brother like you?"

Pale with rage, Chet turned on him. "You ain't got him anymore." He raised his gun and fired.

The sound snapped O'Brien out of his trance. He looked at Mike squirming on the ground, and his hand flashed to his holster. His bullet hit Chet in the chest, and he stumbled and fell. He lay there, the blood leaking from his chest, looking with wonder at his father. His eyes stayed on him until they went dull.

Slocum bent to Mike. He'd been hit in the side, not a mortal wound.

O'Brien didn't look at Chet, but went to White Flower. He took the gag from her mouth. He studied her face.

"Migod," he said, "you look like Sunbird. And something like Mike." He paused. "Sunbird is your mother?"

"She's gone. She said, 'Go find your father— Sean O'Brien.'"

"She said that?" O'Brien's voice was choked.

He stared hungrily at her. Then he stared at Chet on the ground. *"Lost a son—got a daughter."*

Swallowing painfully, he put his arms out.

She moved into his embrace.

Mike, who was conscious, looked at them, and his face twisted in a smile.

The sun was going down, huge and yellow, in a flame-streaked sky.

They were in front of the big white house, the ranch stretching miles behind them. Slocum was standing next to his newly washed and curried roan.

In a beautiful white dress, White Flower was looking with glowing blue eyes at Slocum.

"Won't you stay, Slocum. How can I feel safe— without you?"

"You've got a brother and a father. You'll be safe. And you have that map of Apache gold, just in case."

"I'll miss you, Slocum. All the excitement. Now I have to live like a paleface."

"Now, you are Daisy O'Brien—like I said."

She came close. "But it's you I love, Slocum. Can't you stay?"

"And do what? No, I must go. But I'll surely be passin' through here again."

He swung over the roan and waved.

She watched him ride down the trail, sitting tall in the saddle, against a flaming sunset. She watched until he was lost to sight.

JAKE LOGAN

J.D. HARDIN

"THE MOST EXCITING
WESTERN WRITER SINCE
LOUIS L'AMOUR"
—JAKE LOGAN